"*Baseball Bits* will definitely have a desigr
—Ron Blomberg, former Yankee DH and autnor or *Designatea Heorew*

"After reading *Baseball Bits*, I'm convinced Dan Schlossberg got his inspiration from *Temporary Insanity*. He's almost as crazy as I am, but he's lots of fun to read."
—Jay Johnstone, former outfielder and author of *Temporary Insanity*

"*Baseball Bits* can be read from the front, from the back, or from the middle. It's funny, informative, and the kind of book you hate to finish. Yogi was right when he said, 'It ain't over till it's over.'"
—David Kaplan, director, Yogi Berra Museum and Learning Center

"Careers of good pitchers eventually end, but careers of good writers keep going forever. Dan Schlossberg proves that with his latest book, *Baseball Bits*. It's truly a literary home run."
—Ferguson Jenkins, Hall of Fame pitcher

Dan Schlossberg

ALPHA

A member of Penguin Group (USA) Inc.

To the 1957 Milwaukee Braves—my first team and first love.

ALPHA BOOKS

Published by the Penguin Group

Penguin Group (USA) Inc., 375 Hudson Street, New York, New York 10014, USA

Penguin Group (Canada), 90 Eglinton Avenue East, Suite 700, Toronto, Ontario M4P 2Y3, Canada (a division of Pearson Penguin Canada Inc.)

Penguin Books Ltd., 80 Strand, London WC2R 0RL, England

Penguin Ireland, 25 St. Stephen's Green, Dublin 2, Ireland (a division of Penguin Books Ltd.)

Penguin Group (Australia), 250 Camberwell Road, Camberwell, Victoria 3124, Australia (a division of Pearson Australia Group Pty. Ltd.)

Penguin Books India Pvt. Ltd., 11 Community Centre, Panchsheel Park, New Delhi—110 017, India

Penguin Group (NZ), 67 Apollo Drive, Rosedale, North Shore, Auckland 1311, New Zealand (a division of Pearson New Zealand Ltd.)

Penguin Books (South Africa) (Pty.) Ltd., 24 Sturdee Avenue, Rosebank, Johannesburg 2196, South Africa

Penguin Books Ltd., Registered Offices: 80 Strand, London WC2R 0RL, England

International Standard Book Number: 978-1-59257-775-0
Library of Congress Catalog Card Number: 2007941485

10 09 08   8 7 6 5 4 3 2 1

Interpretation of the printing code: The rightmost number of the first series of numbers is the year of the book's printing; the rightmost number of the second series of numbers is the number of the book's printing. For example, a printing code of 08–1 shows that the first printing occurred in 2008.

Printed in the United States of America

Note: This publication contains the opinions and ideas of its author. It is intended to provide helpful and informative material on the subject matter covered. It is sold with the understanding that the author and publisher are not engaged in rendering professional services in the book. If the reader requires personal assistance or advice, a competent professional should be consulted.

The author and publisher specifically disclaim any responsibility for any liability, loss, or risk, personal or otherwise, which is incurred as a consequence, directly or indirectly, of the use and application of any of the contents of this book.

Trademarks: All terms mentioned in this book that are known to be or are suspected of being trademarks or service marks have been appropriately capitalized. Alpha Books and Penguin Group (USA) Inc. cannot attest to the accuracy of this information. Use of a term in this book should not be regarded as affecting the validity of any trademark or service mark.

Most Alpha books are available at special quantity discounts for bulk purchases for sales promotions, premiums, fund-raising, or educational use. Special books, or book excerpts, can also be created to fit specific needs.

For details, write: Special Markets, Alpha Books, 375 Hudson Street, New York, NY 10014.

Publisher: Marie Butler-Knight	**Senior Development Editor:** Phil Kitchel	**Indexer:** Brad Herriman
Editorial Director: Mike Sanders	**Production Editor:** Kayla Dugger	**Layout:** Brian Massey
Senior Managing Editor: Billy Fields	**Copy Editor:** Lisanne V. Jensen	**Proofreader:** John Etchison
Acquisitions Editor: Michele Wells	**Cover/Book Designer:** William Thomas	

CONTENTS

Foreword

I suppose that I'm the typical American male. My earliest memories of baseball coincide with most of my other early memories, but the great home run race between Roger Maris and Mickey Mantle in 1961 hooked me on the game forever. Maris was my first hero—the first player I idolized. I didn't know at age seven in 1961 that Roger was a relatively new Yankee and that Mickey Mantle had been there for many years. I rooted for both of them, and when Mantle bowed out near the end, I rooted like crazy for Maris. To me, his record (of 61 home runs in a season) is pure and still stands. I still refer to Roger as "the people's champ" on the air.

A year later, when the Mets brought National League baseball back to New York not far from our home in Queens, it was easy for me to make the switch. I remember thinking they were created just for me. I remember the comedy, purity, and innocence of the first Mets team. I didn't watch the first game, because it was a night game in St. Louis, and my parents ordered me to bed. When I was getting ready for school the next morning, I asked my dad how the Mets did. He said they lost, and that was it. I was disappointed. I was hooked before I ever saw them play a regular-season game.

The first Mets game I went to was in July 1962 at the Polo Grounds, when Rod Kanehl hit the first grand slam in Mets history and Gil Hodges hit a home run that either tied or passed Ralph Kiner on the all-time list. But the greatest game I saw in the pre-1969 era was played on August 4, 1966.

Juan Marichal was pitching a perfect game for the Giants with two outs in the sixth and the Mets down by a couple of runs. Dennis Ribant was the Mets' pitcher, and manager Wes Westrum—for some reason I still can't figure 41 years later—let him hit. He hit a little groundball through the middle for a base hit, ending the perfect game—and Ron Swoboda hit a home run off Bill Henry in the ninth to win it. I was 12 and so excited that I said to myself, "I'm always going to remember this date and this game."

I have gotten into that pattern over the years, whenever there has been a significant game or event. Because I was so influenced by big games as a kid, I have a tendency to remember years or dates, but I'm not sure that I would call myself a pure historian. A historian is someone who makes a conscious effort to record, preserve, and compile history, anecdotes, and artifacts.

Dan Schlossberg, my longtime press box colleague, shows in this book that he not only knows baseball history but remembers stories and anecdotes that never appeared in published form before. *Baseball Bits* makes readers laugh, learn, and leap at the chance to test the baseball knowledge of their friends. But more than anything else, it brings back memories of the good old days before the designated hitter, wild card, and interleague play. Like Dan, I love baseball but hate many of the recent changes.

Baseball had a perfect system when it had 24 teams. There were two 12-team leagues, each split into two divisions, and teams played division rivals 18 times and the other guys 12 times. It was perfect because it was symmetrical: everybody had the same path to the postseason.

Interleague play is just a gimmick. While it's great to have a Mets-Yankees or Cubs–White Sox series every year, the price you pay (in bad games) distorts the value of the gimmick games. The wild card is even worse. Watching the Braves-Giants divisional battle in 1993, we all knew that it was the last great race. The three-division format was going into play the next year, and we'd never see another race like that again. There are so many things I dislike about the wild card. We've developed a scenario where a team with a very mediocre record can get into the postseason.

I also think that many of our most cherished baseball records have been distorted and diluted. To me, both of Barry Bonds' home run records are tainted. And if Alex Rodriguez or anybody else would hit 61 home runs in a season, I'd question it because of the entire human growth hormone issue and the fact that you can't test for it.

Some records have personal meaning to me. I was there when Tom Seaver struck out 19 men, including the last 10 in a row, so I will always have a connection to that. I still don't understand how four guys left him off their Cooperstown ballot, although I remember Deane McGowan of *The New York Times* saying he didn't vote for anyone the first year they were eligible.

I would also like to see eligibility rules massaged so that a person's entire career can be taken into account—with the playing record separated from the managing record. That would certainly help Gil Hodges, whom I revered but never met. I also think defense gets lost in the equation, which hurts not only Hodges but also Keith Hernandez.

Like Hodges and Hernandez, Dan Schlossberg catches everything when it comes to baseball. In this book, he covers all the bases, from ball clubs and ballparks to players, managers, executives, trades, and special events. He touches on the odd side of the record book—the undiscovered flip side of the game few fans see. This volume is designed to bridge the gap between the last out of the World Series and the first pitch the following February.

Although every season is different, I don't think any team will ever replace the 1969 Mets as my favorite. They defined my life as a kid. After watching all those bad Mets teams for the first seven years but loving them anyway, I felt like I was presented with a gift in 1969. I grew up with those guys and bonded with them. As a kid, when your team is winning, you can put everything else in your life on a shelf and get absorbed in what your team is doing.

Gil Hodges, who managed that team, made the miracle happen. When he signed his first contract as Mets manager, it established a line of demarcation between the early Mets and the serious Mets. Everything changed the minute he became manager. I still look at him as an icon.

I will always feel a fondness for Davey Johnson, because he was the manager when I started doing the pre- and post-game shows in 1987. Initially, he was a bit of a tough guy to crack because I don't think he understood what we needed to do. I had to ask him legitimate questions. It took him a little while to warm up to that, but once he did, we really clicked. I learned so much about baseball sitting in his office before games. Most of it was from discussions that took place before or after the tape recorder was on. Once he found a comfort level with me, he was fine with me asking him anything—on or off the air.

When I covered Yankees home games, I got to know Billy Martin, too. He was a trip. You never knew what you were getting from day to day with Billy. Whenever he addressed anyone with the word "pal," that guy might as well turn and walk out of the room, because it was going to get ugly. When Billy was losing his patience or his temper, he would say, "Now look, pal ..." It always got worse from there. It never happened to me, but I always got a kick out of it.

Billy had a short fuse, and I'm sure working for George Steinbrenner contributed to the problem. I remember how calculating George was in the '70s. When things were unraveling or at a controversial point in a season or a game, George would wander out of his box and stroll to the back of the press box. He knew if he stood there for five seconds, one of the writers or columnists would come up to him. They'd walk off to George's office, and that would be the next day's exclusive for whomever got to him first.

I covered some big stories in my time. I'll never forget the contract dispute that convinced the Mets to trade Tom Seaver in 1977. I was already in the business then, working for WHN radio, and was assigned to cover Seaver's departure from LaGuardia Airport. He was flying to Montreal to join his new team, the Cincinnati Reds.

My assignment was to walk with him right to his gate at the airport. Here I was having to be a professional broadcast journalist while it's tearing my heart out inside. How could they trade that guy? I still don't have very nice things to say about M. Donald Grant for that. (Then again, nor does Seaver.)

The Mets were only 15 years old at the time and had gone from inept infancy to surprise champions, then through another period of mediocrity before winning another pennant. That trade drew another line of demarcation. It was all downhill after that for a number of years. I used to love trades, but they used to be based upon value-for-value. Now, all trades are motivated by financial considerations. As kids, we used to sit on the steps in Bayside and make "trades" every night. Very rarely did we ever consider that fair value had to be given to the other guys.

Although players change constantly, ballparks give the game a sense of stability. The old ones are reminders of our youth—we all get nostalgic and love things that connect us to the time when we were younger. Even today when I see Wrigley Field, my mind drifts back to 1969 and the great race with the Cubs. The ballpark looks virtually identical, save for the lights, to the way it did all those years ago.

When you go to the old ballparks, they're great to watch the games in but they're inconvenient for the fans and for those of us who have to work. I love the parks in Pittsburgh, Philadelphia, and San Francisco. Unlike many of my colleagues, I even like Minute Maid Park in Houston—except for Tal's Hill in center field. It has a lot of quirks, but I like the combination of old-ballpark charm plus a comfortable working environment. That's what I look forward to when the Mets move into Citi Field in 2009.

I also look forward to many more hours of pleasure leafing through this book. In crafting a perfect companion for both the armchair fan and the broadcast professional, Dan Schlossberg has found artwork, photographs, and obscure tidbits, including many gems that media guides missed. His love for the game and its infinite nuances jump off the pages of *Baseball Bits*.

—Howie Rose

Howie Rose, radio voice of the New York Mets, also spent eight years as play-by-play man for Fox Sports New York/MSG. He was with New York radio station WHN when it began an all-sports format as WFAN on July 1, 1987, and was the first host of "Mets Extra," a post-game show launched by the station. Also an accomplished hockey announcer, he has been the voice of the New York Islanders since 1996 for Fox Sports New York. Rose replaced Bob Murphy in the Mets' broadcast booth in 2004.

Introduction

Watching newsreel footage of female riveters working on wartime airplanes reminded me how this book was put together. It was not just written, but assembled—from a million different parts. From the Flying Dutchman to the Bronx Bombers, baseball can be measured by the sum of its parts. Those parts come in different sizes, different colors, and different weights, but fit together in a mosaic that has captured the imagination of millions for more than a century.

Like my friend Howie Rose, who found time to pen the foreword during the stretch drive disaster that decimated his Mets, I was only a kid when baseball swept me off my feet. My first baseball memory is watching the 1957 Milwaukee Braves win the World Series on a small black-and-white TV that got only the three networks plus a handful of local channels. I watched with my dad, a prominent North Jersey radiologist, but without the sound. He explained to me what was happening, and I hung on every word. He didn't talk much, but when he did, people listened. (Especially me, the impressionable nine-year-old.)

Because the Brooklyn Dodgers and New York Giants were leaving town and all my friends rooted for the vanquished Yankees, I figured that the Braves were the best team. By the time the Mets started to play five years later, I was thoroughly hooked on Aaron, Mathews, and Spahn. In fact, it took me a long time to get over the first doubleheader I saw in person on May 12, 1962, at the Polo Grounds. The Mets, en route to a historic 120-loss season, beat the Braves twice—winning one of the games on a Hobie Landrith pop fly that turned into the only home run of his Met career—a two-run, ninth-inning shot that just cleared the wall at the right-field line, 257 feet from home. Hobie is in this book, along with the names of the other 21 players selected by the Mets in the expansion draft. Casey Stengel, who managed those misfits, is here, too—as a player, prankster, and pilot.

Baseball Bits is designed to evoke the excitement of the game. Its anecdotes, stories, and off-the-beaten-path tidbits are woven within a fabric of photographs and artwork—much of it never previously published—plus sidebars, box scores, and graphs guaranteed to entertain the armchair fan as well as the baseball professional. It makes no attempt to cover all the bases—few books can go beyond the 1,000-page compendiums—but tries to capture both the flavor of the game and its humor. It's the kind of book you can read backward or pick up in the middle without missing a beat. There's no continuous story—just hundreds of tales from a game so diverse that no two days at the ballpark are the same.

Baseball Bits begins with the creation and evolution of a game that is barely recognizable today, then delves into the ever-changing world of ball clubs, ballparks, players, and bosses. Trades, traditions, and spring training are included along with All-Star games, postseason play, and postwar progression across the color line and past most of the game's hallowed records.

Unlike football, which to me is three minutes of action in three hours of game, baseball has enough substance to sustain itself 365 days a year (366 days in 2008). It spawns fantasy leagues, water cooler conversations, and trivia contests even during the long, cold off-season. And it breeds organizations like the Society for American Baseball Research (SABR), a group of 7,000 writers, authors, educators, and rabid fans whose research has reversed several long-held baseball records. I've been a card-carrying member since 1981.

More than any other source, SABR has been a godsend to this baseball writer. Its publications, conventions, and conversations have provided considerable material and directed me to places where I could solve baseball mysteries. Nothing is too obscure for that group, nor is anything too obscure for this book. In fact, the whole idea of *Baseball Bits* is to get people to say, "I never knew that!"

It is my hope you'll have that reaction as you review the pages and pictures that follow.

Dan Schlossberg
Fair Lawn, NJ
October 2007

Acknowledgments

The generosity, courtesy, and cooperation of the following people were instrumental in producing this book:

Bill Acree and Brad Hainje, Atlanta Braves; Kevin Barnes, freelance broadcaster; Bill Beck, Florida Marlins; Laura Gaynor, photographer; Sam Bernstein, Society for American Baseball Research (SABR); John Blundell, Major League Baseball; Todd Burke, JetBlue Airways; Debi Dorne, baseball insider; Bill Goff, goodsportsart.com; Dionne and Lewis Grabel, memorabilia collectors; Milo Hamilton, Houston Astros broadcaster; and Brad Horn and Jeff Idelson, Baseball Hall of Fame.

Also, Ronnie Joyner, baseball artist; David Kaplan, Yogi Berra Museum; Kal London and Bob Muscatell, WLIS/WMRD radio; Ed Lucas, baseball writer; Doug Lyons, baseball author; Clay Luraschi, The Topps Company; Bruce Markusen, baseball writer and author; Bill Menzel, baseball photographer; Debbie Mirandi and Howard Goldstein, attorneys at law; and John Pennisi, baseball artist.

Thanks also to Kristin Roberts, Hotel Valley Ho; Jay Horwitz, New York Mets; Larry Shenk, Philadelphia Phillies; Jimmy Stanton, Houston Astros; David Vincent, baseball author; and Jason Zillo, New York Yankees.

This book began with a 10-minute encounter between a writer and an editor during the Perfect Pitch session of the American Society of Journalists and Authors (ASJA) and was nursed to fruition by longtime friend, colleague, and publicist Bob Ibach, formerly with the Chicago Cubs but now the successful president of his own sports public relations firm.

Michele Wells, the pleasant and professional acquisitions editor of Penguin Books, took the time to come to ASJA, sign a "new" Penguin author, and go far beyond the call of duty in preparing this book for publication.

Without Patty Tuthill's help, the author would *still* be trying to figure out what photos or pieces of art go where.

Bill Goff, Bill Menzel, Ronnie Joyner, Wanda Chirnside, and John Pennisi provided most of those photos, artwork, and graphics without charge and even took the time to burn them onto CDs to make the harried author's life much easier. No book works without good art—and those guys are good.

So is smooth-talking Mets radio man Howie Rose, who took time out in the middle of a pennant race to reveal his thoughts on how baseball has changed—for better and for worse—during his five decades as a fan. As author of the foreword, Howie makes a great leadoff man for *Baseball Bits*.

Milo Hamilton, another heavy hitter, provided insights of his broadcast career during an eight-hour round-trip car ride to Cooperstown. He's been a professional sports broadcaster in *seven* different decades—making him almost as old as Julio Franco.

My many friends in SABR provided great support and will supply fodder for future editions when they find fault with this one (hopefully not too much). Their comments are always welcome.

So are comments from friends and family who now know the reason so many September invitations were spurned. Thanks for your patience and for putting up with my impatience.

CHAPTER

1

Origin, Innovation, and Evolution

Although Abner Doubleday, Alexander Cartwright, and Henry Chadwick would not recognize anything about today's game beyond the bat and ball, the three of them left an indelible mark on baseball.

Legend has it that Doubleday "invented" the game of baseball in Cooperstown, New York, in 1839—although history indicates he was a plebe at West Point that year. Because there's no mention of baseball in Doubleday's diaries, using his alleged invention of baseball as the rationale for placing the Baseball Hall of Fame in Cooperstown seems shaky at best.

Cartwright has a legitimate claim to the "father of baseball" title: he wrote the first rules and umpired the first recognizable game—six years after Doubleday's so-called discovery. Chadwick started covering baseball for *The New York Clipper* in 1858, before the advent of the Civil War or the first professional team or league. Searching for a way to rank and compare players, Chadwick invented the box score and developed some of the vital statistics still used today.

The first league, the National Association of Baseball Clubs, was organized in New York in 1857. The league played all their games at the Fashion Race Course in Jamaica, Queens.

By 1869, one-time cricket player Harry Wright had gathered nine other top players to form the Cincinnati Red Stockings, the first professional team. They went undefeated in 69 games (plus a tie) and launched a 130-game winning streak that finally ended on June 14, 1870.

The success of the Red Stockings sparked the establishment of the National Association of Professional Baseball Players (the first pro league) in 1871. But franchise and player shifts, plus the presence of unsavory characters in the ballparks, killed its reputation.

Learning from that fiasco, William A. Hulbert, owner of the Chicago National Association club, and Boston pitcher A. G. Spalding founded the National League (NL) in 1876 and came up with a 70-game schedule for its eight members.

Cartwright's Rules

Alexander Cartwright organized the first regular team, the Knickerbockers, and wrote rules to govern the sport. The capable draftsman designed the diamond and mandated nine players on a side, three outs per inning, and an unchangeable batting order.

Cartwright's rules changed the shape of the field from a square to a diamond, introduced the concept of foul territory, and eliminated the practice of getting rivals "out" by hitting them with thrown balls. Cartwright later developed the concept of a nine-inning game.

The first game played under Cartwright's rules, at the Elysian Fields in Hoboken, New Jersey, on June 19, 1846, ended when the New York Nine scored their twenty-first run (then called an ace) in the fourth inning (called a hand). Although games then ended when a team scored 21 "aces," visiting teams could continue to bat. New York scored twice more before the Knickerbockers took their final turn at bat, and the game ended in a 23–1 defeat for the home team.

By 1849, the Knickerbockers had reached such a level of respectability that they wore uniforms for the first time (straw hats, white shirts, and blue pants).

With no union to protect their players, early NL teams had a salary cap of $2,400 per man and a club ceiling of $30,000. Teams were not bound to pay injured or ill athletes, and rules changed constantly.

For years, batters could "order" pitches as if they were ordering steaks in a restaurant. Batting averages weren't kept until 1871, and only a few teams kept track. When walks counted as hits one year, averages soared. Not until 1889, after decades of discussion, were batters entitled to four balls and three strikes. Home plate did not assume its familiar pentagonal shape until 1900—so that umpires could get better looks at pitches on the corners.

Only after the advent of the American League (AL) in 1901 was a meaningful postseason series played. It began two years later, after the National Agreement between leagues was signed. By then, two AL franchises had shifted—Baltimore to New York and Milwaukee to St. Louis—and Boston had replaced Buffalo. The National League (NL) that year had teams in Boston, Brooklyn, Chicago, Cincinnati, New York, Philadelphia, Pittsburgh, and St. Louis, while the 1903 AL included Boston, Chicago, Cleveland, Detroit, New York, Philadelphia, St. Louis, and Washington.

As league size and membership varied, so did the schedule—reaching 112 games in 1884 and 126 two years later. By 1901, when the AL shattered the NL's monopoly on big-league baseball, the two circuits were playing 140 games each. That increased to 154 games in 1904 and the current 162 during the expansion era that started in 1961.

Early Bits

The first recorded reference to baseball as "the national pastime" was made in an 1857 publication called *The Spirit of the Times.*

◊

Rules changes in 1858 set the distance between bases at 90 feet and the distance from pitcher to plate at 45 feet, restricted the length of games to nine innings rather than 21 runs, and required that outs be made on balls caught without bouncing.

◊

Henry Chadwick created the first newspaper box score, the first system of keeping score, and the first baseball publication. The one-time cricket writer spent 27 years as editor of *Spalding's Official Baseball Guide.* Chadwick, a British national, later became the first foreign-born member of the Baseball Hall of Fame.

A Christmas Day baseball game between two teams of Union soldiers drew a crowd of 40,000 curious spectators in Hilton Head, South Carolina, in 1862.

◇

Although *The Star-Spangled Banner* was first played during the seventh-inning stretch of 1918 World Series Game 1 (during World War I), it did not become a regular pregame feature until 1942, when it was again used to boost wartime morale. Francis Scott Key's 1814 poem, written to the tune of an old British drinking song, became the official national anthem during the Depression in 1931.

◇

The first NL franchises, in 1876, sold for $100 each. Five years earlier, National Association franchises went for just $10. Umpires worked gratis until 1883, then were paid $5 per game by the home team. In 1888, visiting clubs received 15 cents from each paid admission to the ballpark. And clubs deducted $30 per season from players' salaries for uniform costs and 50 cents per day for meal money.

◇

To cope with its biggest problem—constant player movement to other teams—the NL imposed the first reserve rule in 1879. Clubs were allowed to place five men "on reserve" so that other teams would not sign those players for the following year. The list eventually grew from 5 to 15 and finally to the entire roster. Players deemed it an honor to be placed on reserve, because they were considered valuable by their teams and were guaranteed a job. But the reserve clause also allowed owners to slice salaries, because it forbade free player movement.

◇

The smallest crowd ever to attend a big-league game braved a rainstorm to see Chicago beat Troy (NY) on September 17, 1881. Only 12 fans showed up.

◇

In a one-year experiment that didn't take, the NL mandated uniform colors for its teams in 1882: Boston (red), Cleveland (navy blue), Chicago (white), Buffalo (gray), New York (green), Detroit (old gold), Worcester (blue), and Providence (light blue).

◇

Philadelphia zookeeper Jim Murray sent baseball scores to telegraph offices by carrier pigeon every half inning in 1883.

NL President Abraham Mills was hailed as "the Bismarck of Baseball" when he signed the first National Agreement with the rival American Association in 1883. The pact set up an 11-player reserve list, guaranteed territorial rights, set minimum salaries at $1,000, and even created a post-season series between league champions—the first "World Series."

◇

Umpires in the 1880s wore top hats and asked players and spectators their opinions on controversial calls.

◇

Well into the 1880s, batters ordered their own pitches and runners interfered with fielders trying to make plays. Pitchers were obliged to throw underhand until 1881 and faced numerous other restrictions that remained in force until 1884. Their distance from batters was much closer until 1893, when the current standard of 60 feet and 6 inches was introduced by accident. Pitching distance had been 45 feet until 1881, then went to 50 feet, then "60 feet, 0 inches." The surveyor misread the "0" as a "6," and the mistake was never corrected.

◇

In the early days of the game, proximity to home plate allowed hurlers to work more and win more. Old Hoss Radbourn won 60 and lost 12 for Providence in the NL in 1884. In the modern era, it would take a star pitcher three seasons to win that many.

◇

The biggest slugger of the nineteenth century was Roger Connor. He held the lifetime home run record before Babe Ruth with 138 homers, never hitting more than 17 per year, in a career that ended in 1897. Gavvy Cravath hit 119 lifetime, making him the pre-Ruth home run king of the "modern era" that began in 1901. He won six home run crowns from 1913 to 1919.

◇

Roger Connor hit the first grand slam in baseball history on September 9, 1881. It came with two outs in the bottom of the ninth inning of a game that Troy was losing to Worcester, 7–4. Connor, whose Troy team morphed into the New York Gothams (later the Giants) a year later, hit a ball out of the original Polo Grounds on September 11, 1886, thrilling fans so much that they passed a hat and collected enough money to buy him a gold watch. Connor ended his career in 1897 with 138 home runs— a record that lasted until Babe Ruth broke it on July 18, 1921.

Although he later spent 53 seasons as a manager, Connie Mack began his major league career as a light-hitting catcher with the Washington Nationals in 1886. He managed the Pittsburgh Pirates briefly, then took over the Philadelphia Athletics in the new AL in 1901. After hearing John McGraw disparage the idea of a team in Philadelphia (calling it a "white elephant"), Mack made the animal the team's symbol.

The Players League

Because the reserve clause kept salaries at low levels in the 1880s, law school graduate and Giants star John Montgomery Ward started a union called the Brotherhood of Professional Base Ball Players. Ward convinced teams to lift their salary ceilings after the 1888 season, but founded the Players League after owners reneged on their promises. Although the Players League attracted many of the game's top players and put franchises in seven of the eight NL cities, it lasted only one year after its backers bought into the NL.

The collapse of the Players League, coupled with the demise of the weakened American Association, left the NL with an unwieldy 12-club structure dissimilar to the one created by the second wave of expansion in 1969. The original 12-team format was not broken into divisions, thereby enabling a team to suffer the ignominy of a twelfth-place finish. Four NL teams were dropped after the 1899 campaign, restoring the league to eight members.

Long before establishing a reputation as a perennial doormat in the AL, Washington was just as bad in the NL. The team joined the eight-team league in 1886 and immediately finished last—60 games out of first place. It also finished last in both 1888 and 1889.

◇

In 1888, Cap Anson signed the longest contract ever given to a manager. After winning five NL pennants with the Chicago White Stockings from 1880 to 1886, Anson inked a 10-year deal to keep the job. During a base-ball career that started in 1871, Anson played for 27 seasons and managed for 19, creating concepts such as the pitching rotation, platooning, signals, and hit-and-run plays. The longtime first baseman finished with a .329 career batting average.

Frank Selee found Kid Nichols pitching at Omaha in 1889 and brought him to Boston when he became manager of the Red Stockings a year later. In a dozen Boston seasons, the durable control artist won 329 games, often winning 30 games and topping 400 innings pitched per year.

◇

Ed Barrow, best remembered as general manager of the Yankees during the Babe Ruth era, was also the man who discovered Honus Wagner. Barrow was a minor-league general manager scouting Wagner's older brother Butts when he found the shortstop in a Pennsylvania railroad-yard game in 1896.

Honus Wagner won eight batting titles, an NL record later tied by Tony Gwynn, en route to a .329 career mark. The star shortstop of the Pittsburgh Pirates topped .300 in 17 straight seasons and swiped 722 bases, leading the NL five different times.

(Baseball Hall of Fame)

Sound familiar? In 1896, New York Giants pitcher Amos Rusie sat out the entire season because the team attempted to deduct a $200 fine from his contract. A series of lawsuits eventually persuaded the league to cough up the $3,000 he had demanded.

Deadball Bits

The American League appeared for the first time in 1900 as the American Association. When the new circuit began, it announced goals of fostering honest competition without the reserve rule and supporting itself by luring big crowds with low prices and family-friendly ballparks. Created from the remains of the Western League, the AL changed its name on November 14, 1900, and announced a lineup that included Baltimore, Buffalo, Chicago, Cleveland, Detroit, Milwaukee, Philadelphia, and Washington. Playing a 140-game schedule with 14-man rosters, AL teams in both Chicago and Boston drew more fans than NL rivals in those cities.

◇

Joe McGinnity deserved his "Iron Man" nickname. On September 3, 1901, he pitched two complete games for Baltimore against Milwaukee, winning 10–0 and 6–1.

One of the most durable pitchers in baseball history, Joe McGinnity pitched and won three double headers in one month for the 1903 New York Giants. Called "Iron Man" because he once worked in his father-in-law's Oklahoma foundry, McGinnity won 246 games in the majors and more than 200 in the minors, where he lasted until age 54.

(Baseball Hall of Fame)

When the AL began play in 1901, it stole several top stars from NL clubs. The biggest was Napoleon Lajoie, who jumped from the Philadelphia Phillies to the Philadelphia Athletics on February 8, 1901. After hitting an AL-record .422 and winning the league's Triple Crown in his only year there, he was banned from playing in Pennsylvania by court order. The A's sent him to the Cleveland Indians, where he thrived for the rest of his Hall of Fame career. The team was even called the Cleveland Naps after he became its manager in 1905.

◇

Although his given name was George Edward, Rube Waddell earned his nickname because his eccentric behavior was even more pronounced than his curveball. The star pitcher of Connie Mack's Philadelphia A's early in the twentieth century, he was known for pausing during games to watch passing fire trucks—and sometimes chasing them.

A left-hander with a great fastball and colorful personality, Rube Waddell had four consecutive 20-win seasons for Connie Mack's Philadelphia Athletics during the Deadball Era. He also led the American League in strikeouts six straight times.

(Baseball Hall of Fame)

After a rocky coexistence during their first two years, the American and National Leagues agreed in 1903 to stop raiding each other's rosters and stage a postseason World Series. Although the first one, pitting Pittsburgh against Boston, was a success, it wasn't played in 1904 because New York Giants manager John McGraw refused to recognize the upstart AL by playing its champion.

◇

In 1904, the Yankees (then called the Highlanders) missed a chance to win their first pennant because pitching ace Jack Chesbro, seeking his record forty-second victory of the season, uncorked a two-out wild pitch in the ninth inning against the first-place Red Sox in an end-of-season double-header. A New York sweep would have won the pennant, but Boston won 3–2—and the second game was unnecessary.

◇

Cy Young symbolized durability. He had five 30-win seasons, topped 20 wins 15 times, and finished with 511 victories—nearly 100 more than runner-up Walter Johnson—and 316 losses (also a record). He won the Triple Crown of pitching in the AL's 1901 debut season, then pitched the Boston Pilgrims to the first World Series crown two years later.

Although the pitching distance was lengthened during his career, Cy Young didn't skip a beat. A master of control, he had more wins, losses, starts, innings pitched, and complete games than any other pitcher. The Ohio farm product pitched for the Cleveland Spiders, Cleveland Indians, Boston Red Sox, and Boston Braves.

(Baseball Hall of Fame)

Roger Bresnahan of the Giants invented shin guards in 1908 and introduced the first helmet, which he designed after a serious beaning in 1907. Bresnahan was a compact catcher who was versatile enough to play all nine positions during his 17-year sojourn in the majors.

◇

The Cubs got their only run in the Merkle game on an inside-the-park home run by Joe Tinker. The ball was played into a home run by Giants right fielder "Turkey" Mike Donlin, who was slow getting to it because of a leg injury. Had Tinker been held to two bases, the Giants might have won the game and the pennant.

Before Merkle's Boner

There was precedent to the 1908 game in which Fred Merkle failed to touch second base and was called out—nullifying a run, a sure victory for the New York Giants, and a probable pennant.

On September 4, the Cubs and Pirates—tied for second and one game behind the Giants—entered the bottom of the tenth scoreless in Pittsburgh. The Pirates had loaded the bases with two outs when Chief Wilson singled, apparently plating Fred Clarke with the winning run. But rookie Warren Gill, seeing Clarke score, ran directly from first base into the dugout without touching second. Evers called for the ball, touched second, and alerted umpire Hank O'Day. The umpire, working alone, had turned away from the action as soon as Clarke scored and did not see Evers' play. He refused to reverse his decision, and the NL denied the Cubs' protest. Had the New York papers published a more complete account of that game, Merkle might not have tempted fate again in almost the same situation.

By September 23—the date of the Merkle game—the Giants and Cubs were separated by percentage points with Pittsburgh one game out. Batting in the home ninth inning of a 1–1 tie against the Cubs, the Giants had Moose McCormick on first with two men out. Merkle singled, putting runners at the corners, and Al Bridwell ripped a liner past Evers. Fans swarmed the field, thinking the game was over—but Evers called for the ball. When center fielder Solly Hofman made a bad throw, Giants third-base coach Joe McGinnity grabbed it and threw it into the throng. But the determined Evers dived into the crowd to retrieve the ball, stepped on second, and appealed to base umpire Bob Emslie to call a forceout that would send the game into extra innings. Emslie said he missed the play but deferred to the home plate umpire, Hank O'Day. Remembering the Cubs' protest in Pittsburgh, O'Day had gone to the pitcher's mound to watch the action. He saw Merkle miss second and called him out, nullifying the winning run.

On October 4, a Pittsburgh win in Chicago would have clinched the NL flag. But the Cubs prevailed 5–2 to knock out the Pirates and give Chicago a 98–55 record—the same that the Giants posted after winning three makeup games against the Boston Braves. That created a one-game playoff at the Polo Grounds. Chicago won 4–2 behind the stalwart relief pitching of erstwhile starter Mordecai "Three Finger" Brown.

Because he was deprived of a sure victory by Merkle's Boner, Christy Mathewson had to settle for a tie in career victories with Grover Cleveland Alexander, but still holds NL records for wins in a season (37) and career (373). The soft-spoken Bucknell graduate had four 30-win seasons and a streak of 68 straight innings without yielding a walk.

Addie Joss had four straight 20-win seasons for Cleveland while compiling a career ERA of 1.89, second only to Ed Walsh. An off-season sportswriter in Toledo, Joss was just 31 when he died of meningitis early in the 1911 season.

(Baseball Hall of Fame)

A wild pitch once chilled the Chicago White Sox in the heat of a pennant race. On October 2, 1908, with the Sox fighting Cleveland and Detroit for the pennant, 40-game winner Ed Walsh pitched a four-hitter and struck out 15—but his two-strike, two-out spitball in the third broke off the glove of catcher Ossie Schreckengost and allowed a runner to score. Cleveland's Addie Joss pitched a perfect game to win 1–0.

◇

Because the Polo Grounds' clubhouses were located under the scoreboard in deep center field, players had long walks—and often had to run for their lives—when hostile fans swarmed the diamond. After the Cubs won the 1908 NL pennant by beating the Giants in New York, Chicago players Joe Tinker, Frank Chance, and Jack Pfiester were injured in altercations with angry fans. Chance, hit in the throat, lost his voice for several days while Pfiester suffered a knife wound in his shoulder.

Walter Johnson was called "The Big Train" because his fastball was reputed to match the speed of the fastest locomotive in the early 1900s. Johnson started his career in 1907 and won 416 games, second only to Cy Young on the lifetime list. He would have won many more with better support, but he usually had bad teams behind him. Johnson, who pitched exclusively for Washington, had to end his 21-year career after breaking his ankle during spring training batting practice in 1928.

Walter Johnson's 20-year tenure with the Senators started in 1907. Johnson pitched in the 1924 and 1925 World Series, winning his (and Washington's) only world championship in 1924.
(Baseball Hall of Fame)

The third baseman in Connie Mack's "$100,000 Infield," Frank "Home Run" Baker acquired his famous nickname by homering in consecutive World Series games against Rube Marquard and Christy Mathewson in 1911.

◇

Ty Cobb won his only Triple Crown in 1909 by leading the league in hitting, home runs, and runs batted in (RBI). Three years earlier, when Cobb became a regular in the Tigers outfield, he started a streak of 23 consecutive .300 campaigns.

Because he played most of his games in Detroit, Ty Cobb made frequent use of this team-issued sweater. It certainly kept his bat hot. Cobb was such a luminary that his team was called the "Ty-gers" in his honor.

(Baseball Hall of Fame)

Before June 26, 1916, fans had to identify the players without the benefit of a scorecard. That changed when the Cleveland Indians took the field for a game against the White Sox and wore numbers on their sleeves. Although the experiment was short-lived, the Yankees became the first club to wear numbers permanently 13 years later.

CHAPTER

2

Ball Clubs

Even before the advent of the American League (AL) in 1901 marked the dawn of baseball's modern era, teams were created by a combination of scouting, coaching, signing, and trading. In a year-round competition with league rivals, managers, general managers, and owners used all the resources they had—especially money—in an effort to put together teams that could win.

Teams in major markets—such as the New York Yankees—or teams with magnanimous ownership—including the Boston Red Sox—had an advantage over small-market rivals that still persists today. The era of free agency accelerated the process, because teams with the most money offered veteran stars the most incentives and were able to land more than their share of top-tier players.

On the other hand, winning still requires a dose of good fortune. Hot rookies, cold veterans, or unanticipated injuries can change pennant races in a hurry. Weather, umpiring, and the vagaries of the various ballparks play major roles, too.

Some teams are memorable. The 1906 Chicago Cubs went 116–36, yielding a record .763 winning percentage while posting a 1.76 ERA. The 2001 Seattle Mariners matched that win total but did it during the 162-game schedule. The 1954 Cleveland Indians won 111—the most by an AL club in the days of the 154-game format. Amazingly, none of those teams followed their record regular seasons with a world championship.

Bad ball clubs also have a legacy. Only a last-week spurt helped the 2003 Detroit Tigers avoid tying or beating a 41-year-old record for futility. The original New York Mets of 1962 won 40, lost 120, and finished 60½ games out of first place. They never even bothered to make up two rainouts.

Only one team was worse. The 1899 Cleveland Spiders won 20, lost 134, had a .130 "winning" percentage, lost 24 games *in a row*, and finished a mind-boggling 84 games behind the Brooklyn Superbas in an NL that then consisted of 12 clubs and no divisions. Caught in a web of political maneuvering, the Spiders vanished in 1900 along with three other NL clubs—but Cleveland, Washington, and Baltimore returned as members of the new AL.

Like players, teams have a tendency to move around. New York City had three teams for years, then had one, and now has two. Washington has had three different teams—two called the Senators—but never at the same time. The Braves and Athletics twice found greener pastures, with the former moving from Boston to Milwaukee to Atlanta and the latter migrating from Philadelphia to Kansas City to Oakland.

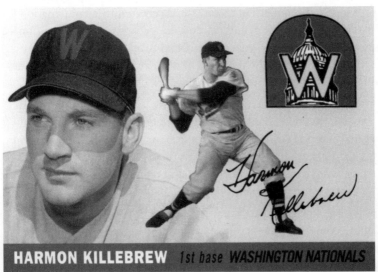

HARMON KILLEBREW 1st base *WASHINGTON NATIONALS*

Hall of Famer Harmon Killebrew won his first home run crown with the Washington Senators and five more for the same franchise after it became the Minnesota Twins in 1961.
(The Topps Company)

The baseball map has had a myriad of other moves, too. Just since the Braves went to Wisconsin, the St. Louis Browns became the Baltimore Orioles; the Philadelphia A's moved to Kansas City and then Oakland;

and the New York Giants and Brooklyn Dodgers—archrivals—went west together to San Francisco and Los Angeles, respectively. That wasn't all. The Washington Senators transferred to Minneapolis–St. Paul as the Minnesota Twins, leaving behind a second-edition Senators expansion team that later became the Texas Rangers. The Seattle Pilots, another expansion team, lasted only a season before moving to Milwaukee as the Brewers—filling the void created when the Braves moved to Atlanta. The Brewers made a different type of move, crossing league lines to accommodate the latest wave of expansion in 1998.

To fight the challenge of Branch Rickey's Continental League, new teams popped up in several proposed Rickey cities, including New York (Mets), Houston (Colts), and Denver (Colorado Rockies). Expansion also added the Los Angeles Angels, Montreal Expos (now the Washington Nationals), Toronto Blue Jays, Kansas City Royals, San Diego Padres, Seattle Mariners, Florida Marlins, Tampa Bay Devil Rays, and Arizona Diamondbacks.

All teams have two goals: winning the pennant and winning the World Series. Both became tougher after Major League Baseball (MLB) split the leagues into divisions, creating scheduled playoffs to determine World Series opponents.

Team Bits

Hoping to spread international goodwill, teams of major-league players, coaches, and managers made world tours in 1874, 1888–1889, 1913–1914, 1924, 1931, and 1934.

◇

Brooklyn has had teams in eight different leagues, starting with the Atlantic League in 1861. Brooklyn was in the National Association in 1871, the Interstate League in 1883, the American Association in 1884, the National League and the Players League in 1890, and the Federal League in 1914. The current Brooklyn Cyclones joined the New York–Penn League in 2001 as a farm team of the New York Mets.

◇

The Dodgers nickname is a shortened version of Trolley Dodgers, a reference to denizens of Brooklyn early in the twentieth century. When Ned Hanlon managed the pennant-winning Brooklyn team of 1900, the team was also known as Hanlon's Superbas after a turn-of-the-century acrobat act featuring the Hanlon brothers.

Baltimore had a big-league team long before the St. Louis Browns moved there in 1954. The first Baltimore Orioles played in the NL from 1892–1899, then had a short-lived franchise in the embryonic AL for its first two seasons, 1901 and 1902.

◇

Although the 1906 White Sox were known as the "Hitless Wonders" for their ability to win with pitching, speed, and defense, the 1908 White Sox were even more powerless. They hit only *three* home runs during the entire season, yet finished a game and a half out of first place.

◇

The 1911 New York Giants carved a niche in the record books by scoring 10 first-inning runs before any outs were recorded. It happened during a May 13 game against the St. Louis Cardinals. The Giants won 19–5 with Rube Marquard fanning more men in a regular-season relief role than any pitcher before or since (14 in eight innings).

◇

The Boston Braves of 1914, 11½ games out of first place in July, won the 1914 NL flag by 10 games and swept the favored Philadelphia Athletics in the World Series. Historians still wonder how "Boston's Miracle Braves" won after finishing 31½ games behind the previous year.

◇

The Giants twice retired jerseys without retiring numbers. Neither Christy Mathewson, the team's star pitcher early in the twentieth century, nor longtime manager John McGraw wore numbers during the time they were active with the team.

◇

The 1916 New York Giants won a record 26 games in a row. The only other teams to win at least 20 in succession were the 1935 Chicago Cubs (21) and the 2002 Oakland Athletics (20).

◇

After the Chicago White Sox won the 1917 World Series, they went 88 years without winning another.

◇

The year 1919, although best known for the Black Sox Scandal that gave Cincinnati a tainted world championship, was also the year when things went south for the Philadelphia Phillies. During a 27-year stretch that started in 1919, the Phillies finished last or next to last 23 times under 16 different managers. One of them, Doc Prothro, was a practicing dentist who later fathered National Football League (NFL) head coach Tommy Prothro.

The only triple header in baseball history was played on October 2, 1920. The Cincinnati Reds beat the Pittsburgh Pirates in the first two games, but the Pirates won the finale—called after six innings because of darkness.

◊

The St. Louis Browns once scored six two-out runs in the ninth *after the umpire called the game-ending out.* It happened on May 20, 1922, when the Browns were playing the Yankees at the Polo Grounds. New York led 2–1 when the Browns exploded for a seven-run rally and won 8–2. The last six runs were scored after a decision by first-base umpire Ollie Chill was reversed.

◊

The Chicago Cubs beat the Philadelphia Phillies 26–23 in a game at wind-blown Wrigley Field on August 25, 1922. The combined total of 49 runs remains a major league record.

◊

Playing at Shibe Park on June 15, 1925, the Philadelphia Athletics beat the Cleveland Indians 17–15 by scoring *13 runs* in the bottom of the eighth.

◊

The New York Yankees started their domination of the AL in the 1920s, winning 27 pennants in 42 years from 1923 to 1964.

With Babe Ruth and Lou Gehrig anchoring the third and fourth spots in their batting order, the 1927 Yankees stormed through the AL and smothered the Pittsburgh Pirates in the World Series. Because their bats struck so suddenly, rivals referred to their lineup as "Murderer's Row"— borrowing the name from a notorious New York prison where killers were kept.

(American League)

The St. Louis Cardinals once had two 10-run innings in the same game. It happened in the second game of a double header on July 6, 1929, when they hit the 10 spot in the first and fifth frames en route to a 28–6 win over the Philadelphia Phillies. No other NL team has ever scored that many runs in a game.

◇

The 1935 St. Louis Browns had a *season attendance* of 88,113—smaller than the size of the crowd that attended a "Roy Campanella Night" exhibition game at the Los Angeles Coliseum in 1959.

◇

The 1937 Brooklyn Dodgers showed their colors by switching from blue to green caps, socks, and shirtsleeves. They also switched from gray to tan uniforms on the road. The changes didn't prevent the team from finishing sixth in an eight-team league.

◇

The 1938 Pittsburgh Pirates had such a late-August lead over the Chicago Cubs that they expanded their press box, expecting a crowd for the World Series. But the Cubs won 30 of their final 42 while the Pirates barely treaded water at 20–24. The turning point came in the final week when the Cubs swept a series from Pittsburgh at Wrigley Field. The key blow came in the middle game on September 28, which began with the Cubs trailing by a half game. Pittsburgh blew a 5–3 lead, allowing two Cub runs in the eighth and another in the ninth—on a home run by Chicago player-manager Gabby Hartnett just before the game would've been stopped by darkness. With two outs and two strikes, Hartnett homered to left, knocking the Pirates out of first place for the first time since July 11. They never regained the top rung, thanks in part to the so-called "Homer in the Gloamin'." Pittsburgh had led the NL race by seven games as late as September 1.

◇

Defending their 1941 NL crown, Brooklyn led St. Louis by 9½ games on August 15 and won 25 of their remaining 42 games, including the final eight. But the Cardinals were already rolling, well into a streak that gave them 43 wins in their final 52 games. That left St. Louis in first place at season's end by two games.

◇

When White Sox pitcher Ted Lyons pitched for a Navy team in Guam during World War II, his first game was against an Army team anchored by Joe DiMaggio. "I left the country to get away from DiMaggio," Lyons quipped, "but here he is!"

With many top players in wartime military units, Cubs owner Phil Wrigley created the All-American Girls Professional Baseball League in 1943. The league, which drew a million fans one season, lasted until 1954 and inspired the movie *A League of Their Own*.

Teams showed their patriotism during World War II by admitting uniformed servicemen free.
(Cincinnati Reds)

◇

The St. Louis Browns won their only AL pennant in 1944, finishing one game over Detroit and six over New York. The Browns finished strong, winning four straight from the Yankees, but went into the final day tied with Detroit. Last-place Washington topped Tigers titan Dizzy Trout (27–14) as the Browns wrapped up the Yankees series and the pennant. An overall poor quality of play helped the Browns win; a dozen of their own players had been rejected by draft boards as unfit for military service.

◇

Hank Greenberg, just back from a four-year military tour, cracked a ninth-inning grand slam in the opener of a double header against the Browns to clinch the 1945 pennant for Detroit. Had the Tigers dropped both games, they would have had a one-game playoff against Washington.

◇

Thinking they would improve nighttime visibility for fans under the primitive lighting systems then in use, the Boston Braves tried satin jerseys in 1948.

Although the St. Louis Browns won only one pennant, facing the cross-town Cardinals while rosters were depleted by wartime military assign-ments in 1944, they gave their fans many moments to remember.

(Ronnie Joyner)

Both the owner and the manager of the world champion Cleveland Indians of 1948 were younger than some of the players. Owner Bill Veeck was 32 and player-manager Lou Boudreau was 30.

◇

The St. Louis Cardinals, the first team with a farm system, once had 33 Minor League affiliates.

◇

For three years in succession, the Brooklyn Dodgers and the Philadelphia Phillies hooked up for pennant-deciding battles in the final days of the season. In 1949, the Cardinals beat the Cubs and would have tied for the pennant if Philadelphia had beaten Brooklyn. During the next season, the Philadelphia Whiz Kids frittered away a big lead. In the decisive final game, Richie Ashburn's ninth-inning throw nipped Cal Abrams at the plate, sending the game against Brooklyn into the tenth inning and set-ting the stage for the Dick Sisler home run that won the pennant for the Phillies. Had the Dodgers won the season-ending game, the Phillies and the Dodgers would have needed a playoff. Dodgers manager Burt Shotton, criticized for not replacing Abrams (a poor baserunner), was dropped that winter. In 1951, Jackie Robinson's extra-inning homer for Brooklyn beat the Phillies and sent the Dodgers to their famous three-game playoff with the Giants.

Duke Snider (second from right) relaxes on the Dodger bench before a 1954 game against the Milwaukee Braves. The Duke of Flatbush was the leader of the "Boys of Summer" team that won NL pennants in 1952, 1953, and 1956 plus Brooklyn's only world title in 1955.

(Milwaukee Sentinel)

When the St. Louis Browns became the Baltimore Orioles in 1954, the new owners threw the old uniforms out on the street.

Why Whiz Kids Won

The 1950 Philadelphia Phillies had an average age of $26\frac{1}{2}$ but wouldn't have won anything without workhorse reliever Jim Konstanty. At age 33, he led the league with 74 appearances (then a record) and finished with a 16–7 mark, 22 saves, and a 2.66 ERA. After the World Series, which the Whiz Kids lost to the Yankees, Konstanty became the first reliever to be voted Most Valuable Player in his league.

The 1950 New York Giants finished third—five games behind Philadelphia—but couldn't get untracked in 1951. After winning their opener, they lost 11 straight and seemed dead. As late as August 11, the Giants trailed the Dodgers by 13½ games. But the performance of rookie Willie Mays, the transfer of Bobby Thomson to third base, and the leadership of Leo Durocher produced a sudden turnaround. New York went 39–8 down the stretch while the Dodgers plodded along at .500 and almost blew the pennant *without* a playoff.

Dandy Dodger Decoy

On the last day of the 1951 season, with the Brooklyn Dodgers desperate to stave off the charging New York Giants, the Philadelphia Phillies played host to the Dodgers. The game was tied in the eleventh, but Phillies pitcher Robin Roberts represented the winning run at third base. Eddie Waitkus slapped a liner up the middle that Jackie Robinson appeared to reach with a lunging dive. But did he? Not according to Roberts, who had a clear view of the play. "Running in, I could see it," Roberts remembered. "It appeared to me that he trapped the ball. As he rolled, he tried to throw it to second for a force—and he threw it behind Pee Wee Reese. It wasn't even close. In my mind, the game was over when I touched home. Then I saw my team running out on the field. (Umpire) Lon Warneke said Jackie had caught it." Three innings later, Robinson won the game for Brooklyn with a home run, setting up the three-game playoff ended by Bobby Thomson's "Shot Heard 'Round the World."

The 1954 Yankees won 103 games but finished eight games behind front-running Cleveland.

◇

Needing a partner to join him on the West Coast, Dodgers owner Walter O'Malley convinced Giants owner Horace Stoneham that California would not only prolong the Dodgers-Giants rivalry but would also provide greener pastures for both teams. The Brooklyn Dodgers and New York Giants played their final seasons in 1957.

The 1960 Chicago White Sox, owned by the innovative Bill Veeck, were the first team to wear their names on the backs of their jerseys.

◇

The best record ever compiled by an expansion team in its first season was a 70–91 record by the 1961 Los Angeles Angels.

The Go-Go Sox

The 1959 Chicago White Sox ended a string of four straight Yankees pennants by blending speed, defense, and a potent bullpen. Called the "Go-Go Sox" because Comiskey Park fans yelled "Go! Go!" when one of their speedsters reached base, the White Sox led the AL in triples, stolen bases, ERA, and saves.

Three of the fourteen expansion teams in baseball history later relocated to other cities: the 1961 Washington Senators, who became the Texas Rangers in 1972; the 1969 Seattle Pilots, who became the Milwaukee Brewers in 1970; and the 1969 Montreal Expos, who became the Washington Nationals in 2005.

◇

The .250 winning percentage of the 1962 New York Mets was 11 points lower than the composite NL *batting average* that year.

◇

With ace southpaw Sandy Koufax idled for the season with a finger circulatory ailment diagnosed in July, the 1962 Los Angeles Dodgers couldn't hold off the September surge of the San Francisco Giants. Los Angeles dropped 6 of its last 7 and 10 of 13 to force a rerun of the best-of-three pennant playoff they had lost to the Giants 11 years earlier. History then repeated itself. After losing the first game and winning the second, the Dodgers had a 4–2 lead in the final inning of the finale when the Giants erupted for four runs.

◇

The 1965 Milwaukee Braves set an NL record when six players hit at least 20 homers: Hank Aaron, Eddie Mathews, Joe Torre, Felipe Alou, Mack Jones, and Gene Oliver.

When he broke in with the 1952 Boston Braves, Eddie Mathews had no idea he would be the only man to play for the same team in three different cities. He moved to Milwaukee with the Braves in 1953 and went to Atlanta when the Braves headed south in 1966.

(Atlanta Braves)

Collapse of the Phillies

Three years after their record 23-game losing streak left them with a record of 47–107 and a 46-game deficit in the standings, the 1964 Phillies parlayed a youth infusion and a few shrewd trades into a pennant-contending club. Seeking their first NL flag since 1950, the Phillies compiled a 6½ game lead with 12 games to go. But manager Gene Mauch, overworking pitching aces Jim Bunning and Chris Short, watched his team drop 10 straight—including a crucial three-game series to the suddenly awake Cardinals and Reds. On October 1, the Cards—fueled by an eight-game winning streak—led Cincinnati by a half game and the Phillies by two and a half. But the hapless Mets knocked off St. Louis 1–0 and 15–5 on successive days while the Phillies won one game from the Reds, 4–3. That left St. Louis tied with Cincinnati and one game ahead of Philadelphia with a single day left on the schedule. The Phillies beat the Reds again, 10–0, but St. Louis beat the Mets. Had the Cardinals lost, all three would have wound up with identical 92–70 marks—forcing the first three-team playoff in baseball history.

Before the 1965 Milwaukee Braves moved to Atlanta, their largest public stockholder was a local automobile dealer named Bud Selig.

◇

With a magic number of "1" on the last day of the 1966 season, the Los Angeles Dodgers were forced to use star southpaw Sandy Koufax. Either a win by the Dodgers in either game of a doubleheader with the Phillies or a loss by the Giants against the Pirates would give the pennant to the Phillies. Koufax settled matters quickly. In what would be his last regular season start, he won the game.

◇

Many historians believe that baseball's best pennant race occurred in 1967, when the Boston Red Sox finished one game ahead of the Minnesota Twins and Detroit Tigers (who tied for second), and three ahead of the Chicago White Sox. Under rookie manager Dick Williams, the Sox overcame 100 to 1 odds to ride from ninth in the 10-team league the year before to pennant winners, clinching on the final day. Boston's run was dubbed "The Impossible Dream" after a hit song from *Man of La Mancha*, a popular musical that made its debut the same year.

The Miracle Mets

In August 1969, the Chicago Cubs looked like shoo-ins for a divisional title. They had hitting, defense, and a 9½-game lead. But they couldn't match the young pitching or determination of the New York Mets. Riding the pitching prowess of Tom Seaver and Jerry Koosman, the upstart Mets narrowed the Chicago lead to 2½ games on September 8, when the slumping Cubs came to Shea Stadium for a two-game series. The Mets won both, moved into first place the following day, and romped down the stretch to finish with 100 wins and an eight-game lead in the new NL East (divisional play began in 1969). The 1969 "Miracle Mets" were certainly a surprise. The 1962 expansion team had never finished better than ninth in a 10-team league, and were 24 games out of first place the previous season.

Both the 1967 Boston Red Sox and the 1969 New York Mets won the pennant after finishing ninth in a 10-team league the year before.

◇

A 1972 gold pass prepared by the AL for "The President and His Party" was never used by Richard Nixon because the Washington Senators became the Texas Rangers.

Although the Pittsburgh Pirates powered their way to world championships both times they reached the World Series—against the Baltimore Orioles in 1971 and 1979—they lost the NL Championship Series four times in between. Cincinnati, which advanced to the Fall Classic four times, and Pittsburgh were the only major-league teams that managed six first-place finishes during the decade of the '70s.

Blanket Statement

Five of the six clubs in the 1973 NL East were so tightly bunched in the final week that Phillies manager Danny Ozark said, "You could put a blanket over the whole bunch." With four days left in the season, there was even a chance that all five could finish with identical 80–82 records. The standings at that point were as follows:

Team	W	L	PCT	GB
New York	80	78	.506	–
Pittsburgh	79	79	.500	1
St. Louis	78	81	.491	2½
Montreal	77	82	.484	3½
Chicago	76	82	.481	4

Remaining games: New York (4) all at Chicago; Pittsburgh (4) three vs. Montreal and a one-game makeup vs. San Diego if needed; St. Louis (3) all vs. Philadelphia; Chicago (4) all vs. New York; Montreal (3) all at Pittsburgh.

Resolution: The need for a playoff never developed. With a 6–4 win over the Cubs on the final day, the Mets clinched the title with an 82–79 record and .509 percentage—the lowest ever recorded by a championship club. Although one of their Chicago dates was cancelled by rain, they finished 1½ games ahead of St. Louis, 2½ ahead of Pittsburgh, 3½ ahead of Montreal, and 5 up on the Cubs. They went on to beat the favored Reds in the NLCS and took the A's a full seven games in the 1973 World Series before bowing. One of the great comeback teams in baseball history, the Mets had been last in the division and 12 games behind on July 8 before rebounding to win.

The 1974 Atlanta Braves, hoping that Hank Aaron would break Babe Ruth's home run record at home, planned to keep the slugger benched during a season-opening three-game series in Cincinnati. Commissioner Bowie Kuhn intervened, ordering manager Eddie Mathews to use Aaron in the same manner that he normally would during the season. As a result, Aaron tied Ruth's record in the first inning of the first game—connecting against Jack Billingham—but did not start the second game. Aaron returned to the lineup for the Sunday game, and the Braves held their breath—rooting *against* Aaron's chances of hitting a home run. When the team came home on Monday, Aaron broke the record in the fourth inning against Al Downing of the Los Angeles Dodgers.

◇

The Chicago White Sox were the only team to hold Hank Aaron homerless. He faced the Chisox only in his last two seasons, which he spent as a designated hitter for the Milwaukee Brewers.

◇

Boston blew a probable pennant in 1978. On July 17, the Red Sox owned a 14-game lead over the New York Yankees, but fortunes quickly changed. A series of injuries slowed the Hub's pennant express to a crawl while the Yankees regrouped under low-key manager Bob Lemon, who replaced Billy Martin on July 25. The teams ended the season tied, forcing a one-game playoff at Fenway Park that was the first divisional playoff game in baseball history. Bucky Dent's three-run homer was the difference in a 5–4 Yankees victory. The Yanks went on to win both the ALCS and the World Series.

◇

Although both were best known for their exploits with other teams, Reggie Jackson and Mark McGwire once held the Oakland club record for home runs.

◇

The 1982 New York Yankees had to defend not only their AL pennant but the mercurial moves of their owner. George Steinbrenner employed five different pitching coaches, four different hitting coaches, and three different managers.

◇

There were several surprise champions in 1982. The Milwaukee Brewers won their first AL East crown after beating Baltimore on the final day of the season, while the Atlanta Braves won their first divisional title since 1969, also on the last day of the season. The Braves, under new manager Joe Torre, had won 13 straight at the outset—a feat duplicated by the Brewers five years later.

The 1984 Detroit Tigers never gave rivals a chance. They went 35–5 to open the season, finished with 104 wins, and went 7–1 in postseason play against the Kansas City Royals and San Diego Padres.

◇

The Houston Astros clinched the 1986 NL West flag with a no-hitter by Mike Scott. It was the only time a team clinched a title with a no-hit game.

◇

Firing the manager does not always help. The 1988 Baltimore Orioles lost their first 21 games, even after Frank Robinson replaced Cal Ripken Sr. at the helm six games into the streak. Not surprisingly, the team lost 107 games thanks primarily to the pathetic start—the worst record in baseball history.

◇

The Oakland A's (Dave Stewart) and Los Angeles Dodgers (Fernando Valenzuela) were the only teams to win no-hit games on the same day: June 29, 1990.

◇

Broadcaster Jack Brickhouse once said of the Chicago Cubs, "Anybody can have a bad century."

Worst to First

Before two teams did it during the 1991 season, no major league club had vaulted from last place one season to first place the next. But six teams did it in the 1990s, with free agency being the great equalizer that allowed bad ball clubs to rebuild in a hurry. The worst-to-first Braves of 1991, for example, had the worst record in the majors (65–97) the year before jumping to the head of the pack with a 94–68 mark. Teams that wound up in first place a year after finishing last:

Atlanta Braves, 1991
Minnesota Twins, 1991
Philadelphia Phillies, 1993
San Francisco Giants, 1997
San Diego Padres, 1998
Arizona Diamondbacks, 1999
Arizona Diamondbacks, 2007
Colorado Rockies, 2007
Chicago Cubs, 2007

The 1991 Toronto Blue Jays were the first team in any sport to top 4 million in attendance.

In 1993, the last year before baseball initiated a three-division format that featured wild card winners, the game enjoyed its last pure title chase. The Braves, powered by the midyear arrival of slugger Fred McGriff, overcame a 10-game deficit in the NL West to finish with 104 wins. The Giants, last-day losers, won 103 and went home for the winter. Had it existed at the time, the wild card would have destroyed the daily suspense, because both teams would have advanced to the postseason.

With Pedro Martinez and John Wetteland on the mound and Larry Walker, Moises Alou, and Marquis Grissom at the plate, the 1994 Montreal Expos seemed well on their way to their first pennant when the season was suspended by a player strike. When play stopped, the team led the majors with a .649 winning percentage and 74–40, six games better than the Atlanta Braves in the NL East. By the end of the 234-day strike, financial realities set in. Wetteland went to the Yankees, Walker to the Rockies, Grissom to the Braves, and good times went out the window.

Before they became the Washington Nationals, the Montreal Expos retired uniform numbers worn by Gary Carter, Andre Dawson, Tim Raines, and Rusty Staub.

Although they opened the decade with a last-place finish, the Atlanta Braves won 74 more games during the 1990s than any other club. They were also the only team to take five pennants during the decade.

The Cincinnati Reds postponed their opener on April 1, 1996, after home plate umpire Larry McSherry, starting his twenty-sixth season, suffered a fatal heart attack seven pitches into the game.

Mike Piazza, who won All-Star Game MVP honors while representing the Los Angeles Dodgers when the 1996 game was played in Philadelphia, often attended Phillies games at Veterans Stadium during his youth in the 1970s. His dad had season tickets.

◊

Although the Kingdome was a covered ballpark, it rained home runs in Seattle during the 1997 season. The Mariners smacked 264 home runs— a major league record.

The 1998 Yankees clinched a playoff berth earlier than any other team (August 29) and reached 100 wins sooner (September 4). With 66 more wins than losses, the 1998 Yanks also tied the club record held by Babe Ruth's 1927 team. Their 22-game margin over the second-place Boston Red Sox in the AL East was the biggest in league history and second only to the 1902 Pittsburgh Pirates, who finished 27½ games ahead of the Brooklyn Dodgers.

◇

The Arizona Diamondbacks, a 1998 NL expansion team, went 65–97 in their first year, but 100–62 in their second for a reversal of fortune. Although their 35-game turnaround was the best in baseball history, they couldn't get by the New York Mets in the first round of the playoffs.

◇

Between 1996 (when Derek Jeter became a regular) and 2007, the Yankees sold 38 million tickets—more than the entire population of Canada.

◇

The only team to play in four different divisions was the Milwaukee Brewers. In their one-year incarnation as the Seattle Pilots in 1969, they were in the AL West. After they moved to Milwaukee, they were placed in the AL East. When the leagues adopted a three-division format in 1995, the Brewers bounced to the AL Central. Three years later, Milwaukee became the first team of the modern era to switch leagues, moving to the NL Central when the NL needed a second team to pair with the expansion Arizona Diamondbacks. Another expansion team, the Tampa Bay Devil Rays, took the spot vacated by the Brewers in the AL. Even though that left the AL with 14 teams and the NL with 16, the moves made scheduling easier because both leagues had an even number of teams.

◇

When the Cleveland Indians beat the Seattle Mariners 15–14 on August 5, 2001, it marked the third time a team overcame a deficit of at least 12 runs. Although there were 40 hits and 29 runs in the game, Ichiro Suzuki failed to score, Bret Boone failed to drive in a run, and Robbie Alomar got no hits. When the game started, Ichiro led the majors in runs scored, Boone led the AL in RBI, and Alomar was the league's leading hitter.

◇

The 2001 Atlanta Braves, with a magic number of "1," were so determined to clinch the NL East title on October 5 that they exploded for 10 runs in the first inning en route to a 20–3 win over the Florida Marlins.

A three-way ownership trade left the 2002 Montreal Expos orphans, operated by the other 29 clubs under the aegis of Major League Baseball. The situation was created when Jeffrey Loria, the New York art dealer who had owned the Expos, bought the Florida Marlins after Florida owner John Henry became the principal owner of the Boston Red Sox. The Expos, drawing few fans to much-maligned Olympic Stadium, played 22 "home games" in San Juan, Puerto Rico, in their final two years (2003 and 2004), lasting only three seasons under MLB ownership before becoming the Washington Nationals.

◇

After spending their first 10 years apologizing for the frequency of high-scoring games in Denver, the 2002 Colorado Rockies introduced a $15,000 humidor designed to keep baseballs from shrinking, hardening, and losing friction because of the thin air in the Mile High City. Temperature control devices were also mandated for the other 29 clubs by Major League Baseball, which added a directive that game balls must be from the current year only. Baseball officials said the move was made to keep all balls in line with the specifications of the manufacturer, Rawlings Sporting Goods.

◇

Rain once erased seven home runs in one game. It happened on May 11, 2003, when the St. Louis Cardinals were playing the Chicago Cubs at Wrigley Field. With a 23-mph wind blowing out to right, Moises Alou (Cubs) homered in the bottom of the first. Albert Pujols (Cardinals) hit a grand slam in the second before Corey Patterson (Cubs) led off the home second with a home run. Tino Martinez (Cardinals) connected in the third, as did Troy O'Leary (Cubs). Martinez hit another in the fourth with two men on, but Alex Gonzalez (Cubs) answered in the same frame with a two-run shot. Then it rained in the top of the fifth, negating the 11–9 St. Louis lead and all player records from the game.

◇

When rain wiped out an interleague game between the Mets and Yankees on June 21, 2003, the teams agreed to make it up with a day-night double header *that used both ballparks* a week later.

◇

In addition to those played by Canada-based teams, big-league games outside the United States since 1996 have been played in Las Vegas, Mexico, Hawaii, Japan, and Puerto Rico. Teams opened the season in Tokyo twice: in 2000 (Cubs vs. Mets) and 2004 (Yankees vs. Devil Rays).

When snow prevented play in Jacobs Field, an open-air park, the Cleveland Indians moved an April 2007 series against the Los Angeles Angels of Anaheim to Milwaukee's Miller Park, a domed stadium unoccupied because the Brewers were on the road.

◇

Although the Orioles spent millions on free-agent relievers prior to the 2007 season, the Baltimore bullpen combined to allow 53 earned runs over an eight-game stretch in August. That was the worst performance of any relief corps in baseball history, topping the eight-game mark of 47 earned runs yielded by the 1928 Philadelphia Phillies.

Looney Linescore

				R	H	E
Texas	0 0 0	5 0 9	0 10 6	30	29	1
Baltimore	1 0 2	0 0 0	0 0 0	3	9	1

In Baltimore on August 22, 2007, the Texas Rangers set a modern-day mark with 30 runs in a game, topping 29-run games by the Boston Red Sox and Chicago White Sox. Although eight previous teams scored at least 30 times in a game, no team did it since June 28, 1897, when Chicago routed Louisville 36–7 in an NL game. Marlon Byrd and Travis Metcalf had grand slams, while Jarrod Saltalamacchia and Ramon Vasquez both had two-homer games and seven RBI.

The Tampa Bay Devil Rays and Texas Rangers played a three-game series at Disney's Wide World of Sports in May 2007. The Rangers had averaged 8,000 fans per game at Tropicana Field, and the Devil Rays—eager to expand their fan base—were confident they could fill Disney's 11,000-seat stadium, which stands in Lake Buena Vista, 90 minutes east of St. Petersburg.

◇

Although they were en route to their first playoff appearance in 14 years, the 2007 Philadelphia Phillies became the first team to lose 10,000 games.

◇

The 2007 Washington Nationals failed to score a first inning run in April.

Hawaii native Shane Victorino hit a game-winning home run for the Phillies on the same night that his team gave away a Shane Victorino hula doll—complete with grass skirt and bare feet.

The Tie That Binds

There has never been a three-way tie in baseball history. But that doesn't mean teams didn't come close. Heading into the last day of the 2007 season, four teams could have finished with identical 89–73 records—forcing two extra playoff games before the *scheduled* playoffs.

These were the standings:

National League East	W	L	PCT	GB
Philadelphia Phillies	88	73	.547	–
New York Mets	88	73	.547	–
National League Wild Card	**W**	**L**	**PCT**	**GB**
San Diego Padres	89	72	.553	–
Colorado Rockies	88	73	.547	1
Philadelphia Phillies	88	73	.547	1
New York Mets	88	73	.547	1

The Mets hosted the last-place Florida Marlins while the Phillies hosted the Washington Nationals. In the wild card race, the Padres were on the road against the Milwaukee Brewers and the Rockies were home against the Arizona Diamondbacks. If the Mets, Phillies, and Rockies had won and the Padres lost, all four clubs would have been 89–73—forcing a Mets-Phillies playoff for the NL East title and a Rockies-Padres playoff for the wild card. As it turned out, the Phillies and Rockies won and the Mets and Padres lost, eliminating the Mets but forcing a Rockies-Padres showdown for the wild card. Colorado won, 9–8 in 13 innings, and advanced to the NL Division Series against Philadelphia.

The 2007 New York Mets managed the biggest September collapse in baseball history. Ahead by seven games with 17 to play, they finished one game behind the Philadelphia Phillies in the NL East. The Mets occupied first place in the NL East from May 16 until September 28, regained a tie on September 29, then lost on the last day of the season. The Mets went 5–12 down the stretch while the Phillies went 13–4 over the same span.

The Alaska Goldpanners, a semi-pro team comprised of collegians with promise, play a Midnight Sun game every June on the date of the summer solstice—the longest day of the year. Because of its northerly location and the fact that the summer sun never sets in Fairbanks, the team starts its Midnight Sun game at 10:30 and plays without lights. Past participants in the Midnight Sun game included Tom Seaver, Dave Winfield, and Barry Bonds.

◇

The San Diego Padres were one strike away from clinching the NL West title on September 29, 2007. But Tony Gwynn Jr.—son of the longtime San Diego standout—tripled in the tying run in a game his Brewers eventually won. That kept the Padres lead at a game over the Colorado Rockies but left their magic number at "1" with one day left in the season. Either a San Diego win or Colorado loss could have clinched the crown. Neither happened.

◇

Followers of the San Diego Padres questioned rookie manager Bud Black's decision not to pitch Jake Peavy in the final game of the 2007 season. Peavy, en route to the Triple Crown of pitching (league leadership in wins, strikeouts, and ERA), could have worked the finale at Miller Park in Milwaukee on September 30 but was withheld by Black for a potential playoff game the following day. Black was banking on the Padres maintaining the one-game lead they took into the final day, but Brett Tomko blew the lead, the Brewers beat the Padres, and the Colorado Rockies closed the gap with a win over the Arizona Diamondbacks. Peavy, pitching on normal rest, yielded six runs to the Rockies in the playoff game. Colorado won 9–8 in 13 innings with a three-run uprising against Padres closer Trevor Hoffman.

◇

The 2007 Colorado Rockies went 14–1 in their last 15 games, tying the 1983 Philadelphia Phillies and 1965 Los Angeles Dodgers for the best finish in NL history. Of the 10 teams that won at least 13 of their last 15, six reached the playoffs, two won pennants, and two (the 1965 Dodgers and the 2007 Rockies) reached the World Series.

◇

Through the 2007 season, 11 teams finished first after overcoming deficits of at least 11 games during the season.

Teams That Tanked

The following teams blew September leads that looked insurmountable:

2007 New York Mets: Went 1–6 in final homestand to blow an NL East lead that had stood at seven games with 17 to play on September 12.

1934 New York Giants: Seven games up on September 6, but it wasn't enough.

1938 Pittsburgh Pirates: A seven-game, September 1 bulge on the Chicago Cubs evaporated, capped by Gabby Hartnett's "Homer in the Gloamin'."

1964 Philadelphia Phillies: Blew a 6½-game lead with 12 to go by dropping 10 straight starting on September 20.

1951 Brooklyn Dodgers: A once-enormous lead dwindled to 6½ by September 8 and wasn't enough against the charging New York Giants.

1995 California Angels: On September 4, their AL West lead over Seattle stood at 6½ games.

CHAPTER

3

Ballparks

Ballparks are as different as houses. Each has its own size, shape, and personality with quirks and angles included, and no two are alike. If Ted Williams had played home games at Yankee Stadium and Joe DiMaggio had played his at Fenway Park, both would have broken Babe Ruth's records. Instead, DiMaggio's right-handed drives often died in Death Valley—an area of left-center field at Yankee Stadium defined by its distance from home plate—while the left-handed shots of Williams seemed more suited for the Bronx than Boston. While symmetrical parks might make baseball records more comparable, they would also change the nature of the game.

The first stadiums were made of wood and had limited capacities, inadequate outfield fences, and barriers to guard against freeloaders. Many parks had a special admissions gate for horse-drawn (and later horseless) carriages, which were allowed to park in the outfield. When fans exceeded a park's capability to seat them, they were also permitted to stand behind roped-off sections of outfield, creating the need for special ground rules governing balls hit into the crowd. After a number of fires, concrete and steel stadiums began to replace wooden ballparks, which faded into history with the last game at Robison Field in St. Louis on June 6, 1920.

Early twentieth-century parks were shoe-horned within existing city blocks, making it easier for fans to ride streetcars to games—while later park designs considered such factors as parking, weather, and whether or not a dome or retractable roof would be suitable to prevent postponements. Some parks favored hitters, others favored pitchers, and many were subject to the vagaries of wind and weather.

Today, the ballpark provides continuity—especially since the era of free agency created a climate conducive to unprecedented player movement. Teams that can't always keep star players can keep star ballparks. Nearly a century later, both Fenway Park and Wrigley Field survive as relics of another era. The memories of lost fields linger: the horseshoe shape of the Polo Grounds, the angles of Ebbets, the winds of Candlestick Park, the Crosley Field terrace, and so many more. When Yankee Stadium meets the wrecking ball before the 2009 season, only the Boston and Chicago ballparks will still be able to trace their roots to Babe Ruth's heyday. In fact, Dodger Stadium (circa 1962) will become the third oldest active ballpark.

In its first three seasons, the future Wrigley Field had three names. North Side Ball Park (1914) gave way to Weegham Park for Federal League club owner Charles Weegham and then Whales Park a year later for the Chicago Whales of the Federal League. The stadium became Cubs Park in 1916 but was also called Wrigley Field after chewing gum magnate William Wrigley bought the Cubs in 1918. Both the Whales and the Cubs won their debuts in the friendly confines.

(Library of Congress)

Stadium Bits

The first ballpark, Union Grounds in Brooklyn, existed seven years before the Cincinnati Red Stockings became the first professional team in 1869 and 15 years before the NL's first season in 1876. Admission was 10 cents.

◇

In 1887, the Philadelphia Nationals opened their new Baker Bowl on April 30, when 14,500 fans watched the team beat New York 15–9. Construction cost for the park was $80,000 (the average player's salary in 1978).

The New York Giants were forced to vacate the Polo Grounds because of the extension of 111th Street, forcing the team to open the season on borrowed ground across the Hudson River in Jersey City. Some "home" games were played on Staten Island before the new Polo Grounds, at 155th Street and 8th Avenue, was dedicated on July 8, 1889.

◇

The Players League of 1890 put its New York ballpark so close to the NL's Polo Grounds that Mike Tiernan of the Giants hit a home run from one park into the other. When the Players League collapsed, the Giants moved into their horseshoe-shaped park and remained there until leaving for San Francisco in 1958. The park had two more years of major-league service as home of the expansion New York Mets in 1962 and 1963.

◇

A dozen league games in 1902 and 1903 were played outside cities that banned Sunday baseball. The Indians left Cleveland for contests in such cities as Canton, Columbus, and Dayton, Ohio, and played two games in Fort Wayne, Indiana. The Boston Braves played a "home" game in Providence, Rhode Island, and the Detroit Tigers visited Columbus and Toledo, Ohio, and Grand Rapids, Michigan.

◇

During Ty Cobb's day as a great base stealer, rival clubs trimmed their infield grass before Detroit came to town so that Cobb's bunts would reach fielders more quickly.

◇

Only 2 of the 16 ballparks in use the first half of the twentieth century were symmetrical. The others had individual angles and peculiar quirks, but that was their charm.

◇

Ball clubs used ballparks to their advantage. Connie Mack froze balls before slugging clubs came to town and frightened visiting hitters by ordering his groundskeepers to build a 20-inch mound for ace pitchers Lefty Grove, George Earnshaw, Chief Bender, and Eddie Plank. Washington manager Joe Cantillion, taking the opposite approach, trained his pitchers to work on a flat mound; rival pitchers hated to pitch in the Senators' park.

◇

Construction cost of Forbes Field was $1 million—a lot of money in 1909. Center field seemed so distant at the Pittsburgh ballpark (457 feet) that the batting cage was kept there—in fair territory.

Shibe Park, named for original Philadelphia A's owner Benjamin Shibe, hosted the Athletics from 1909 to 1954 and the Phillies from 1938 to 1970. The first triple-decked stadium, it was also the site of the first AL night game on May 16, 1939. It was renamed Connie Mack Stadium in 1952 over Mack's objections.
(Library of Congress)

Ben Shibe and Connie Mack paid $150,000 for a brickyard where they built Shibe Park (later Connie Mack Stadium) in 1909, but they worried that they might have ventured too far from downtown Philadelphia. The city not only caught up with the park but overran it, forcing the Phillies to build Veterans Stadium in time for the 1971 season.

◇

Baker Bowl's 280-foot right-field line helped left-handed batter Chuck Klein of the Phillies but was even more beneficial for visiting sluggers. In 1930, when the Phillies hit .315 as a team, Klein hit 40 homers, knocked in 170 runs, and batted .386. But the team won only 52 times because its pitchers allowed rivals an average of 6.71 earned runs per game—a dubious major-league record.

◇

The Phillies played in Baker Bowl until 1938, when they joined the A's in Shibe Park because Connie Mack needed the revenue. Shibe's right-field fence was originally 10 feet high, allowing tenants of apartments facing the park to have an unobstructed view. Fans inside the ballpark weren't so lucky; they often found themselves in seats behind steel support pillars.

◇

Without established standards, teams built parks to suit their own needs. Because their lineup featured left-handed slugger Babe Ruth, the New York Yankees built Yankee Stadium with a short right-field porch—just 296 feet from home plate. The park had long dimensions from home to center and left-center field, but was called "The House That Ruth Built" with good reason. He hit most of his shots to right, as did Roger Maris when he broke Ruth's one-season record by hitting 61 home runs in 1961.

Although George Burns—no, not that George Burns—got the first hit in Yankee Stadium, Babe Ruth hit the first home run. His three-run shot in the third inning gave the Yankees a 4–1 win over the Red Sox in a game witnessed by 74,200 fans (more than 25,000 more couldn't get in). Because Ruth's popularity enabled the Yankees to afford the $2.5 million park, writer Fred Lieb was quick to call it "The House That Ruth Built."
(The Baseball Bulletin)

The Yankees reached into their bag of tricks by raising or lowering a huge green curtain in center field of Yankee Stadium. If a power pitcher worked for New York, the curtain was up so that enemy batters had trouble picking up the ball against a sea of white shirts. If an ordinary pitcher was on the mound, the curtain went down to help the Yankees batters.

◇

Braves Field was the largest ballpark in the country when it opened in 1915. The Boston ballpark, one mile from Fenway Park, held 40,000 fans—many of whom rode the streetcar right into the stadium.

◇

The Boston Braves and Boston Red Sox played World Series games in each other's parks—even though they weren't playing each other. The 1914 "Miracle" Braves played in two-year-old Fenway Park because it was larger than South End Grounds, where the Braves played at the time. In both 1915 and 1916, the Red Sox played their home World Series games at Braves Field, which held more fans than Fenway.

◇

Braves Field was so big that no ball cleared its left-field barrier in its first 11 seasons.

The New York Giants hit four inside-the-park homers at Boston's Braves Field on April 29, 1922.

◊

The 1946 Boston Braves played early-season games at Fenway Park, because the freshly painted Braves Field hadn't dried properly. Fans who attended the opener got green paint all over their clothes in an incident that pundits dubbed "the wearing of the green" in heavily Irish Boston. The Braves had to pay $6,000 in cleaning bills.

◊

The last game at Braves Field in 1952 drew only 8,822 people, because fans didn't realize the team was on the verge of moving from Boston to Milwaukee. Brooklyn won, 8–2.

◊

The grandfather of President John F. Kennedy threw out the first ball at Fenway Park. John F. "Honey Fitz" Fitzgerald was mayor of Boston when the park opened on April 20, 1912.

◊

Fenway Park once featured a steep incline in front of the left-field wall. The incline, which rose 10 feet, was nicknamed "Duffy's Cliff" after Red Sox left fielder Duffy Lewis, who became adept at climbing the slope in pursuit of balls. It lasted from 1912, when the park opened, until it was remodeled in 1934.

◊

Fenway Park has always been known as a pitcher's nightmare. In 1950, the Boston Red Sox beat the St. Louis Browns by back-to-back scores of 20–4 and 29–4. Three years later, the Sox scored a record 17 runs *in one inning*. They also won and lost 24–4 in 1940 (vs. Washington) and 1923 (vs. the Yankees).

◊

Although Boston writer Hy Hurwitz dubbed Fenway Park "Williamsburg" because it seemed like Ted Williams owned the place, the nickname was applied to right-field bullpens added in 1940 to help the left-handed Williams hit home runs. The new bullpens cut the distance from home plate to right field by 23 feet.

◊

The bluegrass removed from Fenway Park's left field after a 1967 resodding wound up as Carl Yastrzemski's lawn in Lynnfield, Massachusetts.

◊

Although Wrigley Field is in Chicago, its brick outfield wall is covered by *Boston* ivy vines. They were originally planted by Bill Veeck in 1937.

U.S. Cellular Field and Wrigley Field, linked by Chicago's Red Line subway, are closer together than any other big-league parks today. They are separated by only 9.81 miles, just short of the 10.04 miles separating Yankee Stadium and Shea Stadium in New York.

◊

Wind is almost always a factor in games played at Wrigley Field. When it blows in off Lake Michigan, the wind blows fly balls back into play, keeping scores respectable. When the wind blows out, however, games become blowouts, too. The Cubs won 26–23 and 23–22 games and got a record three 60-homer seasons from Sammy Sosa.

◊

Five years passed between the first night game in the minors and the first night game in the majors. The Reds beat the Phillies 2–1 in that game on May 24, 1935. The Crosley Field lighting system cost $55,000.

◊

Night ball played tricks on the eyes of batters for years—especially in its first 20 years, when teams played more often by day than by night. On June 15, 1938, Johnny Vander Meer of the Reds became the only man to pitch back-to-back no-hitters but was helped considerably in the second effort by the dim lights of Brooklyn's Ebbets Field. It was that park's first night game.

◊

Rain cancelled the first night game in the majors and proved an equal opportunity destroyer 53 years later by wiping out the first night game in the last park to light up. Rain and cold wiped out the first one at Cincinnati's Crosley Field on May 23, 1935, while wet weather forced postponement of the first game under the lights at Chicago's Wrigley Field, which had been scheduled for 8–8–88 to make it more memorable.

◊

The last game at Ebbets Field in 1957 drew only 6,700 fans. Even at capacity, the home of the Brooklyn Dodgers held just 32,000 people in cramped seats. The park, which was active for 44 years, was squeezed into a city block in Flatbush, leaving inadequate room to park (700 spaces).

◊

Playing the carom off the right-field wall at Ebbets Field was a challenge: there were nearly 300 different angles. The bottom of the barrier was concrete, the scoreboard was metal, and the screen was made of wire. The distance from home plate to the right-center corner was gradually shortened from the original 500 feet to 403 feet.

Duke Snider always denied that he was the chief beneficiary of Brooklyn's short right-field dimensions. Snider said the 40-foot height of the scoreboard took away as many homers as the 297-foot distance provided. But he still hit 56 percent of his career home runs at home.

◇

The lights of Ebbets Field found a home for years in New York's Downing Stadium on Randall's Island, near the junction of Manhattan, Queens, and the Bronx. The Ebbets Field flagpole still stands on Utica Avenue in East Flatbush. The pole, which stood in center field at the Brooklyn ballpark, stands in front of the Canarsie Casket Company.

◇

Before Fenway topped it for longevity, Sportsman's Park (renamed Busch Stadium in 1953), enjoyed the longest life span of any major league field. The St. Louis ballpark, first used by the Cardinals in the NL's initial 1876 season, was reinforced with concrete and steel in 1908 and remained in regular service until May 8, 1966. (It was unoccupied from 1878 to 1884, when the city had no club.)

◇

Many fans heading to the 1955 All-Star Game at Milwaukee County Stadium took the Wells Street trolley car for the whopping fare of 20 cents.

◇

Richie Ashburn of the Phillies won the 1955 NL batting crown partly because his bunts down the third base line never rolled foul. They coasted to a stop in fair territory because of "Ashburn's Ridge," an inclined foul line raised slightly above the rest of the infield level.

◇

Two modern clubs, the Brooklyn Dodgers and the Chicago White Sox, borrowed a pre-1900 concept of playing "home" games at a neutral site to hike attendance. The Dodgers played seven games in Jersey City's Roosevelt Stadium in both 1956 and 1957 before moving to Los Angeles, while the Chisox occupied unused Milwaukee County Stadium, vacated by the Braves after 1965, for 9 games in 1968 and 11 games in 1969.

◇

During its brief tenure as home of the Dodgers from 1958 to 1961, the Los Angeles Coliseum had the largest capacity and most unusual dimensions in baseball. The football-designed Coliseum measured 251 feet to the left-field foul line and 320 feet to the left-center power alley, but 385 feet to right-center field. Duke Snider, who never adjusted, wasn't the same home run threat he had been at Ebbets Field—but Wally Moon, another left-handed hitter, learned to go the opposite way and deposit "Moon Shots" over the 40-foot screen that topped the left-field wall. The park held 93,600 for baseball and nearly reached that figure three times during the 1959 World Series against the White Sox.

◇

The biggest crowd in baseball history came to an exhibition game. It happened on May 7, 1959, when the Dodgers played the Yankees in a game to raise funds for the care and treatment of paralyzed Dodgers catcher Roy Campanella. The game, played at the Los Angeles Coliseum, drew 93,103 fans.

◇

The Washington Senators helped slow-footed third baseman Harmon Killebrew, their top slugger, by letting the Griffith Stadium infield grass grow enough to slow balls hit his way. They got the idea from the Cleveland Indians, whose excessive watering turned the hot corner into the warm corner. There was good reason: slugger Al Rosen broke his nose *nine times* on hard-hit balls.

Moving with his team from New York to San Francisco cost Willie Mays a chance to beat Babe Ruth in career home runs. He found the swirling winds of Candlestick Park a deterrent to his power.

(Dan Schlossberg)

Bill Veeck gave birth to the idea of using the scoreboard as an attraction to lure customers. In 1960, his exploding scoreboard delighted White Sox players and fans but irritated the opposition (Cleveland center fielder Jimmy Piersall once threw a ball at the noisy monolith).

◇

Richard Nixon and Ty Cobb were among the celebrities who attended the first game at Candlestick Park, on April 12, 1960. The home-team Giants won on a wind-blown triple.

◇

There were two Wrigley Fields used by big-league clubs in 1961, the first year of AL expansion. The new Los Angeles Angels played home games in a California-based Wrigley Field, also built by the chewing gum magnate who owned the Chicago Cubs. After a year at Wrigley, which was also used in the TV show *Home Run Derby*, the Angels shared Chavez Ravine (now Dodger Stadium) for four years before relocating to Anaheim.

◇

The tape measure came out on consecutive nights at the Polo Grounds in 1963 when Lou Brock, then with the Cubs, and Hank Aaron of the Braves became only the second and third hitters ever to reach the distant center field bleachers in the Polo Grounds. The ancient New York ballpark tantalized batters with short distances to the right- and left-field seats but agonizingly long distances to center field. Joe Adcock of the Braves was the first man to reach the bleachers with a 475-foot shot in 1953, but no one duplicated the feat until Brock, with only seven career home runs at the time, found the range. Aaron did it with the bases loaded.

 ## Dome on the Range

Called "The Eighth Wonder of the World" when it opened, the Houston Astrodome cost $31.6 million, stood 18 stories high, had room for 30,000 cars, and generated $30,000 monthly air-conditioning bills. The first park with theater seating, the Astrodome had an initial capacity of 46,217 (later expanded to 54,816). Fans were entertained by indoor fireworks, a scoreboard "home run spectacular" featuring a snorting bull, and a grounds crew dressed in spacesuits.

In the first game at the Houston Astrodome on April 9, 1965, Mickey Mantle's homer helped the New York Yankees beat the newly named Houston Astros (née Houston Colts) 2–1 as President Lyndon B. Johnson, a Texan, watched. The Astros also lost the first regular-season game 2–0 to Philadelphia on April 12.

◇

Things didn't always work as planned at the Astrodome. The 4,500 plastic skylights caused a glare that resulted in fielders "losing the ball" in the roof. After conditions deteriorated to a point where outfielders wore helmets for day games, the team painted the skylights and reduced the day lighting by 25 to 40 percent. The subsequent lack of sunlight killed the original grass turf, which was replaced a year later by the artificial Astroturf. In addition, the hard surface created the new problem of turf injuries: shin-splints, sore knees, and other wear and tear.

◇

Mike Schmidt lost a tape-measure homer when his long Astrodome shot to center against Claude Osteen in 1974 struck a loudspeaker 329 feet from the plate and 117 feet above the field. Under prevailing ground rules, the Philadelphia slugger had to settle for a single—arguably the longest single in baseball history.

◇

When Atlanta-Fulton County Stadium opened in 1966, Atlanta's Opening Day battery was pitcher Tony Cloninger and catcher Joe Torre. Both men also appeared in the stadium's last contest, Game 5 of the 1996 World Series. Torre was manager of the Yankees and Cloninger was his bullpen coach.

◇

Charges of partisan groundskeeping were hurled at the Houston Astros when they moved into the Astrodome in 1966. Ed Kranepool of the Mets noticed that the air-conditioning was blowing out when Houston hitters took their swings but that the breeze stopped when the visitors came to bat. He made the deduction by watching the flag in the outfield.

◇

The Philadelphia Phillies got a new ballpark in 1971 when they moved from Connie Mack Stadium (née Shibe Park) to a cookie-cutter model slightly larger than its cross-state rival, Three Rivers Stadium in Pittsburgh. Veterans Stadium, called "The Vet" for short, held 56,371 at its opening but squeezed in several crowds of 62,000 for big games.

Three other fields also opened during the decade: Royals Stadium, the first park with its own waterfall, in 1973; and both the Seattle Kingdome and Montreal's Olympic Stadium three years later. The Canadian ballpark became the home of the Expos after the 1976 Olympics.

Cookie-Cutter Architecture

Build it and they will come. That theory, expressed so vividly in the film *Field of Dreams*, also applied to the wave of new ballparks that sprang up during the 1970s. The symmetrical new parks, which looked like they could have been produced from the same cookie-cutter, held more people than the fields they replaced and carried with them the air of novelty.

Nobody was more surprised to land a franchise than the city of Montreal. Given an NL franchise in 1969, the city scrambled to find a suitable stadium before deciding to convert Jarry Park, formerly used by amateur teams.

Because Montreal was a surprise selection for an NL expansion team in 1969, Jarry Park had to be rushed into service. Neither the park nor the team proved instant successes, however, and the club never reached the World Series during its 36-year existence.

(Dan Schlossberg)

Facelift in the Bronx

The 1974–1975 remodeling of Yankee Stadium, originally projected to cost $24 million, ended up with a $100 million price tag—more than triple the cost of building Royals Stadium, which opened in Kansas City in 1973. Redoing the 50-year-old Bronx ballpark was the only option open to New York City in 1972 when it appeared the team would join the football Giants in a baseball/football park in Hackensack, New Jersey—less than 5 miles from Manhattan but more accessible for fans than Yankee Stadium.

Fans have packed Yankee Stadium since its inception in 1923. The team set a new single-season attendance record in 2007, drawing more than 4 million fans for 81 home games.
(Bill Menzel)

The Toronto Blue Jays drew so well after opening their futuristic SkyDome in 1989 that they became the first team to draw 4 million fans in a season.

◇

Before poor attendance forced them to become the Washington Nationals, the Montreal Expos played in Olympic Stadium, originally built to house the Summer Olympics. The much-maligned ballpark featured a "technical ring" with a central opening that measured 600 feet by 300 feet. Not surprisingly, snowouts were a problem before the roof was completed in 1987. There were other problems, too. A game was postponed when explosions caused a fire in the tower; a windstorm later tore holes in the roof; and a 50-ton slab of concrete fell to the promenade, forcing the Expos to play their final 26 games of 1991 on the road.

◇

Playing their first game in Denver's hastily converted Mile High Stadium, an enormous football field, the Colorado Rockies drew a record Opening Day crowd of 80,227 on April 9, 1993. When Coors Field opened two years later, the stadium sparked the resurrection of the rundown LoDo (Lower Downtown) area that surrounded it. Hideo Nomo is the only man to pitch a no-hitter in Coors Field. Nomo, who later pitched a no-hitter in the AL, was with the Los Angeles Dodgers at the time.

◇

In 1998, 10 fields had artificial surfaces and 5 had covers.

◇

Todd Jones not only threw the last pitch at Tiger Stadium, but kept a seat and home plate from the old Detroit park as part of his memorabilia collection.

◇

The Houston Astrodome, in service from 1965 to 1999, sparked a string of imitations—some with retractable roofs. One of them, now called Minute Maid Park, replaced the Astrodome in 2000.

◇

Turner Field got its name because television magnate Ted Turner invested heavily in a moribund franchise that was considering relocation to another city. The ballpark, originally built for the 1996 Summer Olympics, replaced Atlanta-Fulton County Stadium as home of the Braves in 1997.

 Bonanza in the Bronx

Pitchers with perfect games at Yankee Stadium:

Don Larsen, October 6, 1956, vs. Brooklyn (World Series)
David Wells, May 17, 1998, vs. Minnesota
David Cone, July 18, 1999, vs. Montreal

A fatal crane accident prevented the Milwaukee Brewers from moving into Miller Park as planned in 2000. The team spent an extra year in Milwaukee County Stadium instead.

◇

The Yankees and Mets played a double header *that used both New York ballparks* on July 8, 2000. The Yankees won both games with 4–2 scores, taking the afternoon game at Shea and the night game in the Bronx—but the big story was the beaning of Mets slugger Mike Piazza by Roger Clemens. The catcher had to be hospitalized with a concussion.

◇

Shortly after the Philadelphia Phillies occupied Citizens Bank Park in 2004, pitchers started calling it "Coors Field East." The compact South Philadelphia stadium quickly developed a reputation as one of the most hitter-friendly parks in the NL.

After a 33-year tenure at Veterans Stadium, the Phillies moved to a new park built next door in South Philadelphia. Pitchers soon complained that the new Citizens Bank Park favored home run hitters.

(Philadelphia Phillies)

Disney's Wide World of Sports, where the Tampa Bay Devil Rays played three games in 2007, was the smallest ballpark used for a major league game since the Oakland A's opened the 1996 season with six games in Las Vegas. Disney's listed capacity of 9,500 seats was just slightly larger than the 9,000-seat Cashman Field. Oakland opened there while waiting for repairs to be completed on the Oakland-Alameda County Coliseum.

◇

The 2007 Cleveland Indians played their home opener in Milwaukee after a scheduled four-game series with the Seattle Mariners was snowed out. While the Mariners waited out the weather in Cleveland, their *covered stadium* in Seattle stood empty. Miller Park, which also has a retractable roof, was available because the Milwaukee Brewers were also playing on the road. Only twice previously—in 2004 and 2005—were games shifted to new locations because of weather (Florida hurricanes).

◇

Seattle suffered six postponements on the road in April 2007: four to snow, one to rain, and one to a Texas tornado watch.

◇

To reach McCovey Cove, the area of San Francisco Bay directly behind the right-field stands at AT&T Park, a ball has to clear a 22-foot fence that stands 309 feet from home plate at the foul-pole and travel 55 feet more. Barry Bonds, en route to becoming baseball's home run king, did it 34 times in the ballpark's first seven-and-a-half years. Only 10 home runs hit by others reached McCovey Cove (officially known as China Basin Channel) during that time span.

◇

Although it has fewer seats, the $610 million cost of Nationals Park, where the Washington Nationals began playing in 2008, is $10 million more than the cost of Citi Field, where the New York Mets will move in 2009.

◇

Citi Field will have the look of Ebbets Field but the feel of a rush-hour subway to fans trying to get tickets. Instead of holding 56,000 fans (the capacity of Shea Stadium), the new ballpark will fit only 45,000.

◇

The estimated cost of building the new Yankee Stadium, scheduled to open in 2009, is $1.02 billion—making it the most expensive ballpark of all time. Hot dogs figure to be ridiculously expensive, too.

A smaller, twenty-first–century version of Yankee Stadium, built in the Bronx near the current ballpark, will open in time for the 2009 season.
(Bill Menzel)

Although snow, ice, and cold often accompany spring and fall to Minneapolis, the Minnesota Twins will move from a domed stadium to an open-air ballpark in 2010. The new $522 facility will hold 40,000 people. The Twins have played in the covered Hubert H. Humphrey Metrodome since 1982.

◇

During their tenure in Oakland, the A's played in Oakland-Alameda County Stadium, McAfee Coliseum, and Network Associates Coliseum without ever moving. The stadium's name changed as the team sold naming rights. When their newest park, the $500 million Cisco Field, opens in Fremont in 2011, it will have the smallest seating capacity in the majors (32,000).

CHAPTER 4

Batters and Pitchers

Baseball without its players is like the beach without its sand. The game revolves around the talented men in uniform, each of whom brings something different to the mix. Some players can run, some can hit, some can throw—and a select few can do everything. Size doesn't matter, especially for those players who get maximum mileage out of minimal skills.

Being a hitter means being able to "swing a round bat at a round ball and hit it square," as Ted Williams said. For pitchers, it means being able to throw that round ball in such a way that hitters can't make contact.

What makes baseball so appealing is that anyone can play. The rules are easy to understand and there are no restrictions on height, weight, race, or religion.

Batter Bits

Ross Barnes, who hit the first home run in National League (NL) history, for the Chicago White Stockings on May 2, 1876, hit only one more the rest of his career.

◇

Honus Wagner never made much as a player but his baseball card is worth millions. The T206 Wagner, part of a 1909 American Tobacco set, was pulled because Wagner eschewed tobacco products. Only a half dozen or so survived, driving up the price, and one of them sold for $1 million in

2000. One of them, given an 8 out of a possible 10 by Professional Sports Authenticators, has doubled in price every time it has sold. Once owned by hockey star Wayne Gretzky, it was purchased by a California collector for $2.35 million in 2007.

◇

Negro Leagues star John Henry "Pop" Lloyd was such a superlative short-stop that he was often called "the black Honus Wagner." Asked about the nickname, Wagner said it was an honor to be compared to Lloyd. Barred from the big leagues by the color line, Lloyd played for the Chicago American Giants, New York Lincoln Giants, and Atlantic City Bacharach Giants from 1906 to 1932.

◇

Cool Papa Bell, a standout in the Negro Leagues, played professional baseball for 29 summers and 21 winters. He was said to be so fast that he could turn out the lights in his hotel room and be asleep before the room got dark.

◇

Of the seven men who produced .400 seasons since the 1901 advent of the modern era, three of them were repeaters: Ty Cobb and Rogers Hornsby three times each and George Sisler twice.

◇

Pete Rose and Tony Gwynn share the NL record for most years leading the league in hits (seven) but they couldn't catch major league leader Ty Cobb, who led the American League (AL) eight times during his long tenure (1905 to 1928).

◇

The career of catcher Hank Gowdy was interrupted by service in both world wars.

◇

Joe Jackson got his Shoeless nickname in the minors, when he played a game in his socks after a new pair of shoes gave him blisters.

◇

Shoeless Joe Jackson used one bat throughout his career. The 40-ounce hickory bat, nicknamed Black Betsy, helped Jackson compile a .356 career average. The mark was expunged from the record books when Jackson was banned for life after the 1919 Black Sox Scandal.

◇

Shoeless Joe Jackson, allegedly part of the scheme to fix the 1919 World Series, hit the only home run in that best-of-nine against the Cincinnati Reds. He also batted .375, hardly the mark of someone trying to throw games.

The film *Field of Dreams* was wrong to portray Shoeless Joe Jackson as a right-handed batter. The outfielder was such a good *left-handed* hitter that fellow lefty Babe Ruth copied his swing.

◇

As a minor league outfielder, Casey Stengel entertained fans by sliding into his defensive position in center field. An insane asylum was located right behind the ballpark and, after one inning, his manager pointed to the building and said, "It's only a matter of time, Stengel."

◇

When Babe Ruth hit 29 home runs for the Boston Red Sox in 1919, he broke Gavvy Cravath's single-season record of 24, set four years earlier.

◇

Babe Ruth not only set the one-season home-run record four times, but in 1920, his first year with the Yankees, he out-homered all seven opposing *teams.*

They never met, but Babe Ruth and Josh Gibson could have compared notes about the titanic home runs both hit at Yankee Stadium. In a 2007 portrait, famed baseball artist Bill Purdom imagined what such a meeting might look like.

(Copyright 2007 by Bill Purdom. Reprinted with permission of SportsLithographs.com.)

Babe Ruth actually hit 60 homers six years *before* he set the official record in 1927. In 1921, he lost a sure home run when he hit a ball to right at the Polo Grounds, then the Yankees' home field, but saw it called a double after a fan reached out to grab it. Umpires Tommy Connolly and Ollie Chill made the call after a short conference. He finished the year with 59 home runs.

◇

Twice in the 1930 season, Babe Ruth hit home runs that were ruled doubles. Though separated by five months, both occurred in Philadelphia's Shibe Park when the baseballs cleared the fence, struck loudspeakers, and bounced back onto the field.

◇

Although widely considered a buffoon whose only talents fell between the white lines, Babe Ruth played the piano and the saxophone. He was also such a good golfer that he won more awards on the links than he did on the diamond.

◇

Babe Ruth may have lost his single-season and lifetime home run records but he still owns major league marks for most seasons leading a league in slugging (13), homers (12), and runs (8).

◇

In 1927, the year Babe Ruth hit 60 home runs, teammate Lou Gehrig received the Chalmers Award, forerunner of the AL MVP created four years later.

◇

Joe Sewell fanned twice in the same game in 1930—and once in the rest of the season. He batted 353 times.

◇

Before he became a feared and durable Yankee slugger, Lou Gehrig was a Columbia University pitcher who fanned a school record 17 men in a game against Williams College. P.S.: He was also the *losing* pitcher.

◇

Even his wedding couldn't interrupt Lou Gehrig's streak of 2,130 consecutive games; he played on the day he got married.

◇

Lou Gehrig lost three triples in five innings at Washington during a 1934 game cancelled by rain before the home fifth could be completed.

◇

Like Ted Williams, who would later do it twice, Lou Gehrig missed winning the MVP award in a Triple Crown season. Detroit's catcher/manager Mickey Cochrane hit .320 with only two homers and 76 runs batted in for the 1934 season but brought his club home first. In New York, Gehrig led the league with a .363 average, 49 homers, and 165 RBI. His slugging percentage was a resounding .796. But the Yankees finished second, seven games behind.

Although overshadowed by Babe Ruth on the Yankees, Lou Gehrig was one of the great sluggers of baseball history. He had a record five seasons with at least 400 total bases, two years with more than 100 extra base hits, and 23 grand slam home runs, another mark. Although he lasted only 13 full years before illness idled him, he had an average of 147 RBIs per year. The native New Yorker was the first American Leaguer to hit four home runs in a game.

(Baseball Hall of Fame)

Lou's Lost Crown

Yankee slugger Lou Gehrig, trotting around the bases with an apparent game-winning homer, lost the 1931 home run crown when teammate Lyn Lary proceeded from third base to the dugout rather than completing the circuit to home plate. Gehrig was ruled out for passing Lary and was credited with a triple, as he had touched only three bases safely. That year, Gehrig and Babe Ruth finished with 46 home runs each to share the home run title.

Lou Gehrig wore the first number retired by the Yankees. His No. 4 was honored at a 1941 memorial game played a month after he died at age 37.

Gehrig Out After 2,130 Games

LouBenched At His Own Request

Dahlgren Chosen As Replacement For 1st Sacker

Once he sat out, Lou Gehrig never played again. Felled by a neurological disorder now called "Lou Gehrig's Disease," he played in 2,130 consecutive games, a record that stood nearly six decades before Cal Ripken Jr. topped it.
(Dan Schlossberg collection)

Two Cardinals, Jim Bottomley (1936) and Mark Whiten (1993), share the record for RBI in a game. Both had 12, one more than Tony Lazzeri, who knocked in an AL-record 11 in 1936.

The first man to hit two grand slams in a game, Tony Lazzeri was a slugging second baseman who starred for the "Murderer's Row" Yankees of the 1920s. Before reaching the majors, he became the first player to produce a 60-homer season in professional baseball—for Salt Lake City of the Pacific Coast League in 1925.
(Baseball Hall of Fame)

For more than a dozen seasons, the Pittsburgh Pirates pounded rivals with two left-handed-hitting outfielders named Waner (Paul and Lloyd). The Waner brothers were in the majors from 1927 to 1945—long enough to hit well over .300 and earn separate plaques in the Hall of Fame. When they hit consecutive homers, against Cliff Melton of the New York Giants on September 15, 1938, they became the only brothers to do that. Lloyd never connected again.

◇

Bill Terry lost the 1931 NL batting crown by three one-thousandths of a percentage point because he lost a base hit in a game canceled by darkness. Playing a doubleheader in Brooklyn, the New York Giants first base-man singled in his first at-bat of the second game. Confident he had won the batting title in a tight three-way race with Jim Bottomley and Chick Hafey, he left the lineup. But Brooklyn's Fresco Thompson set fire to several scorecards as a signal that it was too dark to continue. Umpire Bill Klem spent considerable time looking for the culprit, then called the game. None of the records counted.

The First Hammerin' Hank

Long before Jackie Robinson broke baseball's color line in 1947, another talented young player survived a slew of threats and epithets en route to a Hall of Fame career. The son of Jewish immigrants from Rumania, Hank Greenberg signed with the Tigers in 1930, reaching the majors three years later. Opponents riled Greenberg, who once marched into the Yankee clubhouse after a game to challenge the race-baiters. No one would take him on. The six-foot-four, 215-pound Greenberg found few challenges on the diamond, either. He helped the Tigers take consecutive pennants in 1934 and 1935, earning his first MVP Award. Three years later, he stood two shy of Babe Ruth's 60-homer mark with five games to go, but received a steady diet of intentional walks because pitchers didn't want a Jew breaking Ruth's record. Although he missed nearly five seasons because of wartime military service, Greenberg finished with four home run crowns and two MVP awards while hitting .313 with 331 homers.

Stan Musial, signed as a pitcher, was 18–5 in 1940, his third minor league season. But he hurt his shoulder doing double duty as an outfielder and became a full-time position player. The results included seven batting crowns and three MVP awards. He also finished second in the MVP voting four times.

◊

Joe DiMaggio's 56-game hitting streak was not his first long streak: he hit in 61 straight for San Francisco in the Pacific Coast League in 1933.

◊

Joe DiMaggio's salary *for his entire 13-year career* was $704,769—less than Mike Piazza earned for 100 at-bats in 1999.

Not Getting Rich

Reggie Jackson's father, Martinez, earned $7 a game with the 1933 Newark Eagles, a Negro Leagues team. Thirty-three years later, Reggie signed a five-year, $3 million contract to play for the Yankees.

In 1941, Vince and Dom DiMaggio became the first brothers to appear as teammates on an All-Star team. Carlos and Lee May were the first brothers to play on opposite sides in 1969.

◊

Voters for AL MVP in 1941 had to choose between Joe DiMaggio's 56-game hitting streak and Ted Williams' .406 batting average. Although Williams actually out-hit DiMaggio during the streak (.412 to .408), DiMaggio won the vote.

◊

Pete Gray was born right-handed but became a lefty after losing his right arm in a truck accident. The 1944 Southern League MVP hit .218 in a 61-game stint with the 1945 St. Louis Browns.

◊

Only a fraction of a percentage point separated Ted Williams from a record third Triple Crown. In 1949, he led the AL in home runs and RBI but batted .3427, a fraction of a point behind George Kell's .3429. Rogers Hornsby and Williams are the only men to win the Triple Crown twice.

When Ted Williams hit .388 in 1957 at age 39, he became the oldest player ever to lead a league in batting. Bobby Doerr was the only Red Sox player to hit for the cycle twice.

◇

The quality of play was so poor in 1945 that the men who finished second and third in the AL batting race—Tony Cuccinello and John Dickshot— were released before the next season started.

◇

Ted Williams was the only man to lead his league in each of the three Triple Crown categories more than twice.

◇

Although Ty Cobb took 11 batting titles, Ted Williams led his league in on-base percentage more often (12 times). Both are major league records.

◇

After hitting 10 homers against subpar pitching in 1945, George (Snuffy) Stirnweiss needed seven more seasons to hit 10 more.

◇

Although Yogi Berra made No. 8 so famous it was eventually retired in his honor, the longtime Yankee catcher wore No. 38 as a rookie and No. 35 in his second year.

◇

Because his bat was so potent, Yogi Berra sometimes got a break from the rigors of catching by playing left field. He was there one day when a streaker ran across the outfield right in front of him. Play was halted for several minutes while the offending fan was corralled and cloaked. After the game, a writer asked Yogi whether the streaker was male or female. "How should I know?" he said. "He had a bag over his head."

◇

After Jackie Robinson broke baseball's color line in 1947, nine of the next 13 MVP winners were black.

◇

John Neves, a minor league outfielder in 1951, wore a one-of-a-kind uni- form number that season: a reverse 7. After all, he reasoned, Neves spelled backwards is seven.

◇

Nellie Fox was the toughest man to fan in the majors in a record 14 seasons.

◇

Ernie Banks, who twice won MVP awards while his team finished fifth in the eight-team NL, began his baseball career with a black barnstorming team that paid him $15 a game. He was with the Kansas City Monarchs, a

Negro Leagues team, when the Cubs made him their first black player in 1953. He went on to hit 512 home runs, including an NL-record five grand slams in 1955.

◇

The Milwaukee Braves spent $10,000—a pittance by modern standards—to purchase Hank Aaron's contract from the Indianapolis Clowns, a Negro Leagues team, in June 1952.

◇

Less than a year out of high school, Eddie Mathews built a reputation as "the next Babe Ruth" with tape measure home runs in the minors. Playing for the Atlanta Crackers in Ponce de Leon Park, Mathews belted a drive that landed in the giant magnolia tree, which stood in fair territory 462 feet from home plate and halfway up an embankment. Only Ruth had reached the tree previously, and that was on a one-bouncer in an exhibition game.

◇

Although too poor to own his own bat, future home run king Hank Aaron learned to play baseball in a pecan grove in his hometown of Mobile, Alabama. Aaron, who developed his legendary strength by working on an ice truck as a teenager, left home with two sandwiches, two dollars, and two pairs of pants packed into a cardboard suitcase.

Because of his quiet personality and the fact he never played for a New York team, Hank Aaron spent most of his career in obscurity. He never hit more than 47 home runs in a season but was such a model of consistency that he passed Babe Ruth on the career home run list in 1974. Aaron was an All-Star every year he played except for his first (1954) and last (1976).

(Dan Schlossberg)

Hank Aaron hit the first grand slam of his career the day after hitting the home run that clinched the 1957 pennant, the first of two in a row won by the Milwaukee Braves.

◊

When Hank Aaron broke Babe Ruth's record for lifetime home runs on April 8, 1974, he did it on the fourth pitch of the fourth inning in the fourth game of the fourth month in a year divisible by four, against a pitcher wearing his own No. 44 (Al Downing). The four-time home run king matched his uniform number with four 44-homer seasons, including one in which he tied for the league lead with fellow No. 44 Willie McCovey.

◊

In his lengthy career, Hank Aaron combined with Eddie Mathews to hit the most home runs by teammates (863) and with Tommie Aaron to hit the most home runs by brothers (768). The Aaron brothers homered in the same game three times in one season (1962) and once did that in the same inning (the ninth inning on July 12).

Small World Department

The opposing right fielder when Hank Aaron hit his last career home run on July 20, 1976, was Bobby Bonds, father of the man who eventually broke Aaron's record of 755 home runs. Aaron, playing for the Brewers at Milwaukee County Stadium, hit his farewell homer against Dick Drago of the California Angels.

Although the Aarons out-homered all other brothers—including several trios—the three Alous played the most games. The Waners had the most hits, while the DiMaggios had the most runs batted in.

◊

Tony Lazzeri and Tommy Heinrich both wore No. 7 for the Yankees, but the last man to wear it before Mickey Mantle was Bob Cerv.

◊

Sent to the minors for more seasoning during his 1951 rookie season, a despondent Mickey Mantle might have quit if his father hadn't talked him out of it.

◊

The Gold Glove Award was created by Rawlings and *The Sporting News* in 1957 as a way to honor defensive stars. The first recipients were decided by a panel of 19 sportswriters.

Defensively challenged first baseman Dick Stuart once got a standing ovation from Red Sox fans after making a clean catch of a windblown hot dog wrapper.

◇

Three-time MVP Roy Campanella was permanently paralyzed in January 1958 when his car skidded off an icy road, flipped over, and slammed into a telephone pole. The slugging Brooklyn catcher was unable to join his teammates in the move to Los Angeles a few months later.

◇

When Angels pitcher Ted Bowsfield was getting battered at Yankee Stadium in 1961, his center fielder suddenly disappeared. Jimmy Piersall ducked behind the monuments—then in fair territory in deep center field. Manager Bill Rigney, seeing no one in center, called time and trotted out in search of Piersall. He found him cowering behind the granite tablets. "I've got nine kids," Piersall explained, "and I'm not about to risk my life out here."

◇

The only home run of Jack Reed's big league career was a twenty-second-inning shot that gave the Yankees a 9–7 win over the Tigers on June 24, 1962. The game lasted 7 hours and 22 minutes.

◇

Los Angeles won a pair of All-Star Game MVP awards in 1962, the first year the award was given. Maury Wills of the Dodgers won in the first of two All-Star Games played that year, while Leon Wagner of the Angels won in the other.

◇

Roberto Clemente claimed he lost two batting titles because of bad decisions by official scorers.

◇

Willie Stargell, whose Pirates finished two-and-a-half games behind in 1973, was bypassed for MVP honors when writers named batting champion Pete Rose as the NL's MVP. Stargell had hit 44 homers, driven home 119 runs, and recorded a .646 slugging average, while Rose had only 5 homers and 64 RBI to go with his .338 average. But Cincinnati was a winner.

◇

The only man with at least 500 games at five different positions, Pete Rose also holds career records for singles (3,215), at-bats (14,053), and games played (3,562). He also made more outs than any other player.

◇

Pete Rose made 11 cents per day—hardly enough to pay his $50,000 fine for tax evasion—in the machine shop of the Marion, Illinois, federal prison in 1991. The career hits king also served five months for tax evasion, three months in a halfway house, and had to perform 1,000 hours of community service.

◇

During an eight-year span spent with five different teams, Al Oliver's uniform number was "O," though he insisted it was the first letter of his surname and not a zero. He was the first man to wear 0 in the majors, the first to wear it for a Canadian club, and the first to wear it while representing teams from two different countries in the same season. Rey Ordonez, Junior Ortiz, Oddibe McDowell, and Oscar Gamble liked Oliver's idea and followed suit.

◇

Al Kaline's second season was his best: he led the AL with a .340 average and 200 hits, both career peaks, in 1955. Just 20 at the time, Kaline became the youngest batting champion in baseball history. Although Kaline never lived up to his initial image as Detroit's Mickey Mantle, his 11 Gold Gloves, 15 All-Star selections, and 3,007 lifetime hits helped him win election to the Hall of Fame.

◇

Although limited to 102 games in 1968 by a broken arm suffered when he was hit by a pitch in May, Al Kaline squeezed into the Tiger lineup in time to help win the World Series. Manager Mayo Smith, desperate to add offense, moved Mickey Stanley from center field to shortstop, allowing Jim Northrup to switch from right to center and Kaline to return to his regular spot in right. Kaline's bat was the key: he hit .379, homered twice, and led both teams with eight runs batted in as the Tigers won in seven games.

◇

Bobby Bonds was faster than his son Barry and had a better throwing arm. He had a record five 30/30 seasons (at least 30 homers and 30 steals).

◇

The only man to win batting crowns in three different decades, George Brett also had a flair for dramatic home runs. He connected three times against Catfish Hunter in the 1978 ALCS, gave Kansas City its first pennant with an upper-deck blow against Goose Gossage at Yankee Stadium two years later, and produced a pair in the pivotal third game of the 1985 ALCS versus Toronto—allowing the Royals to reach the World Series and win their only world championship.

◇

George Brett wore No. 5 for Kansas City because fellow third baseman Brooks Robinson, who wore it for Baltimore years earlier, was his role model.

Tiny Fred Patek had only 41 career homers but hit three of them *in the same game.* The five-foot-four Kansas City shortstop did it at Boston's Fenway Park in 1980.

◇

Although Ron Blomberg never lived up to his reputation as "the next Mickey Mantle," he carved his niche in history by becoming the first designated hitter for the New York Yankees against the Boston Red Sox at Fenway Park on April 6, 1973.

RON BLOMBERG
First Base

Ron Blomberg, a lefty-hitting first baseman with a plethora of physical prob-lems, became the first designated hitter on Opening Day 1973.
(New York Yankees)

Minnie Minoso was 53 when he squeezed into three games for the 1980 Chicago White Sox. Those appearances enabled him to play in five different decades.

◇

Don Mattingly hit a record six grand slams in 1987 … but never hit another in eight more seasons.

◇

Award winners usually come from contending clubs, but there are exceptions. Andre Dawson of the 1987 Cubs and Alex Rodriguez of the 2003 Texas Rangers were Most Valuable Players whose teams finished last.

Cal Ripken Jr. was supposed to be a pitcher. At Aberdeen (Maryland) High, he had a 7–2 record, 0.70 ERA, and 100 strikeouts in 60 innings. Since he also hit .492 with 29 RBI in 20 games, the Baltimore Orioles gave young Ripken a choice. He said, "A pitcher gets to play once every five days. I want to play every day." Thus, the second-round draft choice became a shortstop.

◇

The man who replaced Cal Ripken Jr. after his 2,632-game playing streak ended in 1998 was a rookie named Ryan Minor. "He refused to go into the game," said Ripken, a 19-time All-Star whose career stretched 21 years and included two MVP awards. "He thought it was a rookie prank. We couldn't convince him that I really was going to sit out. Finally, when the whole team was on the field, he went out to third base." Ripken's streak started on May 30, 1982, and ran through September 20, 1998. He broke Lou Gehrig's 56-year-old durability record on September 6, 1995.

◇

In the AAA International League in 1981, future Hall of Famers Wade Boggs and Cal Ripken Jr. played in the longest game in the history of professional baseball—a 32-inning encounter that lasted two days. The Pawtucket Red Sox beat the Rochester Red Wings, 3-2, in a game that consumed 8 hours and 25 minutes, included a 32-minute blackout when the lights failed, and took two days to complete.

◇

Wade Boggs, not a home run hitter, remains the only man to collect his 3,000th hit with a home run.

◇

Ty Cobb's prowess as a base stealer had a profound impact upon Rickey Henderson, who became the single-season and career leader. During his minor league days at Modesto, Henderson was intrigued by films of Cobb in action. "The man did it right," he said. "He went into those bases hard every time. I've never forgotten."

◇

A chat with Ted Williams at the 1992 All-Star Game convinced Tony Gwynn to increase his bat's length from 32½ inches to 33 and decrease his bat's weight to 30½ ounces. Ted's tips must have helped: Gwynn hit .353 over the next five seasons.

◇

Tony Gwynn not only tied Honus Wagner for the most batting titles in NL history (8) but also tied his record of four in a row. Gwynn not only hit a career-peak .394 in 1994 but finished with more .300 seasons (19) than anyone not named Ty Cobb (23).

Two AL outfielders, Fred Lynn (1975) and Ichiro Suzuki (2001), won the MVP award and the Rookie of the Year award in the same season.

◇

Although he pitched and played third base at Stanford, Bob Boone made his mark in the majors by catching more games than anybody else. He moved from third because the Phillies were set at that position with Mike Schmidt.

◇

In 1992, the Boones became baseball's first three-generation family when Bret, son of Bob and grandson of Ray, made his debut. The Bells became the second three years later when David, son of Buddy and grandson of Gus, reached the majors.

Fathers and Sons

Fathers and sons who played for the same team at the same time:

Ken Griffey Sr. and Ken Griffey Jr., Seattle Mariners, 1992
Tim Raines Sr. and Tim Raines Jr., Baltimore Orioles, 2001

Mookie Wilson is Preston Wilson's uncle *and stepfather.* Mookie married Preston's mom, who had been Mookie's sister-in-law.

◇

Mark Whiten is the only switch-hitter to hit four home runs in a game. He did it on September 7, 1993 in the second game of a doubleheader for the Cardinals against the Reds.

◇

How things change: Marquis Grissom, one of 15 siblings, grew up so poor that his Georgia home lacked both running water and air-conditioning. A millionaire before age 26, Grissom built homes for his parents and 12 of his 14 brothers and sisters.

◇

Joe Mauer was the only man named *USA Today* high school player of the year in both football (2000) and baseball (2001).

◇

Thanks to a personal peak of 73 home runs in 2001, Barry Bonds became the only man to hit his 500th and 600th home run in successive seasons.

Barry Bonds and Babe Ruth had a cosmic connection. On August 16, 2001, he hit his fifty-third home run on the fifty-third anniversary of the death of Babe Ruth, who died at age 53. It was also the fifty-third multi-homer game for in Bonds' career. The final score, not surprisingly, was 5–3.

◇

Hank Aaron, Babe Ruth, and Willie Mays all reached the 600-homer plateau in their eighteenth seasons. Barry Bonds needed only 17.

◇

When Willie Mays played winter ball in Puerto Rico in 1954, future Giants teammate Orlando Cepeda was his batboy.

◇

Willie Mays was the first man with consecutive 30/30 seasons (1956 and 1957).

◇

Sadaharu Oh, who hit a world-record 868 home runs while spending his entire career in the Japanese major leagues, was originally signed as a *pitcher*. Oh later won 13 straight home run crowns in Japan, plus five MVP awards and a pair of Triple Crowns.

◇

Frank Robinson is the only man to hit his 499th and 500th home runs in the same game.

◇

Frank Robinson and Orlando Cepeda were the only unanimous Rookies of the Year who later became unanimous MVPs.

◇

Dale Murphy is the only man to top a decade in total bases but not win election to the Baseball Hall of Fame. He did it during the 1980s, when he led the NL in hits, runs, and runs batted in and produced a 30/30 season (that many home runs and steals in a year).

40-40 Men

These players had at least 40 home runs and 40 stolen bases in the same season:

Jose Canseco, 1988 Athletics
Barry Bonds, 1996 Giants
Alex Rodriguez, 1998 Mariners
Alfonso Soriano, 2006 Nationals

Future home run king Barry Bonds was the *sixth* overall pick in the 1985 draft of amateur free agents. *Sixth.*

◇

Ron Gant's home run on April 20, 1997, was the only major-league homer ever hit in Hawaii.

◇

Ken Griffey and his son, Ken Griffey Jr., were the only father-and-son tandem to hit consecutive home runs. It happened on September 14, 1990, when both played for the Seattle Mariners.

◇

Nearly 350 fraternal pairs have played in the majors, but the first father and son to play at the same time were the Griffeys, on different teams in 1989 and together in 1990. They are also the only father and son to win MVP honors in the All-Star Game (12 years apart).

◇

John Olerud hit for the cycle twice, in 1997 and 2001. Both times, the triples he hit in the "cycle" games were the only ones he hit that year.

◇

Mark McGwire hit a then-record 70 homers in 1998, but it should have been 71. On September 20, his first-inning drive to left-center field in Milwaukee was touched by a fan, costing the St. Louis slugger a home run although replays showed the ball would have cleared the fence.

◇

During his 70-homer season in 1998, Mark McGwire failed to make contact (walks plus strikeouts) 42.3 per cent of the time he came to the plate, and never homered on a 3–0 count.

◇

Mark McGwire was not only the first player with four straight 50-homer seasons but also the first man to have more RBI than hits in a season.

50-Homer Yankees

Players who had 50-homer seasons for the Yankees:

Babe Ruth (1920, 1921, 1927)
Mickey Mantle (1956, 1961)
Roger Maris (1961)
Alex Rodriguez (2007)

Before Alex Rodriguez topped 50 home runs in 2007, Mike Schmidt and Adrian Beltre shared the record for home runs by a third baseman.

◇

Chipper Jones and Lance Berkman share the single-season record for home runs by a switch-hitter (45).

◇

Fernando Tatis, the only man to hit two grand slams in an inning, victimized Chan Ho Park both times. Before Tatis turned the trick on April 23, 1999, major leaguers had hit 4,777 slams without ever accomplishing that feat.

◇

Future MVP Miguel Tejada was 3 when Hurricane David destroyed his Dominican home, leaving 10 people homeless. Eight years later, he went to work in a garment factory where he washed clothes to support his family. He spent six years there before signing his first pro contract at 17.

◇

Although the odds are 300,000 to 1 against a fan being hit by a ball, according to Ripley's *Believe It or Not*, Baltimore outfielder Jay Gibbons *injured his own wife* with a foul ball in 2006. Before the incident, Gibbons had been asking team management to provide better protection for women and children in the family section of Camden Yards.

◇

Philadelphia first baseman Ryan Howard made the most of his first full season in 2006: he led the majors with 58 home runs and 149 RBI, then edged Albert Pujols in the voting for NL MVP.

◇

Only two catchers ever won batting crowns: Joe Mauer, who hit .347 for the 2006 Minnesota Twins, and Ernie Lombardi, who won titles with the 1938 Cincinnati Reds (.342) and 1942 Boston Braves (.330).

◇

Sammy Sosa is the only player to produce three three-homer games *in the same season* (2001).

◇

In 2001, Colorado's Todd Helton became the first man with back-to-back seasons of 400 total bases.

◇

Seattle's Mike Cameron collected only four RBI with his four-homer game on May 1, 2002. All four shots came with nobody on base.

◇

Travis Hafner is the only man to hit five grand slams before the All-Star break (2006).

Four-Homer Games

American League

1. Lou Gehrig, Yankees, June 3, 1932
2. Pat Seerey, White Sox, July 18, 1948
3. Rocky Colavito, Indians, June 10, 1959
4. Mike Cameron, Mariners, May 2, 2002
5. Carlos Delgado, Blue Jays, September 25, 2002

National League

1. Chuck Klein, Phillies, July 10, 1936 (10 inns.)
2. Gil Hodges, Dodgers, August 31, 1950
3. Joe Adcock, Braves, July 31, 1954
4. Willie Mays, Giants, April 30, 1961
5. Mike Schmidt, Phillies, April 17, 1976 (10 inns.)
6. Bob Horner, Braves, July 6, 1986
7. Mark Whiten, Cardinals, September 7, 1993
8. Shawn Green, Dodgers, May 23, 2002

Although Hall of Famer Ryne Sandberg was named after former Yankee reliever Ryne Duren, 2007 Peoria Chiefs second baseman Ryne Malone was named after Sandberg—his manager that year.

◇

Former big league third baseman Mike Coolbaugh was killed by a line drive after he retired. Coolbaugh, 35, was coaching first base for the Double-A Tulsa Drillers when he was struck in the head by a line drive in the ninth inning of a game at Little Rock on July 23, 2007.

◇

During his youth, Curaçao native Andruw Jones kept in shape for baseball by slinging a sledgehammer three times a week.

◇

Ichiro Suzuki, winner of seven straight batting crowns and three MVP awards in Japan's major leagues, is the only player ever to start his U.S. big league career with six straight 200-hit seasons.

◇

Slugging Brewers third baseman Ryan Braun, the son of an Israeli immigrant, was 7 years old when he came to the United States. In 2007, he became the first Jewish player to win the Rookie of the Year award.

Red Sox outfielder Jacoby Ellsbury, a rookie who became a World Series star in 2007, is the first Navajo Indian in big league history.

The Hit Parade

Players with the most hits in a season:

Player	Hits	Year
Ichiro Suzuki, Seattle Mariners	262	2004
George Sisler, St. Louis Browns	257	1920
Lefty O'Doul, Philadelphia A's	254	1929
Bill Terry, New York Giants	254	1930
Al Simmons, Philadelphia A's	253	1925
Rogers Hornsby, New York Giants	250	1922
Chuck Klein, Philadelphia Phillies	250	1930

An intelligent player with a degree in engineering, George Sisler made a smooth transition from pitcher to hitter. A two-time .400 hitter, his 257-hit season in 1920 lasted more than 80 years as the best ever produced. The left-handed first baseman had a 41-game hitting streak and .340 career average, mostly for the St. Louis Browns.

(Baseball Hall of Fame)

Pitcher Bits

Although he eschewed alcohol, Walter Johnson was discovered by a traveling liquor salesman. The salesman spotted the 17-year-old Johnson pitching for a semi-pro team in Idaho and notified Washington manager Joe Cantillon. Johnson didn't drink, smoke, or swear and didn't even play cards until late in his career.

◇

Eight years before he and Jim (Hippo) Vaughn pitched no-hitters against each other in the same game, Fred Toney pitched a *17-inning no-hitter* in the minors, with Winchester (Kentucky). He pitched his gem on May 10, 1909, walking one and fanning 19 Lexington batters.

◇

After Smokey Joe Wood was discovered while pitching for a women's barnstorming team in 1912, he went 34–5 for the Red Sox during the regular season and won three World Series games. Three years later, however, his arm went bad after a thumb injury and he had to find another position. In 1918, he started a five-year stretch as a major league outfielder.

◇

Rube Marquard of the New York Giants won 19 games in a row in 1912.

◇

Babe Ruth had consecutive 20-win seasons as a *pitcher* for the Boston Red Sox but switched to the outfield by 1920 because of his booming bat. Ruth won 92 games as a pitcher.

◇

Yankee *pitcher* Ray Caldwell hit pinch-homers in consecutive at-bats in 1915.

◇

Babe Ruth won his big league debut on July 11, 1914 when Duffy Lewis *batted for him in the seventh and delivered a pinch-single that led to the winning run*. The rookie Red Sox lefthander, later a prolific Yankee slugger, got credit for a 4–3 win.

◇

Even though Lefty Grove's 16-game winning streak in 1931 ended with a 1–0 loss, he was the AL's first MVP. His selection, along with the choice of Cardinal second baseman Frankie Frisch in the NL, set a precedent of picking players from championship clubs. Prior to 1931, when the Baseball Writers Association of America created the MVP, each league occasionally rewarded its outstanding player on an annual basis. League awards were given from 1922 to 1929 and, prior to that, Chalmers Awards (automobiles) from 1911 to 1914.

Fatal Pitch

During an afternoon game at New York's Polo Grounds on August 16, 1920, Yankee pitcher Carl Mays, a sidearming submariner with a reputation for pitching inside, hit Cleveland shortstop Ray Chapman in the head with a fastball. Mays, en route to a 26–11 season, thought he had hit Chapman's bat. When the ball bounced to him, the pitcher picked it up and threw it to first. Only then did he realize umpire Tommy Connolly was calling for a physician. Chapman died after a midnight operation—the only on-field fatality in major-league history.

Players did not wear helmets in 1920, though some American Leaguers started doing so after the Chapman incident. Helmets did not become mandatory, however, until the NL required all players to wear protective headgear (often cap liners) in 1957. The AL followed suit a year later, but helmets were not required for all professional players until 1971—more than a half century after Chapman's death. It took *another* 23 years before single-earflap helmets became mandatory.

◇

Wes Ferrell holds the single-season and career records for home runs by a pitcher. He hit nine during the 1931 season and 38 in his career.

Almost Blew It

When Johnny Vander Meer threw successive no-hitters in 1938, he faltered in the ninth inning of the second game. He walked the bases loaded, giving him eight walks (against only seven strikeouts), but kept the Dodgers from scoring. The Reds capped the first night game at Ebbets Field with a 6–0 victory before a standing-room-only crowd of 40,000. Four days earlier, on June 11, the 22-year-old Cincinnati southpaw, in his second season, had stung the Boston Bees with a 3–0 no-hit gem. Control problems kept "The Dutch Master" from posting a winning lifetime record; he led the NL in walks in both 1943 and 1948.

FINAL EDITION THE CINCINNATI ENQUIRER **WEATHER**

VOL. XCVIII. NO. 68—DAILY   THURSDAY MORNING, JUNE 16, 1938   24 PAGES   THREE CENTS

VANDER MEER IN SECOND NO-HITTER; REDLEGS DEFEAT BROOKLYN, 6 TO 0

FIVE BALLS

Hit To Outfield.

Sensational Hill Feat
Viewed By 38,748

At Dodgers' First Night
Game—McCormick Homers
With Two On Bags

The first night game at Ebbets Field became an even more historic event when Cincinnati southpaw Johnny Vander Meer became the only pitcher to throw consecutive no-hitters.

(Cincinnati Enquirer)

The brothers Dean talked a good game, too. Jay Hanna, called "Dizzy" before Paul joined him with the Gashouse Gang Cardinals of 1934, was less than successful in hanging the nickname "Daffy" on his younger brother, but he made good his preseason promise that they would combine for 45 victories. Dizzy won 30 games and Paul 19—plus two apiece in the winning World Series against Detroit—and engineered a double shutout against Brooklyn that included a nightcap no-hitter by rookie Paul. "Why didn't you tell me you wuz gonna throw a no-hitter?" asked Dizzy, who allowed three hits in his game. "I woulda throwed one, too."

◇

Carl Hubbell, crack left-hander of the New York Giants, won a record 24 straight games over a two-year span. The streak started on July 17, 1936, with a 6–0 shutout against the Pittsburgh Pirates.

◇

Bob Feller was a 17-year-old high school senior when he fanned 15 St. Louis Browns in his 1936 big league bow with the Cleveland Indians. Two years later, at 19, he was an AL All-Star, sharing a locker room with Jimmie Foxx and Hank Greenberg.

◇

Although the odds of being hit by a ball are enormous, Bob Feller's mother was hit by a ball fouled off by a White Sox batter from a Feller pitch. The incident happened on Mother's Day in 1939.

◇

A two-out, eighth-inning walk to Luke Appling was the lone blemish on Bob Feller's 1940 no-hitter—the only one ever pitched on Opening Day. Feller said later he had a feeling that the pesky Appling was going to get a hit. Feller pitched the gem for the Cleveland Indians against the White Sox at Comiskey Park.

Sigh Young

Bob Feller attended Cy Young's funeral but never won a Cy Young award. The pitching trophy was created in 1956—the year Feller retired—because writers felt that pitchers were overlooked in the voting for Most Valuable Player.

Bob Feller won eight battle stars for his exploits in the Navy during World War II.

Bob Lemon wore No. 6 as an outfielder-third baseman, No. 21 as a pitcher, and No. 77 as manager of the 1977 New York Yankees.

Although a 1941 hunting accident nearly ended his career, Rip Sewell not only recovered but resurrected his career in an accidental way. Forced to favor his injured foot, the right-hander adopted an over-the-top delivery that yielded the eephus pitch—a high-arching changeup that rose 25 feet off the ground before dropping through the strike zone. Only Ted Williams was able to time it for a home run (in an All-Star Game). Sewell won 20 games twice and 143 overall.

Tommy Lasorda—yes, *that* Tommy Lasorda—fanned 25 men in a 15-inning game while pitching for Schenectady (Canadian-American) against Amsterdam on May 31, 1948.

Satchel Paige threw a shutout for his first complete game in the majors. The ancient Cleveland rookie blanked Chicago on August 10, 1948. Satchel Paige was at least 50 years old when he defeated Columbus for Miami in an International League game in the Orange Bowl in 1956. Attendance for the game was 57,000.

Satchel Paige answered fan mail on a portable typewriter while sitting in his Pullman berth.

Still lean and lanky well into his 60s, former Negro Leagues legend Satchel Paige coached Pat Jarvis (33) and other Braves pitchers in 1968 while picking up needed service time to trigger pension benefits.
(Dan Schlossberg)

Although the Cy Young Award was created in 1956 to mollify pitchers who perceived MVP voting as favoring position players, first-year winner Don Newcombe of the Brooklyn Dodgers also was named NL MVP. Newcombe remains the only man to win the Rookie of the Year Award, Most Valuable Player Award, and Cy Young Award.

◇

Robin Roberts, who spent most of his Hall of Fame career with the Phillies, was the only pitcher ever to yield more than 500 home runs.

◇

If consistency counted, Warren Spahn would be at the top of the list. He led NL pitchers in wins 14 different times, three more than runner-up Walter Johnson and five more than Christy Mathewson. Spahn won more regular season games than any left-handed pitcher.

The first lefty with nine 20-win seasons, Warren Spahn finished his career with 13—and more wins than any other southpaw. He starred for the Braves in both Boston and Milwaukee.

(The Topps Company)

**SPAHN BLAZES
SOUTHPAW TRAIL**
WARREN SPAHN
SEPTEMBER 17, 1958

As teammates with the Milwaukee Braves from 1953 to 1961, Warren Spahn and Lew Burdette were the best pitching tandem in the game. During that time they ranked first and second in 15-win seasons, Spahn with nine and Burdette with eight. No one else in the majors had more than six. Spahn and Burdette combined to give the Milwaukee Braves a total of 407 victories.

◇

Warren Spahn liked symmetry: he finished his career with 363 wins and 363 base hits. He hit 35 home runs, most by a pitcher in NL history, and was one of two Braves (with Hank Aaron) to homer in more than 15 consecutive seasons.

Of all pitchers who worked at least 3,000 innings since 1900, Lew Burdette issued the fewest walks (628).

◇

The losing pitcher in Lew Burdette's 1–0 no-hitter against Philadelphia on August 18, 1960, was Gene Conley, his teammate with the world champion Milwaukee Braves three years earlier.

◇

Star Cleveland right-hander Herb Score seemed en route to a Hall of Fame career when he was struck in the eye by a line drive hit by Yankee infielder Gil McDougald on May 7, 1957. The AL's Rookie of the Year in 1955, when he fanned a rookie-record 245 men, Score was never the same. He pitched only two more full seasons, in 1959 and 1960, before retiring at age 29.

◇

Phillies pitcher Jim Hearn lost a game two months after he retired. Hearn was the starting pitcher for the Phils against Pittsburgh on May 10, 1959, but left the game as pitcher of record on the losing side. When the suspended game was completed in July, he was charged with the loss.

Longtime Cardinals relief ace Lindy McDaniel was named after famed aviator Charles (Lucky Lindy) Lindbergh.

◇

Tom Cheney holds the record for strikeouts in a game. He fanned 21 Orioles for the second edition Washington Senators in a 16-inning game on September 12, 1962.

◇

Jim Bunning's perfect game on Father's Day 1964 was appropriate: the Philadelphia right-hander, who beat the New York Mets at Shea Stadium, had nine kids.

◇

Dodgers great Sandy Koufax won 13 straight games against the New York Mets before Tug McGraw finally beat him, 5–2, on August 26, 1965. The future Hall of Famer had a 21–6 record going into the game, while McGraw had only a 1–2 mark.

◇

Sandy Koufax was the only man to win a Cy Young Award in his last season.

◇

Vida Blue's big league debut was ignored in the Oakland paper because it coincided with Neil Armstrong's walk on the moon. The date was July 20, 1969.

◇

Jim Bouton bounced back to the major leagues as a knuckleball pitcher eight years after his retirement. The one-time Yankee fireballer actually won a game for the Atlanta Braves, the only team willing to give him a chance in 1978.

◇

Long after leaving baseball, Jim Bouton became commissioner of the Vintage Baseball Federation. It also left him exposed to hate mail from the rival Vintage Baseball Association, which claimed the Federation was not following the appropriate nineteenth-century rules. When some of the mail turned vicious, Bouton referred to the senders as the "Talibat."

◇

Earl Wilson wasn't the only man to hit a home run while pitching a no-hitter; Rick Wise hit two while holding the opposition hitless.

◇

Mickey Lolich threw left-handed because he broke his collarbone in a fall from his tricycle at age 3.

After Roberto Clemente lost his life in a New Year's Eve plane crash while attempting to deliver supplies to Nicaraguan earthquake victims, Pirate teammate Steve Blass delivered the eulogy at his funeral. Blass, a 19-game winner and All-Star during Clemente's final season in 1972, was never the same again. Suddenly unable to throw strikes, he went 3–9 with a 9.85 ERA in 1973 and retired a year later without winning another game. To this day, pitchers with unexplained wildness are said to be suffering from "Steve Blass Disease."

◇

Rich Reuschel and Frank Tanana were the only pitchers to surrender home runs to both Hank Aaron and Barry Bonds.

◇

Rick Reuschel and brother Paul produced the only combined shutout ever thrown by brothers during their brief time together with the Chicago Cubs.

◇

Pitcher Terry Forster has the best batting average of any player who appeared in 500 games. The hefty lefty, often used as a pinch-hitter, hit a whopping .397.

Ah, What a Relief!

Four years before earning his doctorate in exercise physiology from Michigan State, Mike Marshall parlayed his knowledge of kinesiology into a record-breaking season. Pitching for the 1974 Los Angeles Dodgers, he pitched in 106 games, finished 84 of them, worked 208 innings in relief, and made 13 consecutive appearances—all major league records. He worked 12 more innings in postseason play. Marshall, who worked at least 90 games in two other seasons, won one Cy Young Award and was runner-up in the voting for another.

Three former All-Stars were 20-game losers in 1974: Mickey Lolich lost 21 games while Randy Jones and Steve Rogers dropped 22 apiece.

◇

George (Doc) Medich, a medical student at the time, jumped into the Baltimore stands in 1978 to save the life of a 61-year-old fan stricken by a heart attack before a game. The Texas pitcher applied heart massage until paramedics arrived.

The only home run of Joe Niekro's career cost brother Phil a victory in 1976. The Niekro brothers still managed to win more games than any other pitching brothers.

◇

Phil and Joe Niekro combined to win 539 games, 10 more than Gaylord and Jim Perry and a record for brothers. The Niekros pitched more innings than any other brother tandem, while the Perrys recorded more strikeouts. The Perrys combined for 39 wins in their only season as teammates (with the 1974 Indians)—and, six years later, were the only brothers to pitch against each other in the same All-Star Game. They are also the only brothers to win Cy Young Awards.

◇

Get those men a cane! When Phil Niekro and Don Sutton opposed each other on June 8, 1987, their combined age was 90 years and 135 days—making theirs the oldest matchup of starting pitchers in baseball history.

Like Hoyt Wilhelm before him, knuckleballer Phil Niekro proved pitchers can win without throwing hard. He and his brother won more games than any brother tandem.
(Dan Schlossberg)

After grandson Len Barker pitched a 1981 perfect game, Tokie Lockhart said, "Tell Len I'm very proud of him. I hope he does better next time."

Tom Seaver, the longtime face of the Mets franchise, won his 300th game in New York—pitching for the Chicago White Sox at Yankee Stadium on August 4, 1985. It was the only time Yankee fans rooted against their own team.

◇

Although Bert Blyleven had more career strikeouts than Walter Johnson, Bob Gibson, or Tom Seaver, he won only one strikeout crown.

◇

Bruce Sutter was the first pitcher to get into the Hall of Fame without ever starting a game.

◇

Dennis Eckersley of the 1990 Oakland Athletics was the first pitcher to record more games saved (49) than base runners allowed (45).

◇

Minnesota lefty Frank Viola was a near-perfect pitcher whenever he saw a banner that read, "FRANKIE SWEET MUSIC VIOLA." In 1987, he went 15–0 with four no-decisions (all Twins wins) whenever the banner appeared, won the first and last games of the World Series with the banner displayed, and won the Series MVP award. To keep the streak going, Viola gave the banner's creator, Mark Dornfeld, tickets to Minnesota home games in the World Series that year.

Stingy Pitchers

Pitchers with at least 50 consecutive scoreless innings:

1. Orel Hershiser (59, 1988)
2. Don Drysdale (58, 1968)
3. Walter Johnson ($55\frac{2}{3}$, 1913)
4. Jack Coombs (53, 1910)

Nolan Ryan, who pitched a record seven no-hitters in the majors, was 12 when he pitched his first no-hitter—in Little League ball in Alvin, Texas.

◇

Any challenger to Nolan Ryan's strikeout record of 5,714 would have to fan an average of 285.7 hitters a year for 20 years.

When Nolan Ryan retired in 1993, he held or shared 53 records, including 27 seasons played, 19 low-hit games, 5,714 strikeouts, 2,795 walks, and six 300-strikeout seasons. The 11-time K king also had the most strikeouts in a season (383) and the most per nine innings by a starting pitcher in a season (11.48) and career (9.55). Ryan was 43 when he won his last strikeout crown but 44 when he pitched the last of his seven no-hitters.

◇

Nolan Ryan and Rickey Henderson had to share back page headlines on May 2, 1991, the day after Ryan threw his record seventh no-hitter and Henderson passed Lou Brock to become the career leader in stolen bases. P.S.: The 44-year-old Ryan fanned 16 men in his no-hitter for Texas against Toronto.

◇

Nolan Ryan is the only player to have his number retired by three different teams (the Angels, the Astros, and the Rangers).

◇

Although Nolan Ryan had more strikeout crowns (16) than any other pitcher, he also set major league marks for most years leading in walks (13 times) and wild pitches (11 times).

Life Begins at 40

Pitchers who hurled no-hitters at age 40:

Cy Young
Warren Spahn
Nolan Ryan
Randy Johnson

Anthony Young lost a record 27 games in a row. The streak ended on May 6, 1994, when the Cubs beat the Pirates 10–1.

◇

Cuban defector Orlando "El Duque" Hernandez got his chance when 1998 Yankees starter David Cone was bitten by a dog and forced to miss a start.

◇

Yankees lefty David Wells pitched a perfect game and started the All-Star Game in the same season (1998). He also took the mound wearing a valuable Babe Ruth cap but was forced to remove it after one inning.

Though he's pitched no-hitters in both leagues, Randy Johnson has also finished on the wrong end of a no-hitter. It happened in 1999, when Jose Jimenez of the St. Louis Cardinals beat the Arizona Diamondbacks, 1–0, in Phoenix on June 25.

◇

Jesse Orosco, often used as a situational southpaw, worked more often than any other pitcher.

◇

St. Louis southpaw Rick Ankiel threw nine wild pitches in four innings during the 2000 playoffs. Plagued by continued wildness in 2001 and elbow problems in two succeeding seasons, Ankiel resurfaced in 2004 but never recaptured the promise he had shown in the minors. Because he could hit, however, Ankiel made a successful conversion to the outfield, leading the minors in home runs in 2007 and joining the Cardinals in time for the stretch drive. His torrid stroke rejuvenated the team and projected it into contention for the NL Central crown.

◇

Roger Clemens fanned 20 men in a nine-inning game twice—and did it 10 years apart. He did it on April 29, 1986, and September 18, 1996, both while pitching for the Boston Red Sox. Kerry Wood of the Chicago Cubs also fanned 20 in nine innings, on May 6, 1998, versus Houston, while Randy Johnson of the Arizona Diamondbacks had 20 K's in an 11-inning game against the Reds on May 8, 2001.

◇

Roger Clemens of the 2001 Yankees was the first 20-game winner without a complete game.

◇

Gaylord Perry was the first man to win Cy Young awards in both leagues. Randy Johnson, Pedro Martinez, and Roger Clemens have done it since.

◇

Roger Clemens, Greg Maddux, and Steve Carlton won 15 Cy Young awards without a no-hitter, while Nolan Ryan had seven no-hitters without winning a Cy Young.

◇

Bird brains: during the 2006 season, Kansas City's Paul *Byrd* pursued Doug *Bird*'s club record for most innings pitched without a walk.

◇

Shortly after his team was eliminated from postseason play, Yankees pitcher Cory Lidle lost his life when his small plane crashed into a Manhattan high-rise on the Upper East Side. Lidle, just 34 when he was

killed on October 11, 2006, was the second Yankees player killed in a private plane crash while active in the majors. Thurman Munson, the team's
catcher and captain, died on August 2, 1979, while practicing takeoffs and
landings in Akron, Ohio.

◇

Chase Wright, a rookie with the 2007 Yankees, became the second member of an ignominious club: pitchers who have surrendered four straight
homers in a major league game. The other man to do it, Paul Foytack, was
a tough act to follow, though: pitching for the Angels against the Indians
on July 31, 1963, he threw gopher balls to the 8–9–1–2 hitters: Woodie
Held, Pedro Ramos, Tito Francona, and Larry Brown.

◇

After winning the first game of the 2006 World Series, St. Louis pitcher
Anthony Reyes went 0–10 in his first dozen starts of 2007 and found himself back in the minors.

◇

Two Cardinals pitchers died within a five-year span: starter Darryl Kile
(coronary artery blockage) in June 2002 and reliever Josh Hancock (car
crash) in April 2007.

◇

Trevor Hoffman's dad, Ed, a successful singer before settling in Anaheim,
was known as "the singing usher" during his days as an Anaheim Stadium
employee. He carried a tuner in his pocket and often filled in for National
Anthem performers who failed to show up on time.

◇

Andy Pettitte is the only active pitcher as of the end of the 2007 season
who worked at least 10 seasons without ever having a losing record.

◇

Although rookie Don Mattingly wore No. 46 for the Yankees, the number gained fame after it was issued to left-handed pitcher Andy Pettitte.
Mattingly switched to No. 23, half of his original issue.

◇

It may not be an appropriate name for a pitcher, but the 2007 Reds had a
hurler named Homer Bailey. P.S.: It wasn't a nickname.

◇

The real first name of Joba Chamberlain, the late-season rookie sensation
of the New York Yankees, is Justin.

◇

Good bloodlines: the mother of star Boston closer Jonathan Papelbon, a
postseason hero in 2007, was a pitcher on the first Louisiana State softball
team.

CHAPTER 5

Bosses

Baseball has many bosses. Managers pick coaches, handle players, and dictate game strategy, while general managers are responsible for contract negotiations, trades, and creating the best 25-man rosters. Owners have the ultimate authority at the team level, but the game's hierarchy is headed by a commissioner who is empowered to make decisions that he considers "in the best interest of baseball." Umpires, hired by the commissioner's staff, enforce the rules of the game on the field.

Managers

Managers are hired to be fired. When a talented team fails to win or a franchise spends too many seasons mired in the lower depths of the standings, owners invariably react. Because it's easier to fire (and replace) a manager than 25 players, the position is not known for its tenure. Common reasons for a manager's dismissal include the inability to win, failure to communicate with or control the players, availability of a better person, or less-than-cordial relations with ownership (often exacerbated by managerial salary demands). There are exceptions, however: Connie Mack managed the Philadelphia Athletics for more than a half century because he owned the team and was not likely to fire himself.

Only 8 other men managed at least 25 years in the majors: John McGraw (33), Tony LaRussa (30), Bucky Harris (29), Bobby Cox (27), Gene Mauch and Sparky Anderson (26), and Casey Stengel and Bill McKechnie (25). Others who managed at least 20 years include Joe McCarthy and Leo Durocher (24), Walter Alston (23), Jimmie Dykes, Dick Williams, and Tommy Lasorda (21 each), and Cap Anson, Clark Griffith, and Ralph Houk (20 each).

Many men have run more than one club. Frank Bancroft managed seven different teams, and three others—Jimmie Dykes, Dick Williams, and John McNamara—had six each. Dykes was even traded for another manager when Detroit sent him to Cleveland for Joe Gordon in 1960. More than 40 managers have run three teams each since the turn of the century, and Bucky Harris actually had eight terms as a pilot (including three with Washington and two with Detroit). Managers feel enormous pressure to succeed. Three were actually fired after winning a pennant but failing to win a world championship: Bill McKechnie, known for his ability to handle pitchers, was dropped by the Cardinals in 1928; Casey Stengel by the New York Yankees in 1960; and Yogi Berra by the Yankees in 1964. Stengel had won 10 pennants in 12 years as manager of the Yankees but was ostensibly dismissed because of his old age (70). Stengel sat out a year, then took over the expansion New York Mets of the National League (NL) for their first four seasons. Eight years after Stengel retired, Yogi Berra, who followed him from the Bronx to Queens, became one of six managers to win pennants in both leagues (Joe McCarthy, Alvin Dark, Sparky Anderson, Dick Williams, and Tony LaRussa were the others).

For all pilots, strategy is critical. Skilled managers gamble by sending runners for extra bases, utilizing the stolen base (and the double steal), and employing the suicide squeeze play and the hit-and-run. Inserting the proper pinch-hitters and relief pitchers is also vital to a team's success.

Managers play to win on the road and tie at home. The time-tested theory is that familiar surroundings, partisan fans, and the sudden-death advantage of the bottom of the ninth (or any subsequent innings) will enable the home team to break the tie and go on to victory. Contending clubs know that they must play .500 against the top teams and murder the tail-enders. A championship cannot be forged without a high winning percentage, and few clubs can maintain a high ratio of wins to losses against top-flight opposition.

Some managers carry an extra burden. Billy Martin, hired five times by mercurial Yankee owner George Steinbrenner, always said his main job as manager was to keep the five players who hated him away from the five who were undecided.

Manager Bits

Early in 1943, Casey Stengel was struck by a car on a rainy night in Boston's Kenmore Square. Idled by a broken leg, Stengel temporarily yielded the reins of the Boston Braves to co-managers George Kelly and Robert Coleman.

◇

The Chicago Cubs tried a rotating college of coaches for five seasons starting in 1961 but junked the idea when players complained they were getting conflicting advice from the rotating head coaches.

Player-Managers

In the early years of baseball, managers were also players. Some were even part owners of their teams, and many handled such general manager functions as trademaking and contract negotiations. Brooklyn boss Charles Ebbets, an early advocate of the player-manager, said he preferred a man who could lead by example. So did Connie Mack, who spent more than half a century with the Philadelphia Athletics as owner, manager, and general manager.

Adrian (Cap) Anson, player-manager of the Chicago NL club from 1879 to 1897, was not only one of the great players of the nineteenth century but also baseball's first great showman. He dressed his teams in colorful Navajo bathrobes, dark blue bloomers, form-fitting pants, and even dress suits for one game.

◇

Cap Anson and Frank Selee were the most successful managers of the nineteenth century. Each won five NL pennants: Anson with the Chicago White Stockings and Selee while managing both Boston and Chicago.

◇

John McGraw, Miller Huggins, and Bucky Harris all took command of their clubs while still on the active list. Cleveland's Tris Speaker hit .388 and won the World Series in 1920. Rogers Hornsby hit .317 as second baseman and manager of the world championship Cardinals of 1926 and one year earlier hit .403 with 39 homers and 143 runs batted in after replacing Branch Rickey as manager early in the campaign.

Ty Cobb managed the Tigers for six seasons without much success but continued to hit the ball hard. In 1922, he hit .401—the high mark for a player-manager in the American League (AL).

◇

Bill Terry, John McGraw's successor with the New York Giants, zoomed from seventh to first in 1933—his first full season as pilot—and kept the team in contention with his strategy as well as batting heroics for two more seasons. After bad knees forced him to retire as a player in 1936, however, the Giants sank in the standings, dropping 10½ games from the top by mid-July. Disobeying doctors' orders, Terry went back on the active list and tripled home the winning run that same day. The inspired Giants launched a 15-game winning streak and went on to win the pennant.

◇

Lou Boudreau was a 24-year-old shortstop when Cleveland made him manager in 1942. He'd only been in the majors three seasons but thought that he could translate his enthusiasm and instincts on the field into leadership that his teammates would respect. In 1948, his club won the world championship after beating Boston 8–3 in a one-game pennant playoff marked by two Boudreau homers and a pair of singles. The last great player-manager, Boudreau's tenure with the Indians lasted through the 1950 season.

◇

The only other player-managers since Boudreau were Phil Cavaretta with the Cubs of the early 1950s; Solly Hemus, who played less than 20 games for the Cardinals in 1959; Frank Robinson, a two-time MVP who took over the Indians in 1975; Joe Torre, who played sparingly for the Mets after replacing Joe Frazier in 1977; Don Kessinger, manager of the White Sox in 1979; and Pete Rose, who took command of his hometown Reds in 1984.

◇

The 1907 Boston Red Sox had *six* managers. The first, Chick Stahl, committed suicide just before Opening Day. Then, owner John Taylor took the job himself until AL president Ban Johnson vetoed that idea. Cy Young was named pitcher-manager until Opening Day, when Taylor hired George Huff. After losing six of eight, Huff was out and first baseman Bob Unglaub was in. He went 9–20 and was booted in favor of Deacon McGuire.

◇

George Stallings of the 1914 Boston Braves was the first manager to use platooning to his advantage during the World Series. He realized that percentages favored a left-handed batter against a right-handed pitcher and vice-versa. Lefty-righty switches have been integral parts of the game since.

Curfews Curtail Carousers

Because a manager must field a team of alert, aggressive players, most employ and enforce curfew rules—especially on the road. During his 30-year tenure as manager of the New York Giants, John McGraw imposed an 11:30 P.M. curfew on the road and a midnight curfew at home.

Rogers Hornsby devised an ingenious one-night plan to catch violators. He handed the only elevator operator a brand-new ball at the stroke of midnight. He bribed the man to get the signature of every player he saw that night—and then hand in the ball the next morning.

John McGraw's 30-year tenure as manager of the New York Giants started on July 19, 1902. Two years later, his team won a pennant, then not only repeated in 1905 but also won a World Series. McGraw retired as manager in 1932 but returned to manage the first NL All-Star team a year later.

(The Topps Company)

Thanks to 10 pennants and 10 second-place finishes, John McGraw won an NL-record 2,840 games. A .334 hitter during his days as a fiery third baseman, McGraw ran the New York Giants for 30 years (1902 to 1932) and preached an aggressive approach in both attitude and technique. His teams used the bunt, the hit-and-run, and defenses that varied according to the opposing hitter. McGraw's teams were also the first to make extensive use of pinch-hitters and relief pitchers.

◇

Most of the game's most successful managers had New York pedigrees. Joe McCarthy and Casey Stengel, best known for their work with the Yankees, won the World Series seven times each while John McGraw, longtime manager of the New York Giants, and Connie Mack, who ran the Philadelphia A's, took five titles apiece.

◇

Connie Mack was the anti-McGraw. Quiet and soft-spoken, he seldom swore and rarely said anything negative to anyone. His gentlemanly approach to managing extended to his dugout outfit: street clothes with a high starched collar. "Talent comprises 75 percent of managing," said Mack, who won 3,776 games as a manager in 53 seasons (both records). "Strategy is 12½ percent, and the other 12½ percent is comprised of what a manager can get out of his team."

Connie Mack, who wore street clothes during most of his 53-season tenure as manager of the Philadelphia Athletics, finished first nine times but lost almost twice as often (17 times). The former catcher, whose father was a Civil War veteran, enjoyed two heydays—winning four pennants from 1910–1914 and three more from 1929–1931. Economic hardships forced him to break up both teams by selling veteran stars.

(Ronnie Joyner)

PHILADELPHIA ATHLETICS   MANAGER

Connie Mack

One of the most successful managers in major-league history once earned 16 cents per hour as a car coupler in a coal mine. Bucky Harris was a 27-year-old second baseman in his fourth major-league season when he was appointed manager of the Washington Senators in 1924. When he proceeded to win the pennant and the World Series, the press referred to him as "the boy wonder"—a name that remained with him through 29 seasons as a big-league manager. Harris won another world championship with the 1947 Yankees but lost a World Series in 1925 when he failed to lift tiring Washington ace Walter Johnson in the late innings of the last game. That turned a 6–4 lead into a 9–7 loss and provoked an angry telegram from AL president Ban Johnson. Harris wired back, "I went down with my best."

◇

A low-key pilot who never played in the majors, Joe McCarthy compiled a record .614 winning percentage while winning eight pennants with the Yankees and one with the Cubs. Called a "push-button manager" by jealous rival Jimmie Dykes because his teams won so easily, McCarthy almost won two more flags with the 1948–1949 Red Sox. Ted Williams, who played for McCarthy in Boston, called him the best manager he ever saw.

◇

Charlie Grimm was the last manager of the Boston Braves, who moved to Milwaukee in March 1953.

Little Big Man

At 5 feet 6 inches tall and 140 pounds, Miller Huggins was smaller than any of his Yankees players. But he had a highly successful tenure as manager from 1918 until his death in 1929. Although the ball club was populated by talented but independent ballplayers who often disregarded training rules and directives from management, Huggins held his own with the support of ownership. When the manager slapped Babe Ruth with an indefinite suspension and a $5,000 fine for a series of infractions in 1925, the star rebelled and the team finished seventh in an eight-team league. Huggins rallied the troops to win three straight pennants, but swirling controversy exacted a toll on the fragile pilot: he died at age 50 before the end of the 1929 season.

Casey Stengel sacrificed a potential career as a left-handed dentist from Kansas City (the "KC" initials inspired his nickname) to become a big-league player and manager. A strategist as well as a showman, Stengel employed the win-at-all-costs tactics of John McGraw, his manager with the 1920s Giants, and mastered the art of platooning. He never mastered the English language, however, and confused interviewers with double-talk gibberish dubbed "Stengelese."

◇

Casey Stengel won 10 pennants in 12 years with the Yankees but struck out at least twice as a talent evaluator. As manager of the Brooklyn Dodgers in 1935, he auditioned diminutive shortstop Phil Rizzuto but couldn't handle his five-foot-six-inch size. He told the Brooklyn-born infielder to go find a box and shine shoes. A couple years later, after Stengel moved to Boston as manager of the Braves, he ordered Warren Spahn to throw at an opposing hitter in retaliation for an earlier hit batsman. Spahn refused and Stengel told him, "You've got no guts. You'll never make it in this game." Without Rizzuto, who won an MVP award that year, Stengel's Yankees wouldn't have won the pennant in 1950. As for Spahn, he merely won 363 games— the most by any left-hander.

◇

Warren Spahn played for Stengel with both the Boston Braves of the 1940s and the New York Mets of the 1960s. Between those stints with bad ball clubs, Stengel had 10 first-place finishes, one second, and one third with the Yankees. "I played for Stengel before and after he was a genius," Spahn said.

◇

Talking to writers before a game in Brooklyn, Leo Durocher spotted Mel Ott, the man he later succeeded as Giants manager. "See Ott?" Durocher said. "He's a nice guy. And nice guys finish eighth." The slightly revised phrase, the only one from baseball in *Bartlett's Familiar Quotations*, was a reference to the eight-team National League of 1948.

◇

After serving a one-year suspension for "activities detrimental to baseball" (associating with gamblers), Leo Durocher returned as Dodgers manager in 1948. But he didn't feel secure in the job, which he had held since 1939. The manager met with Giants owner Horace Stoneham and replaced Mel Ott in New York on July 16. During a Giants tenure that lasted through 1955, Durocher won two NL flags and a world championship.

Although controversy followed him like a shadow, Leo Durocher managed the Dodgers, Giants, Cubs, and Astros long enough to land in the Baseball Hall of Fame. The one-time fiery short-stop, a teammate of Babe Ruth with the Yankees and Dizzy Dean with the Cardinals, even gave the carousing Cards their "Gashouse Gang" nickname. Durocher's teams won 2,008 times, including the playoff game won by Bobby Thomson's ninth inning home run for the 1951 Giants.

(Baseball Hall of Fame)

```
LEO DUROCHER
2,019 Wins
```

Charley Dressen, who piloted five different teams, was much more successful as manager of the Dodgers in the 1950s than he had been with the lowly Washington Senators. In a game where the Senators trailed 22–1 with two outs and nobody on base in the ninth, pitcher Mickey McDermott suddenly announced, "Don't worry, gang. Charley will think of something!"

◇

In 23 seasons as manager of the Dodgers, Walter Alston finished first or second 15 times. He won seven pennants, seven All-Star games, and four World Championships—some with good-hitting clubs, others with teams molded around speed, pitching, and defense. His ability to change as the team changed made him a great manager and earned him 23 one-year contracts. So much for the New York newspapers that headlined, "WALTER WHO?" when Alston was first hired.

Tommy Lasorda, who followed Alston as a Hall of Fame manager with the Dodgers, lost his spot on the 1955 Brooklyn roster to another left-handed pitcher: a green rookie named Sandy Koufax.

◇

Six members of the 1957 Milwaukee Braves later became managers: Joe Adcock, Del Crandall, Eddie Mathews, Del Rice, Red Schoendienst, and Chuck Tanner.

◇

Al Lopez was the only opposing manager to win pennants during Casey Stengel's 12-year tenure with the Yankees. Lopez beat Stengel with the 1954 Indians and 1959 White Sox but finished second 10 times.

◇

Danny Murtaugh was the beneficiary of the Bill Mazeroski home run that won the 1960 World Series for the Pittsburgh Pirates.

Danny Murtaugh had four different terms as manager of the Pittsburgh Pirates. He was at the helm in 1960, when Bill Mazeroski's ninth-inning homer gave the Bucs a world championship.
(Ronnie Joyner)

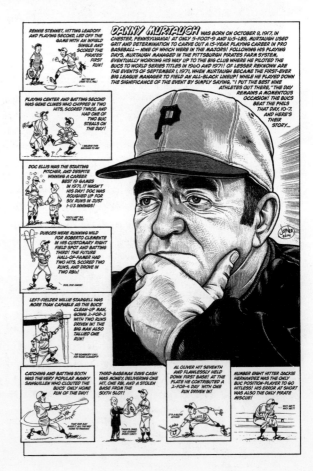

Oriole manager Paul Richards was the first to monitor pitch counts. He started in 1960 when his Baltimore pitching staff was so young they were often called "Baby Birds." Anchors of the rotation were 22-year-old Chuck Estrada plus Milt Pappas, Steve Barber, and Jack Fisher (all 21).

Why Williams Won

Dick Williams was a rookie manager when he brought the 1967 Boston Red Sox home first after the club had finished ninth in a 10-team league the year before. "I was a no-good horse's tail at Boston," he admitted. "I had to be. Hell, I'd been one of them as a player there in 1963 and 1964." Williams won again with the Oakland A's of 1972 and 1973 and took those clubs to the world championship that eluded him in Boston. Williams, elected to the Hall of Fame in 2007, won his final flag with the 1984 San Diego Padres.

DICK WILLIAMS

Dick Williams was manager of the Montreal Expos when the team finished first for the only time in its history. The Expos won the NL East flag during the second half of the 1981 split season (caused by a player strike) but lost to Los Angeles in the ninth inning of the last NLCS game.

(The National League)

When knuckleballer Hoyt Wilhelm was at the peak of his career with Baltimore, Orioles manager Paul Richards designed and deployed an oversized catcher's mitt for Gus Triandos.

◇

Although the Chicago Cubs made Negro Leagues legend Buck O'Neil the first black coach in 1962, it took 13 more years before the Cleveland Indians made Frank Robinson the first black manager.

◇

Phil Linz raised the ire of the usually mild-mannered Yogi Berra by playing his harmonica on the team bus after a tough loss in 1964. Berra managed the Yankees to the pennant that year but was soon replaced by Johnny Keane, whose Cardinals defeated him in the 1964 World Series.

◇

The only man to manage two different teams in one AL city was Joe Gordon, who ran both the Kansas City Athletics and Kansas City Royals.

◇

Gil Hodges once told his players on the Washington Senators that anyone out after curfew the previous evening was to put $100 in the empty cigar box in his office. He said he could name four offenders. When he looked in the box later, he counted $700.

◇

During his first 10 years as manager of the Baltimore Orioles, diminutive but combative Earl Weaver won five divisional crowns and took his team to the World Series three times (1969, 1970, and 1971). Weaver, who had two terms at the helm, was only 56 when he stepped down as Baltimore manager after taking the team to six AL East titles, four pennants, and the 1970 world championship. He said he was getting too old for the stress of managing.

◇

Although Gene Mauch managed a record 26 years without ever winning a pennant, he was widely considered an exceptional manager. A keen student of the game, Mauch managed according to hunches rather than conventional strategy. Dubbed "The Little General" during his time in Montreal, Mauch was said to know the rule book better than most umpires.

◇

A volatile disposition and tendency to cross the front office cost Billy Martin managing jobs in Detroit, Minnesota, and Texas before he won two consecutive pennants with the 1976–1977 Yankees. Martin had won divisional championships with the Twins, Tigers, and Athletics and brought the Rangers home as surprise runners-up.

An explosive temper and a penchant for drinking sabotaged Billy Martin's career as a manager. His list of fights was almost as long as his list of successes, although he did win titles with the Minnesota Twins, Detroit Tigers, Oakland A's, and New York Yankees. Martin, who also did well during a brief tenure with the Texas Rangers, had a record five terms as manager of the Yankees.

(John Pennisi)

First Black Manager

Frank Robinson should have quit after one game. The first black manager would have had a perfect record. At 39, Robinson was still an active player when hired to run the Cleveland Indians in 1975. Baseball's first player-manager since Solly Hemus of the 1959 Cardinals, Robinson relished the role. He even homered in his first at-bat, helping the Indians beat the Yankees 5–3 in his April 7 debut. The only man to win MVP honors in both leagues, Robinson finished his playing career in 1976 with 586 home runs, trailing only Hank Aaron, Babe Ruth, and Willie Mays. He didn't enjoy the same success as a manager mainly because he didn't have the horses. Cleveland went 79–80, fourth in the AL East, in 1975 and 81–78 under Robinson in 1976. Although the team remained fourth, it posted its third winning season since 1959. A year later, however, the situation deteriorated. The Indians were plodding along at 26–31 when Robinson became the first black manager to be fired. He later managed the Giants, Orioles, Expos, and Nationals and served as an executive for Major League Baseball.

Frank Robinson, the only man to win MVP trophies in both leagues, became the first black manager in 1975 with the Cleveland Indians. Still an active player, he marked the occasion by homering in his first at-bat to help his team win.

(Cleveland Indians)

Fired as manager of the Phillies in 1979, Danny Ozark waxed philosophical, saying, "Even Napoleon had his Watergate."

Spring Break

Managers fired during spring training:

Phil Cavaretta, 1954 Cubs
Alvin Dark, 1978 Padres
Tim Johnson, 1999 Blue Jays
Joe Kerrigan, 2002 Red Sox

Whitey Herzog, who had success as a manager in Kansas City and St. Louis, was innovative as well as impulsive. Before one All-Star Game, he noticed that the bus driver assigned to drive the media to the park was inebriated. Seizing both the moment and the steering wheel, Herzog jumped into the driver's seat and drove the bus to the ballpark. He told the writers he wanted to make sure they all got to the game safely.

◊

Sparky Anderson won five pennants and three world championships during his 26-year tenure as manager of the Reds and Tigers. During his first eight years (all with Cincinnati), he won five divisional crowns, four pennants, and two world titles while finishing second twice. His Reds averaged 96 wins per year during that stretch.

◊

Four men were ejected from games in six different decades: Leo Durocher, Frank Robinson, Casey Stengel, and Don Zimmer. All were players before embarking on long careers as managers.

◊

Buck Showalter, first manager of the Arizona Diamondbacks, played with fire in 1998—ordering his pitcher to walk San Francisco's Barry Bonds with the bases loaded and the D'backs leading 8–6. The next hitter worked the count to 3–2 before lining out to end the game. Showalter's strategy had not been used for 54 years, since Giants manager Mel Ott ordered a bases-filled intentional pass for Cubs slugger Bill Nicholson.

◊

Sparky Anderson and Tony LaRussa are the only managers to win world championships in both leagues. But Jim Leyland could have replaced LaRussa had his Tigers defeated the Cardinals in the 2006 World Series.

◊

Although he was voted NL Manager of the Year in 2006, Joe Girardi was fired by the Florida Marlins immediately after the season. Conflicts with owner Jeffrey Loria did not help Girardi's cause. Girardi landed on his feet, though, when he was tapped by the Yankees to succeed Joe Torre for the 2008 season.

◊

After less-than-successful stints as manager of the Mets, Braves, and Cardinals, Joe Torre managed the Yankees into the playoffs in all 12 seasons with the club (1996 to 2007). The string, a record for any manager employed by George Steinbrenner, included nine divisional crowns and three wild card spots.

◊

As the Italian-American manager of the 1998 Yankees, Joe Torre had players from Australia, Cuba, Jamaica, Japan, Panama, and Puerto Rico as well as from the United States.

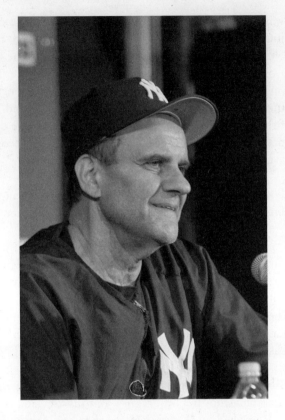

Although Joe Torre never reached the World Series in managing stints with the Mets, Braves, and Cardinals, he won it four times as manager of the Yankees.

(Bill Menzel)

Yankees manager Joe Torre missed nearly two months of the 1999 campaign after being diagnosed with prostate cancer during spring training, but returned to take his team to postseason play and his third world championship.

◇

Joe Torre's tenure with the Yankees ended after his team was eliminated in the first round of the playoffs three years in a row. Insulted when Yankee ownership offered him a new contract loaded with performance clauses— not to mention a pay cut from $7 million to $5 million—Torre walked after the 2007 season, accepting a position with the Los Angeles Dodgers for 2008.

◇

Lou Piniella proved a panacea for the 2007 Chicago Cubs, taking the team to a divisional title on the heels of a last-place finish. Piniella previously piloted the Mariners, Reds, Devil Rays, and Yankees (twice).

In his first year as manager of the Chicago Cubs, Lou Piniella prodded his charges to rise from last place in the 2006 NL Central to first in 2007.

(Bill Menzel)

Before resigning unexpectedly in the middle of the 2007 season, Seattle pilot Mike Hargrove made one of his squawks count. After battling through three snow delays in 4⅔ innings on Opening Day, the Mariners manager complained to the umpires that his hitters couldn't see the pitches from Cleveland's Paul Byrd. The Indians led 4–0 in the top of the fifth but needed one more strike to make the game official. They never got it. The umps called time and play never resumed, costing Cleveland a likely win and Byrd the best performance of his career. The frozen Seattle hitters were unable to muster a single hit.

◇

The career of Bobby Cox has been marked by jubilation and dejection. His Atlanta Braves teams won a record 14 consecutive divisional titles, including a record five pennants in the 1990s, but converted only one of those into a world championship. Cox was also ejected from more games than any other manager, breaking John McGraw's mark of 131 during the 2007 season.

In his second stint as manager of the Braves, Bobby Cox won a record 14 straight division titles—often supported by switch-hitting slugger Chipper Jones. Cox also served as Atlanta general manager for five years before returning to the field in 1990.

(The Topps Company)

BRAVES BOSS AND POWER
BOBBY COX • CHIPPER JONES

Coaches

Most major-league teams carry six coaches, usually hand-picked by the manager. Two flash signs to hitters and direct base-runners from coaching boxes behind first and third base when their team bats; one supervises the bullpen; and the pitching coach monitors pitchers from the dugout, where he shares space with a "bench coach" who serves as an assistant manager and strategy sounding board. One of the base coaches usually doubles as the batting coach.

Coach Bits

Early baseball managers, including John McGraw, preferred to handle all aspects of running their teams. Substitute players manned the coaching boxes, and nonplaying managers frequently filled one of the boxes themselves.

Many modern-day coaches are former managers seeking to find new jobs as pilots or are just-retired players hoping to move into managerial slots without following the traditional route up from the minors.

◇

Coaches use six basic signs: bunt, take, hit-and-run, squeeze, steal, and "forget the previous sign." The third base coach is particularly important because his decisions help or hurt the team in scoring runs. He must gamble often and always make instantaneous decisions, usually with runners in motion. A good third base coach is invariably heir apparent to the incumbent manager.

◇

Johnny Sain, revered as a pitching guru, developed more than a dozen 20-game winners during a long career as a pitching coach in the 1960s and 1970s. In both Minnesota and Chicago, he helped Jim Kaat blossom into a top winner.

◇

Cuban native Fredi Gonzalez, manager of the 2007 Florida Marlins, was with the team before. He was hired as the team's first coach a year before the expansion team started play in 1993.

◇

Yankees coach Frankie Crosetti won so many championship rings that he asked the 1962 Yanks to give him something else. They settled on a pair of shotguns emblazoned with the Yankees logo.

◇

Dave Duncan, longtime pitching coach for manager Tony LaRussa, learned his craft as a catcher.

◇

Former managers often make good coaches. The coaching staff of Joe Torre's 2007 New York Yankees, for example, featured three former managers: Larry Bowa, Tony Pena, and Joe Kerrigan.

Owners and Executives

Baseball owners have one thing in common: they all have plenty of money, most of it earned from other businesses. George Steinbrenner made his fortune as a Cleveland shipbuilder before buying the New York Yankees, while Charley Finley was an insurance magnate from the Chicago area. The Wrigley family made its fortune in chewing gum, Ted Turner thrived when his communications empire took off, and the Busch family used its beer fortune to buy the St. Louis Cardinals. Baseball's ownership ranks have also had a hamburger baron (Ray Kroc of McDonald's fame), a singing cowboy (Gene Autry), and a high-profile legal eagle (Peter Angelos).

Throughout baseball history, owners like Bill Veeck and Calvin Griffith—whose livelihoods depended entirely upon the game—were rare. In fact, owning a team is so expensive today that syndicates and corporations have taken over in many cities. Hands-on owners not distracted by their other business enterprises sometimes serve as their own executives, although that phenomenon is no longer common.

Connie Mack, owner-manager of the Philadelphia Athletics in the first half of the twentieth century, twice broke up championship teams to make ends meet. Years later, after the A's had relocated to Oakland, Charley Finley also made his own deals.

In most cases, however, teams count on hired executives to run day-to-day operations. General managers negotiate contracts, sign free agents, make trades, and hire such key personnel as managers and farm directors.

Executive Bits

The father-and-son tandem of William and Tom Yawkey owned two different teams: the Detroit Tigers and Boston Red Sox, respectively. Tom was only 30 when he bought the Bosox in 1933.

◇

Larry MacPhail's innovations included playing games at night, flying a team for the first time during a pennant race, and increasing fan appeal through the new media of radio and television.

◇

Branch Rickey developed the first farm system, broke baseball's color line, and sparked the expansion era by threatening to launch a third major league. He was best known for discovering the perfect player (Jackie Robinson) for the difficult job of integrating the game. Rickey worked for the Browns, Cardinals, Dodgers, and Pirates.

◇

Walter O'Malley, an engineer and lawyer who was elected to the Hall of Fame in 2007, joined the Brooklyn Dodgers when team attorney Wendell Willkie resigned to run for president on the 1940 Republican ticket. Club president by 1950, O'Malley owned 75 percent of the team when he took the Dodgers to Los Angeles after the 1957 campaign. Using his engineering skills, O'Malley scouted the Chavez Ravine site—once a garbage dump—and correctly estimated that 8 million tons of earth would need to be moved for the building of Dodger Stadium. The ballpark opened in 1962.

A maverick among conservatives, Bill Veeck kept a card box filled with his innovative ideas. He had a midget bat in a game, let fans decide managerial strategy, dressed a team in shorts, and introduced exploding scoreboards and special days for fans. Veeck also brought Negro Leagues legend Satchel Paige to the majors while critics cried that he was too old and set up shop at the winter meetings with an "Open for Business" sign on a lobby desk. "Sportshirt Bill," who eschewed ties, won a World Series with the Indians (1948) and a pennant with the White Sox (1959). He also owned the St. Louis Browns.

(Baseball Hall of Fame)

Bill Veeck, only 30 when he purchased the Cleveland Indians in 1946, integrated the AL a year later, introducing Larry Doby three months after Jackie Robinson's debut in Brooklyn. Veeck was a voracious reader who talked to fans, kept a card file of promotional ideas, and outraged conservative brethren with such innovative ideas as "Grandstand Managers Day" and exploding scoreboards. Nicknamed "Sportshirt Bill" for his aversion to ties, he was also called "The P. T. Barnum of Baseball" because of his penchant for outrageous publicity stunts.

◇

Several Bill Veeck brainstorms were barred by league officials immediately after they occurred. As owner of the minor league Milwaukee Brewers in 1942, Veeck rigged an electric motor to the right-field screen, raising it to a height of 60 feet when the visitors batted but lowering it for the Brewers. Nine years and two teams later, Veeck was the boss of the St. Louis Browns when he sent a midget up to bat in a major-league game. Anticipating the umpire's complaint, manager Zack Taylor produced Eddie Gaedel's standard player contract. Ordered not to swing, Gaedel walked on four pitches and was pulled for a pinch-runner.

Diminutive Eddie Gaedel, who stood less than 4 feet tall, batted in a game for Bill Veeck's Browns on August 18, 1951. Ordered not to swing, Gaedel walked on four pitches and then left for a pinch-runner. His contract was voided by the AL the next day.

(Baseball Hall of Fame)

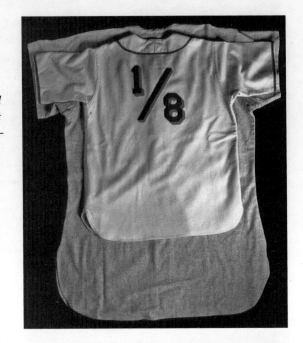

Cardinal jersey No. 85 is the highest retired number in baseball history. It honors longtime owner Augie Busch, who was 85 when he died.

◊

Gene Autry was such a hands-on owner during his tenure with the Angels that he was considered the "26th man" on the roster. The club honored the Singing Cowboy by retiring No. 26—although Autry never actually wore it.

◊

Promotion-minded Oakland owner Charles O. Finley once paid his players $300 each to grow mustaches. One of those who succeeded handsomely was future Hall of Famer Rollie Fingers, whose Snidely Whiplash handlebar mustache became a personal trademark.

◊

Among the innovations pioneered by Charley Finley during his days as owner of the A's were brightly-colored uniforms, mascots, ball girls, and night World Series games.

◊

Although he also played for George Steinbrenner, Reggie Jackson reserved kind words for former owner Charley Finley. "He was the most innovative baseball person I've ever been around," said Jackson of Finley. "He also knew baseball better than any owner I've ever been around."

During his first 25 years as owner of the Yankees, George Steinbrenner changed managers 20 times, general managers 15 times, pitching coaches 37 times, and public relations directors 12 times. After Steinbrenner fired him as manager for the second time in 1985, Yogi Berra boycotted Yankee Stadium for 14 years until broadcaster Suzyn Waldman patched up the quarrel.

◇

An eleventh-hour offer from McDonald's founder Ray Kroc kept the San Diego Padres from moving to Washington early in 1974. During his youth, the piano-playing Kroc had been a bleacher bum in Chicago's Wrigley Field.

◇

Eccentric Cincinnati owner Marge Schott let her pet Saint Bernards roam the field before Reds games. It wasn't always a great idea. "Schottzie pooped at shortstop before a game," said star shortstop Barry Larkin. "In the first inning, I had to dive and I saw this poop right in front of me. When I got up, it was all over the side of my uniform."

◇

Future U.S. President George W. Bush said the biggest mistake he ever made was trading Sammy Sosa. Bush owned the Texas Rangers at the time Sosa was sent to the Chicago White Sox in 1989. Sosa later became the only man to have three 60-homer seasons, all with the cross-town Cubs.

◇

The only naysayer in the 27–1 vote against the three-division format was Bush. He didn't want his Texas Rangers placed in the AL West because all of its road games would be played on the West Coast and start two hours later than home games.

◇

Tom Hicks, current owner of the Texas Rangers, paid the same amount for the entire ball club in 1998 as he did to sign free agent Alex Rodriguez two years later ($250 million).

◇

Just prior to the 2002 season, three teams switched ownership in a move coordinated by Major League Baseball. Montreal Expos owner Jeffrey Loria became the owner of the Florida Marlins; Marlins owner John Henry went to Boston as top man in a syndicate that also included former San Diego owner Tom Werner; and the 29 other clubs assumed ownership of the founding Expos. Three years later, the Expos became the Washington Nationals under a four-man ownership group headed by real estate developer Theodore N. Lerner and his son, Mark.

Washington Nationals owner Ted Lerner, born and raised in the capital, sat in 25-cent bleacher seats at Griffith Stadium while attending
Washington Senators games with his father.

◇

Two general managers of the Los Angeles Dodgers started their careers as
sportswriters: Fred Claire and current GM Ned Colletti.

◇

Before he became team president of the Atlanta Braves after the 2007
campaign, John Schuerholz was the only general manager to win world
championships in both leagues (1985 Kansas City Royals and 1995 Braves).

Commissioners and Officials

Nine different men have been baseball commissioners. The first was
Kenesaw Mountain Landis, who was earning $7,500 per year as a federal
judge in Illinois. He agreed to take the $50,000 job only after baseball club
owners, desperate to repair the game's image in the wake of the 1919 Black
Sox Scandal, agreed to grant him autocratic powers. Landis, who lasted
until 1944, used those powers to ban eight players suspected of involve-
ment in the scandal and impound a Babe Ruth World Series share for
illegal barnstorming. He also slapped Ruth, the game's biggest star, with a
40-game suspension.

Since Landis, the commissioner's chair has been occupied by A.B. "Happy"
Chandler, Ford Frick, Gen. William D. Eckert, Bowie Kuhn, Peter
Ueberroth, Bart Giamatti, Fay Vincent, and Bud Selig. None has had the
authority of Landis, but all have had better paychecks.

Selig earned $14.5 million in 2007 alone. The only commissioner selected
from the owners' ranks, Selig eliminated league presidents—who had dis-
ciplinary power for nearly a century—and consolidated operations under
his office. He also introduced many innovations that infuriated tradition-
alists but delighted teams whose treasuries profited. Interleague play and
expanded playoffs were Selig brainstorms.

Before the commissioner concept was created, baseball was governed by a
three-man commission. But disputes between the NL, which began play in
1876, and the AL, which started in 1901, remained a problem.

Today's disputes are not between leagues but between owners and players,
who formed a formidable union that helped them win free agency and salary arbitration. Decisions by commissioners during the last four decades

have often been overturned by challenges from the Major League Baseball Players Association. In addition, eight work stoppages since 1972 have disrupted the schedule. Even the umpires, who answer directly to the office of the commissioner, are unionized.

Official Bits

With roster raids raging between the established NL and the upstart AL in 1903, Cincinnati Reds President Garry Herrmann suggested a commission to govern the game. In addition to Herrmann, its first members were league presidents Harry Pulliam (NL) and Ban Johnson (AL), both former baseball writers. Because the leagues often took opposite sides on controversial issues, Herrmann was, in effect, the *de facto* first commissioner.

◇

Counting the "Eight Men Out" crew implicated but not convicted in the 1919 Black Sox Scandal, Commissioner Kenesaw Mountain Landis banned nearly 20 players and managers for gambling or other offenses.

◇

Roger Maris hit 61 home runs in 1961 but did it during the first year of the 162-game format, upsetting longtime Babe Ruth chum Ford Frick, who just happened to be commissioner of baseball. Frick ordered an asterisk to be placed next to Maris's name in the record book because Ruth had hit 60 under the 154-game format used in 1927. What Frick didn't say is that Maris actually hit 61 in 153 games (because he didn't hit his first until the tenth game) and that he lost a home run to rain on July 17. Maris and Mantle both reached Hal "Skinny" Brown for homers in a game at Baltimore before rain erased the results in the fifth with the Yanks ahead 4–2.

◇

Bowie Kuhn was Commissioner of Baseball when players won the right to free agency in 1976 through a combination of arbitration decisions and court rulings.

◇

As AL president, Lee MacPhail took four days to rule on the pine tar incident of July 24, 1983. After George Brett hit an apparent game-winning homer in the ninth inning at Yankee Stadium, home plate umpire Tim McClelland sided with Billy Martin's protest and called Brett out, allegedly for having too much sticky pine tar on his bat handle. MacPhail disagreed, reinstating the Brett homer and ordering the game replayed from that point. When play resumed 25 days later, the Yankees protested by playing pitcher Ron Guidry in center field and lefty-throwing first baseman

Don Mattingly at second. The Royals not only wrapped up their victory but enjoyed seeing outspoken Yankee owner George Steinbrenner pay a $300,000 fine imposed by Commissioner Peter Ueberroth. The money was punishment for the owner's comment that Lee MacPhail should go house-hunting in Kansas City if the Yankees lose the pennant (they did, but he didn't).

◇

During his five-year tenure as baseball commissioner, Peter Ueberroth settled strikes by players and umpires, determined that the designated hitter would be deployed during all World Series games in AL parks, suspended nearly two dozen players for substance abuse, and created corporate sponsorships that contributed to the coffers of big-league clubs. He also limited an August 1985 player strike to two days by persuading owners to back off their demand for a salary cap. But his emphasis on fiscal sanity backfired when courts upheld collusion suits by the Players Association, forcing teams to pay $280 million in damages.

◇

Before he could complete his investigation of Pete Rose for allegedly gambling on the game, Peter Ueberroth yielded his job to NL President Bart Giamatti.

Although he spent only 154 days as baseball commissioner, former Yale University president Bart Giamatti will forever be remembered as the man who banned Pete Rose for life. The gut-wrenching decision, which effectively kept the career hit king off the Hall of Fame election ballot, probably contributed to Giamatti's fatal heart attack a week later.

(Major League Baseball)

Although Baseball Commissioner Bart Giamatti gave Pete Rose a lifetime ban for gambling in 1989, effectively ending his eligibility for the Hall of Fame, the all-time hit king denied the accusation for years before confessing in 2004. Giamatti, the former president of Yale University, served only 154 days as commissioner before suffering a fatal heart attack.

Before he was forced to stay neutral as baseball commissioner, Bud Selig rooted for several different teams. The Milwaukee native grew up as a fan of the Chicago Cubs, switched allegiances when the Boston Braves moved to Wisconsin, and led an investment group that turned the Seattle Pilots into the Milwaukee Brewers in 1970.

Barry Bonds was the only player at Bud Selig's table at the 2002 All-Star Gala in Milwaukee. Four years later, however, Selig hired former U.S. Senator George Mitchell (D-Maine) to investigate steroids use in baseball after reading a book that implicated the San Francisco slugger. That book, *Game of Shadows*, was written by *San Francisco Chronicle* reporters Lance Williams and Mark Fainaru-Wada.

The Mitchell Report, issued in December 2007 after a 20-month investigation, identified more than 80 players, both active and retired, suspected of using steroids or human growth hormone.

Missing in Action

Commissioners who failed to attend games in which home run records were broken:

Ford Frick (Roger Maris's 61st, October 1, 1961)
Bowie Kuhn (Hank Aaron's 715th, April 8, 1974)
Bud Selig (Barry Bonds' 756th, August 16, 2007)

Umpires

Umpires are paid to officiate impartially at all games. They decide whether a field is in playable condition, call runners safe or out, and pass instant judgments on balls and strikes at home plate. Umpires are "the law" on the diamond, and their decisions are final.

Modern umpires work in four-man crews, make their own travel and hotel arrangements, handle their own equipment, and dress in a special room far removed from the teams' dressing rooms. Their equipment includes a mask, uniform, and padded chest protector worn under clothing. The old balloon protector, which had to be adjusted before each pitch, gave more protection—but the chest protector pad is far more comfortable.

The strike zone is the chief concern of the umpire. The calls of the home plate umpire make or break no-hitters, preserve or ruin shutouts, win or lose games, and even decide championships. Because of the great variety of pitches and number of pitchers used per game, umpires like to know what each player has in his repertoire. They exchange information often— something that became easier in 2000 after the centralization of all umpires into a single staff, rotated among all 30 ballparks.

Umpire Bits

Umpires started wearing masks in 1882 and chest protectors in 1885.

◇

World Series games had only two arbiters—one from each league—when the classic began in 1903. Regular-season games that year had only one umpire.

◇

Billy Evans, the youngest umpire, was only 22 when he started working for the AL in 1906. The next year, he was severely injured when struck on the head by a thrown bottle and nearly died from a fractured skull.

◇

After New York Giants manager John McGraw called him "a blind robber," umpire Robert Emslie brought a rifle to the ballpark, inserted a dime into a split match at second base, then hit it with a single shot from home plate. McGraw never challenged his eyesight again.

◇

John McGraw had a close relationship with veteran umpire Bill Klem. They were fast friends off the field but archrivals in uniform. The fiery manager once blew his top after a Klem call went against his New York Giants. After a Chicago batter dented the left-field scoreboard, McGraw contended the ball was foul. But the sphere struck a section of board where the vertical line delineating foul territory from fair did not appear. The manager sent a groundskeeper out to check for a dent in the scoreboard— only to learn Klem had made the right call.

When Fans Were Umps

The four umpires who were assigned to work the Pittsburgh-Detroit World Series of 1909 worked in alternating pairs. Bill Klem and Billy Evans of the AL sat in the stands for the opener, but a controversial hit by Max Carey of the Pirates stirred them into action. The ball went into the stands, where a special ground rule designated a specified area as home-run territory—a ball landing elsewhere would be worth two bases. Neither Klem nor Evans could tell where the ball landed, and the umpires on duty weren't sure either. The four umpires, accompanied by both managers, marched out to the stands, and let the crowd convince them that the ball was actually a two-base hit. Evans, deciding fans shouldn't be allowed to substitute for professional umpires, wired AL president Ban Johnson. The next day, all four arbiters were working. The World Series crew was later increased to six, with two umpires monitoring the foul lines.

Frank Chance, manager of the 1910 Chicago Cubs, was the first man ejected from a World Series game.

◇

Casey Stengel was managing the Brooklyn Dodgers when he came out to argue a call. The umpire pulled out his watch, giving Stengel a minute to cease arguing or get ejected. "If I were you," Stengel said, "I wouldn't show that watch in front of this crowd. The owner might recognize it."

◇

Umpire Brick Owens was bitten by a dog during a game in 1912. The dog, which belonged to Honus Wagner, dashed out of the dugout after Wagner was ejected for arguing with Owens.

◇

Red Sox pitcher Babe Ruth challenged umpire Brick Owens so vehemently on a ball-four call to the first Washington hitter on June 23, 1917, that the umpire ejected him. Reliever Ernie Shore came on to retire 26 men in a row plus the man Ruth walked, who was thrown out trying to steal second. That gave Shore the only perfect game that was not a complete game.

For nearly half of his 37 years as an umpire, Bill Klem worked exclusively behind the plate because of superior skills at calling balls and strikes. The first arbiter to use exaggerated gestures to call balls and strikes, he developed that style while taking leisurely horseback rides in the quiet of the seashore pines near Lakewood, New Jersey. Klem, who umpired in a record 18 World Series, also originated arm signals to coincide with verbal calls.

Bill Klem umpired in 18 World Series during his 37-year tenure and was so highly regarded that the New York Giants once honored him with "Bill Klem Night" at the Polo Grounds.
(Library of Congress)

Jocko Conlan started umpiring by accident. A White Sox outfielder in 1935, he was asked to fill in for Red Ormsby, who was overcome by heat. Six years later, he joined the NL umpiring roster.

◇

Although he later became one of baseball's best umpires, Nestor Chylak was blinded for 10 days by a German artillery shell during World War II.

◇

Frank Umont became the first umpire to wear glasses in 1956.

◇

Bill Dinneen was the first man to play in and umpire in the World Series.

◇

The first year six umpires worked the World Series was 1947.

◇

Umpire Bill McGowan was the Cal Ripken of umpiring. He went 16 years without missing an inning (2,541 consecutive games).

◇

Bill Kunkel, who also pitched in the majors, was both an AL umpire and a National Basketball Association (NBA) referee.

Big-league umpires staged strikes in 1970, 1978, 1979, and 1984.

Longtime NL umpire Doug Harvey had a theory about the anonymous role of the umpire. "When I am right," he said, "no one remembers. When I am wrong, no one forgets."

Umpire John McSherry suffered a fatal heart attack on 1996 Opening Day in Cincinnati.

Three of the umpires who worked the April 15, 2000, game between the A's and the Red Sox were the sons of former umpires. They were Jerry Crawford (son of Shag), Mike DiMuro (son of Lou), and Brian Gorman (son of Tom).

Bill Klem and Bruce Froemming both umpired more than 5,000 major-league games. Froemming, who retired after the 2007 campaign, was a major-league umpire for a record 37 consecutive years.

Current umpire salaries range from $87,000 to $357,000 per year, but minor league umps have a ceiling of $3,500 per month. Umpires who work postseason play make nice bonuses: $15,000 for the Division Series, $20,000 for the League Championship Series, and $25,000 for the World Series. Salaries for the regular season range from $85,000 to $355,000 depending on experience.

In 1998, Harry and Hunter Wendelstedt became the first father-and-son combination to umpire the same game.

Eight umpires have done their jobs so well that they are now enshrined in the Baseball Hall of Fame: Bill Klem, Jocko Conlan, Cal Hubbard, Billy Evans, Tommy Connolly, Bill McGowan, Al Barlick, and Nestor Chylak. Hubbard is actually a member of three Halls of Fame: baseball, football, and college football.

CHAPTER

6

Deals and Steals

Trading is what makes baseball different from any other profession. Although all players have contracts, most can be bought, sold, or bartered relatively easily. It's been that way throughout baseball history—or at least since trades became a fact of baseball life in 1889. Trading deadlines were established in 1917 and amended several times over the next five years before the leagues settled on a cutoff date of June 15 (changed to July 31 in 1986). Circumventing the deadline remained possible via waiver trades, although securing waivers for top players was not always possible during pennant races.

Getting waivers means securing permission from other clubs to move a player. After trade deadlines pass, deals may be made when waivers are granted by all other teams, from the bottom of the standings up. The waiving team may then withdraw the waivers or try to work out a deal with the claiming club. If waivers on a player are irrevocable, any team that claims him may keep him for cash.

Without restrictions on trades, teams dive into the talent pool like teenagers on a hot summer afternoon. General managers trade players like kids trade cards—although the art of trading became much more complicated after the advent of free agency–created contracts consisting of seven figures, multiple seasons, and no-trade provisions.

Trades are made for all kinds of reasons. Sometimes a bad team will make a deal in the hope that new faces will bring new fans (or bring back old ones). Salary disagreements and personality clashes force trades—and so does a player's wish to be closer to home or a team's desire to make a local favorite their manager. But every once in a while, a sale, signing, or swap is approved for reasons that fans cannot fathom.

That was certainly the case surrounding the sale of Babe Ruth from the Boston Red Sox, the reigning power of the American League (AL), to the New York Yankees—a team that had never reached the World Series. The World Champion Red Sox of 1918 began swapping stars for bank notes to underwrite owner Harry Frazee's theater productions. With the Yankees office two doors down from Frazee's New York headquarters, he had a short walk and an eager customer. By 1923, 11 former Red Sox stars, including Ruth, were Yankees. For Bostonians, losing the 24-year-old Ruth was the worst event since Paul Revere announced that the British were coming.

Only a handful of players—notably Ted Williams, Mickey Mantle, and Brooks Robinson—spent their entire careers with a single club. Such superstars as Babe Ruth, Rogers Hornsby, Jimmie Foxx, Hank Greenberg, and Warren Spahn experienced at least one trade. Because of trades, Hank Aaron and Willie Mays started and ended their careers in the same cities (Milwaukee and New York, respectively), but with different teams. Nolan Ryan, Randy Johnson, and Greg Maddux switched teams not only through trades but also free agency. Some trades are huge (a 17-man swap in 1954). Some are small (Harry Chiti for a "player to be named later"). And some are blockbusters (the Yankees landing Ruth in 1920 and Alex Rodriguez from Texas in 2004). But virtually all of them make great back-page fodder to keep fans interested in baseball even during freezing weather.

The 1976 advent of free agency reduced trade activity, because it gave rich teams another source of proven talent. Ball clubs willing to open their checkbooks could simply buy players to fill holes without surrendering proven talent to free agents' former clubs. Reggie Jackson, Dave Winfield, and Barry Bonds were among dozens who cemented their Hall of Fame credentials after riding free agency to greener pastures.

Trading Bits

The Boston Red Sox paid only $2,500 to the Baltimore Orioles of the International League to land a left-handed pitcher named Babe Ruth on July 11, 1914.

Orioles Sold Stars to Majors

Before the advent of the farm system, independent minor league teams supported themselves by selling star players to major league clubs. Nobody did it better than Jack Dunn of the Baltimore Orioles. From 1919 to 1925, his team not only won seven straight pennants, but also developed a roster of players who made major impacts in the majors. Dunn, who owned Oriole teams from 1910 to 1928, enjoyed his greatest success after selling Babe Ruth to the Red Sox. His 1921 team went 119–47 (.717 winning percentage) and got a 25–10 season from Maryland native Lefty Grove in his first full year with the club. After Grove followed with 18–8, 27–10, and 26–6 seasons, Dunn sold him to the Athletics for a then-record $100,600—topping by $600 the 1920 Babe Ruth sale.

Two years after posting a 31–4 record and 2.06 ERA for the 1931 Philadelphia Athletics, Lefty Grove was traded to the Boston Red Sox with Max Bishop and Rube Walberg for Harold Warstler, Bob Kline, and $125,000. The deal was motivated by the Depression-era economy, which forced Connie Mack to sell many top stars in an effort to keep afloat.

(American League)

The first five-figure sale in baseball history occurred before the turn of the twentieth century. Mike "King" Kelly, a skilled but zany performer who had helped Chicago win five National League (NL) pennants in seven seasons, was sold to Boston in 1887 for $10,000.

◇

Denton True Young acquired the nickname "Cyclone" after a warmup pitch missed by the catcher splintered a wooden fence. The nickname had been shortened to "Cy" by the time Canton of the Tri-State League sold Young to the Cleveland Spiders. The price, $300 plus a suit of clothes for the Canton owner, was baseball's equivalent of selling Manhattan for $24.

◇

After losing the 1914 World Series to Boston's Miracle Braves, Athletics owner/manager Connie Mack began to break up his team in an effort to keep his stars in the AL rather than the rival Federal League.

◇

When the Cincinnati Reds sought Christy Mathewson as their manager in 1916, the New York Giants obliged by agreeing to a five-player swap that also made Reds of Edd Rousch and Bill McKechnie. The Giants, who landed Buck Herzog in exchange, already had an entrenched manager in John McGraw.

◇

The January 3, 1920, Babe Ruth deal made the Yankees a powerhouse and brought Boston only $100,000 cash plus a $350,000 loan against the mortgage on Fenway Park. The Sox had won more World Series than any team at the time of the deal, but their 86-year drought between 1918 and 2004 was blamed on the "Curse of the Bambino." Ruth hit 54 home runs in 1920, 59 in 1921, and 60 in 1927. Harry Frazee, the man who got more money but less value in a trade than any of his contemporaries, died a broken man in 1929.

◇

Serving as player-manager of the World Champion Cardinals in 1926 wasn't enough to ensure Rogers Hornsby's job. After six batting crowns but only one year as manager, the slugging second baseman upset owner Sam Breadon by demanding a three-year $150,000 contract. Breadon found a willing trading partner in the New York Giants, who gave up local hero Frankie Frisch and pitcher Jim Ring. Hornsby never managed the Giants, where John McGraw was entrenched, but did return to St. Louis as two-term manager for the Browns.

Rogers Hornsby discovered that even superstars aren't immune to trades—especially when salary demands and prickly personalities are part of the package.

(Ronnie Joyner)

The Browns and Senators exchanged future Hall of Fame left-fielders on June 13, 1930. St. Louis sent Heinie Manush and Alvin Crowder to Washington for Goose Goslin.

◇

After a slow recovery from Federal League raids and a wartime economy, Connie Mack's Philadelphia A's made wise purchases that restored their contender status. The best was Bob (Lefty) Grove, who arrived from the International League's Baltimore Orioles for $100,600—supposedly $600 more than the sale price of Babe Ruth. The future 300-game winner cemented a pitching staff that helped the A's win three straight AL flags and two world titles from 1929 to 1931.

◇

The Yankees spent only $50,000 to purchase Joe DiMaggio from the San Francisco Seals of the Pacific Coast League on November 21, 1934.

Trading in the Depression

The Depression made men do desperate things. To keep his Philadelphia A's from folding, Connie Mack used the same tactic he had used to stop Federal League raids: he sold his best players. On December 12, 1933, he sent Lefty Grove, Max Bishop, and Rube Walberg to the Boston Red Sox for Harold Warstler, Bob Kline, and $125,000. Al Simmons, Jimmie Dykes, and Mule Haas had already been sent to the White Sox for $150,000, and Jimmie Foxx arrived in Boston two years later in a $150,000 swap disguised as a four-player trade. Detroit got Mickey Cochrane for $100,000. Pitcher George Earnshaw also wound up with the White Sox. There were other sales, too, bringing Mack a grand total of $900,000. The deals destroyed a potent club and plunged the A's into a long snooze in the AL basement. Only after they moved to Oakland (from Kansas City) in 1968 did the A's revive.

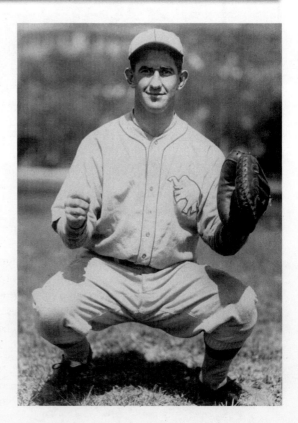

With Philadelphia still buzzing about the Lefty Grove trade three days earlier, catcher Mickey Cochrane followed the star pitcher out of town. Desperate for dollars, Connie Mack sent him to the Detroit Tigers for John Pasek and $100,000 on December 15, 1933.

(American League)

Washington owner Clark Griffith sold one family member (Joe Cronin), but later acquired another (Joe Haynes). He was willing to send Cronin to the Red Sox in 1934 because Boston owner Tom Yawkey offered $250,000—a staggering sum in Depression days—plus Lyn Lary, who replaced Cronin at short. Fourteen years later, he landed Haynes in a deal with Cleveland.

◇

Dizzy Dean wasn't the same pitcher after an Earl Averill liner broke his toe in the 1937 All-Star Game. But he still had high value to a club with post-season ambitions. When the Cardinals put him on the market after the 1937 season, the Cubs—seeking to close the three-game deficit between first and second place that fall—put together an overwhelming package. On April 16, 1938, the team sent pitchers Curt Davis and Clyde Shoun and outfielder Tuck Stainback, plus $185,000, to the Cardinals for the 27-year-old Dean. The right-hander's 7–1 record and 1.80 ERA helped the 1938 Cubs top the Pirates by two games, the Giants by three, and the Reds by six.

Veeck's Victory Strategy

Bill Veeck knew Early Wynn and Mickey Vernon could help his Cleveland Indians win the 1948 AL pennant. But they played for Washington under Clark Griffith, who disapproved of Veeck's gimmicks and outspoken comments. On the other hand, Veeck knew Griffith's son-in-law, Joe Haynes, was a sore-armed White Sox pitcher and definitely available, so he sent catcher Joe Tipton to Chicago for Haynes. Griffith, not wanting his son-in-law to play for Cleveland, sent adopted nephew Calvin to negotiate.

The resulting deal sent Haynes, Eddie Robinson, and reliever Ed Kleimanto to the Senators for Vernon and Wynn. Veeck announced the trade at 4:45 A.M., because he didn't want to give Griffith time to change his mind. Even though Veeck paid for his surgery, Haynes won just 10 games in four years for Washington. Wynn won 163 for Cleveland and 59 more for Chicago (22 of them in 1959, when newly named owner Bill Veeck helped the Sox win their first flag in 40 years). The man Veeck yielded for Haynes didn't do much. But White Sox general manager Frank Lane pulled a coup by sending him to the Philadelphia Athletics for second baseman Nellie Fox, sparkplug of the 1959 White Sox and AL MVP that year. Wynn also won the Cy Young Award that summer.

The acquisition of Ted Williams on December 1, 1937, engineered by general manager Eddie Collins, remains the best deal in Red Sox history. The Sox sent five players and $25,000 to the San Diego Padres of the independent Pacific Coast League for the slugging outfielder. Williams could have gone to the Yankees, but his mother wouldn't accept the team's $500 bonus offer—she wanted $1,000, and the team wouldn't budge.

◊

After the Yankees won their fourth straight AL flag in 1939, the AL passed a rule prohibiting any pennant winner from making trades within the league. The rule, proposed by the Washington Senators, was withdrawn after that single season—even though it worked (the Detroit Tigers won the pennant in 1940).

Although one of his 44 home runs in 1946 was the 300th of his career, Hank Greenberg was placed on waivers by the Detroit Tigers and sold to the Pittsburgh Pirates for $40,000. Although he had spent his whole career in the Motor City, ownership was upset with his salary demands plus his wearing a Yankee uniform—the only one that fit his 6'4" frame—for an exhibition game.

(Baseball Hall of Fame)

After Hank Greenberg led the AL with 44 home runs and 127 RBI for the 1946 Detroit Tigers, he moved across league lines on waivers to join the Pittsburgh Pirates. Greenberg, 35 when the deal was made, teamed with second-year slugger Ralph Kiner, 24, to give the Pirates a solid 1–2 power punch, but the club finished last anyway. Responding to suggestions from Greenberg, however, Kiner more than doubled his power output, leading the NL with 51 home runs. Greenberg hit 25 but retired to join Bill Veeck as general manager of the Cleveland Indians. The 1947 season was the only year Greenberg and Kiner played together.

◇

Trading power for speed and defense helped the New York Giants build their championship club of 1951. The process started on December 14, 1949, when the Boston Braves agreed to swap shortstop Alvin Dark and second baseman Eddie Stanky to New York for third baseman Sid Gordon, outfielder Willard Marshall, infielder Buddy Kerr, and pitcher Sam Webb.

◇

The Boston Braves spent $10,000 to purchase Hank Aaron's contract from the Indianapolis Clowns, a Negro Leagues team, in June 1952. After less than two years in the Braves' minor league system, Aaron reached the majors to stay.

◇

Although Mike Morgan played for more different teams (12) than anyone else, fellow pitcher Bobo Newsom probably made the most return trips. Between 1935 and 1952, he was a member of the following teams, in order: Browns, Senators, Red Sox, Browns, Tigers, Senators, Dodgers, Browns, Senators, Athletics, Senators, Yankees, Giants, Senators, and Athletics. More of a hobo than a bobo, Newsom had three 20-win seasons and three 20-loss seasons but finished with more losses (222) than wins (211).

◇

Red Schoendienst and Alvin Dark both played for the Braves, Giants, and Cardinals but not at the same time. Dark, previously acquired by the Giants from the Boston Braves, moved to the Cards in a nine-man trade that also involved Schoendienst on June 14, 1956. A year later, Schoendienst moved to Milwaukee, then the home of the Braves.

◇

Two-team trades are common, three-team swaps are rare, and four-team trades can be counted on one hand. But they do happen. On February 17, 1953, the Philadelphia Phillies sent pitcher Russ Meyer and cash to the Boston Braves for first baseman Earl Torgeson. The Braves sent Meyer to the Brooklyn Dodgers for infielder Rocky Bridges and outfielder Jim Pendleton. Then the Braves sent Bridges and a player to be named later to the Reds for first baseman Joe Adcock.

After denying Ralph Kiner a bigger contract—and telling him "We could have finished last without you"—Branch Rickey proved the point by trading the home run king to the Cubs. The 10-man deal, announced on June 4, 1953, sent Kiner, Joe Garagiola, Catfish Metkovich, and Howie Pollet to the Cubs for Toby Atwell, Bob Schultz, Preston Ward, George Freese, Bob Addis, Gene Hermanski, and $150,000. Both still battled to keep out of the NL basement, with the Pirates retaining the lowest rung in the standings and the Cubs finishing seventh.

17-Player Swap

General managers Paul Richards of the Orioles and George Weiss of the Yankees engineered the largest two-club deal in the game's history late in the 1954 season. The Yankees received pitchers Don Larsen, Bob Turley, and Mike Blyzka; catcher Darrell Johnson; first baseman Dick Kryhoski; shortstop Billy Hunter; and outfielders Ted del Guercio and Tim Fridley. Baltimore acquired nine players— pitchers Harry Byrd, Jim McDonald, and Bill Miller; catchers Gus Triandos and Hal Smith; second baseman Don Leppert; third baseman Kal Segrist; shortstop Willy Miranda; and outfielder Gene Woodling. Within four years, Larsen pitched a perfect game in the World Series (1956) and Turley won a Cy Young Award and World Series MVP trophy (1958).

After making several bids for New York Giants slugger Bobby Thomson, the Milwaukee Braves succeeded on the eve of the 1954 season. But their glee was short-lived: Thomsom broke his leg during spring training, forcing the Braves to rush a 20-year-old rookie infielder named Hank Aaron. Catcher Sam Calderone, who came with Thomson, was strictly a backup. But the ex-Braves became Giants with a capital G. Johnny Antonelli, a 24-year-old left-hander, went 21–7 with a league-low 2.29 ERA and went all the way to win World Series Game 2. New York also did well with fellow lefty Don Liddle, catcher Ebba St. Claire, infielder Billy Klaus, and the $50,000 the Braves threw in to sweeten the pot.

◇

In 1956, the Cleveland Indians wanted to dump Sal Maglie. General manager Hank Greenberg, asked by the Dodgers' Buzzie Bavasi how much he wanted, said $100,000. "You're nuts!" Bavasi blurted, adding an expletive for emphasis. Greenberg then came down to $10,000. "I don't know," said the sly Bavasi. "I'll have to talk to Walter Alston." After speaking to the manager, Bavasi called Greenberg and told him $10,000 was too much. Greenberg, taken aback, said, "How much are you willing to pay?" They settled on $100—but announced the deal as a $10,000 purchase to save face for the Indians and for Maglie. But Dodger owner Walter O'Malley heard the purchase price was $100,000 and went ballistic before he learned the truth.

◇

Because he refused to part with Brooks Robinson, Paul Richards killed a 1958 deal that would have traded the entire Baltimore Orioles roster for the Kansas City Athletics. Robinson managed to spend his entire 23-year career with the O's.

◇

Waiver-free interleague trading was permitted for the first time after the 1959 season. An interleague trading period was established from November 21 to December 15. Later, the dates were modified to extend the period from five days after the end of the World Series to midnight on the final day of the winter baseball meetings. A spring trading period was added in 1977.

The Rise and Fall of Roger Maris

The man who broke Babe Ruth's single-season home run record was, like Ruth, acquired in trade. To get Maris and backups Joe DeMaestri and Kent Hadley on December 11, 1959, the Yankees sent Hank Bauer, Norm Siebern, Marv Throneberry, and Don Larsen to the Kansas City A's. Maris had started his career in Cleveland. A strong left-handed hitter who liked Yankee Stadium's short right-field porch (296 feet away), Maris hit 39 homers and 112 RBI to win AL MVP honors in 1960 and then won the award again with 61 in 1961—the only time he hit as many as 40. Five years later, at 31, he hit .233 with 13 home runs as the Yankees dropped to last place in the 10-team league. Traded to St. Louis for little-known third baseman Charley Smith, Maris managed his last hurrah when he paced the Cardinals to the 1967 World Championship with a club-leading seven RBI in the World Series.

Cleveland general manager Frank Lane made so many trades he was often called "Frantic Frankie." His worst came in 1960, when he traded AL home run king Rocky Colavito from Cleveland to Detroit for AL batting champion Harvey Kuenn. Irate teenage girls, hurt that their matinee idol was gone, nearly forced Lane to leave town—and the Indians took years to recover.

◇

Just months after trading Colavito for Kuenn on the eve of Opening Day, Frank Lane hooked up with the Tigers again in a historic exchange of managers. Cleveland sent Joe Gordon to Detroit for Jimmie Dykes and got coach Luke Appling as a throw-in. The deal helped neither team.

◇

The original New York Mets of 1962 were willing to accept any warm-bodied players. Two months after landing catcher Harry Chiti from Cleveland for a player to be named later, the Mets named the player—Chiti—and shipped him back. The New York media reported that the team got the bad end of the deal.

◇

The St. Louis Cardinals and Chicago Cubs were archrivals even before the Cubs traded a future Hall of Famer to St. Louis for virtually no return. It happened on June 15, 1964, at the trading deadline. The Cubs sent strikeout-prone speed merchant Lou Brock to the Cards for pitcher Ernie Broglio, an 18-game winner the year before. Chicago also received veteran reliever Bobby Shantz, long past his prime, and backup outfielder Doug Clemens. Broglio, only 28, developed a sore arm and was virtually worthless while Brock established single season and career records for steals before Rickey Henderson surpassed them.

◇

When the Cincinnati Reds surprised the baseball world by sending their top slugger to the Baltimore Orioles during the 1965 winter meetings, general manager Bill DeWitt delivered a parting shot, calling the departing Frank Robinson "an old 30." Robinson repaid him by winning the Triple Crown, bringing Baltimore its first world championship, and becoming the first man to win MVP honors in both leagues. The Orioles won four pennants in Robinson's six seasons with the team. The Reds got Milt Pappas, Jack Baldschun, and Dick Simpson.

◇

After the 1967 season, the New York Mets sent pitcher Bill Denehy to Washington for Senators manager Gil Hodges, first baseman for the original Mets five years earlier. In 1969, his second year at the helm, Hodges led the Mets to their first world championship.

When Bill DeWitt sent Frank Robinson from Cincinnati to Baltimore, he called Robinson "an old 30." The quote came back to haunt him when Robinson won the AL Triple Crown and became the only man to win MVP awards in both leagues.

(Ronnie Joyner)

After he was traded from the St. Louis Cardinals to the Philadelphia Phillies on October 7, 1969, Curt Flood refused to report and began litigation that ultimately erased the reserve clause. Willie Montanez and Bob Browning replaced Flood in the swap, which originally sent Dick Allen, Cookie Rojas, and Jerry Johnson to St. Louis for Tim McCarver, Byron Browne, Joe Hoerner, and Flood.

◇

Only one interleague trade comes close to the Frank Robinson deal as a one-sided swap: the 1971 deal that sent Nolan Ryan from the New York Mets to the California Angels for Jim Fregosi. The Mets, seeking a third baseman, decided they could shift Fregosi, who had been playing shortstop at an All-Star level. But changing leagues and positions didn't work. To make matters worse, the Mets not only traded Ryan for Fregosi but also sent the Angels a power-hitting outfielder in Lee Stanton plus two other players. Fregosi, 29 at the time of the trade, lasted less than two seasons in New York, but Ryan won 19 in his first Angel campaign and lasted for a record 27 seasons.

Bad move: the San Francisco Giants shipped Gaylord Perry to the Cleveland Indians for Sam McDowell in a 1971 trade of pitchers. Perry, 32, was four years older than "Sudden" Sam when the deal was made, but had much more life left in his arm. He eventually joined the 300 Win Club and the Hall of Fame.

◇

Not satisfied with their Perry-for-McDowell move, the Giants pulled another rock by sending little-used outfielder George Foster to Cincinnati for shortstop Frank Duffy and pitcher Vern Geishert. Given a chance to play, Foster was NL MVP in 1977, when he became the league's first 50-homer man since 1965.

◇

Denny McLain's fortunes went south in a hurry. Two years after winning his second straight AL Cy Young Award while pitching for Detroit in 1969, he became a 22-game loser for the last Washington Senators team. Although McLain moved on to the Oakland A's and Atlanta Braves, he was unable to revive his once-brilliant career.

◇

The St. Louis Cardinals shipped out two quality left-handers when salary talks came to an impasse. Steve Carlton, 26, won 20 games in 1971 and Jerry Reuss, 22, won 14 the same season, but both were gone in 1972. Carlton, dealt to Philadelphia for Rick Wise, immediately led the league with 27 victories and a 1.98 ERA, even though his team won only 59 games.

◇

In his first year with the Atlanta Braves after arriving from the Baltimore Orioles, Davey Johnson became a sudden slugger, combining with Hank Aaron and Darrell Evans to give the 1973 Braves the first 40-homer trio in baseball history. After hitting five home runs for the O's in 1972, Johnson hit 43 for the Braves the following year. The Braves had sent Earl Williams and Taylor Duncan to the Orioles for Johnson, Johnny Oates, Pat Dobson, and Roric Harrison.

◇

The Giants and Yankees shocked the baseball world with a 1974 exchange of star outfielders. Bobby Bonds, father of Barry, went to the Bronx for Bobby Murcer.

◇

Shrewd swaps by Gabe Paul recrafted the Yankees as a championship team in 1976 after a 12-year absence from the World Series. Paul, a longtime executive with the Reds, the Astros, and the Indians (twice), engineered deals that brought first baseman Chris Chambliss from Cleveland, second baseman Willie Randolph from Pittsburgh, center fielder Mickey Rivers and pitcher Ed Figueroa from California, and shortstop Bucky Dent from the Chicago White Sox. Randolph had been the unknown factor in a deal that brought veteran pitchers Dock Ellis and Ken Brett to New York from Pittsburgh for Yankee starter George "Doc" Medich.

◇

Fair trades? The Giants swapped Orlando Cepeda to St. Louis for Ray Sadecki in 1966. St. Louis sent Cepeda to Atlanta for Joe Torre in 1969. Five years later, St. Louis sent Torre to the New York Mets for Sadecki.

Bad knees kept Orlando Cepeda from reaching greater heights but he helped the 1962 Giants win a pennant, the 1967 Cardinals win a world title, and the 1969 Braves capture an NL West flag. Traded three times in 17 seasons, Cepeda also played for the A's, Red Sox, and Royals. He was later elected to the Hall of Fame.

(Dan Schlossberg)

Even after Hank Aaron became the career home run king while playing for Atlanta, fellow slugger Dick Allen refused to play there because of perceived racial animosity. Refusing to report after the White Sox dealt him to the Braves on December 3, 1974, Allen waited in baseball limbo before the Braves sent him to back to his original team, the Phillies, on May 7, 1975.

◇

Oakland A's owner Charley Finley, who served as his own general manager, tried to sell his stars before they rode free agency out of town. But Baseball Commissioner Bowie Kuhn intervened, nixing the seven-figure sales of

Vida Blue to the Cincinnati Reds and Rollie Fingers and Joe Rudi to the Boston Red Sox. Fingers and Rudi even donned Red Sox uniforms in anticipation of Kuhn's approval but never actually played for Boston.

◇

Blocked by official baseball from selling his stars, Charley Finley tried to trade them. On April 2, 1976, he sent Reggie Jackson, Ken Holtzman, and more to the Baltimore Orioles for Don Baylor, Mike Torrez, and more. Baltimore only got one season out of Jackson before he declared himself a free agent.

◇

Catfish Hunter signed his seven-figure Yankee contract in 1974 with a 15-cent pen.

◇

Charley Finley landed a player for a manager in 1976, when he acquired veteran receiver Manny Sanguillen plus cash from the Pittsburgh Pirates for A's pilot Chuck Tanner. A year later, he returned Sanguillen to Pittsburgh for several prospects.

◇

A heated salary dispute convinced the New York Mets to trade Tom Seaver to the Cincinnati Reds at the height of his career in 1977. The three-time Cy Young Award winner not only had many productive years left but also pitched his only no-hitter for the Reds. New York received Pat Zachry, Steve Henderson, Dan Norman, and Doug Flynn in the mid-June trade.

◇

In 1977, Dave Kingman became the first man to play for teams in all four divisions (Mets, Padres, Yankees, Angels).

◇

When future Hall of Fame pitcher Nolan Ryan left the California Angels to sign with the Houston Astros after the 1979 season, Angels GM Buzzie Bavasi said, "We'll just go get a couple of 8–7 pitchers."

◇

Although Dave Winfield spent 10 years with the Yankees after signing as a free agent in December 1980, he never played for a world championship team.

◇

Given the power of both manager and general manager by the St. Louis Cardinals, Whitey Herzog engineered one of the biggest deals of the free agent era during the 1980 winter meetings. The swap sent Rollie Fingers, Ted Simmons, and Pete Vuckovich from the Cardinals to the Brewers for Sixto Lezcano, David Green, Dave LaPoint, and Lary Sorenson. A year later, Lezcano was traded again, joining Garry Templeton and Al Olmsted in a move from the Cards to the Padres for Ozzie Smith and Steve Mura.

◇

Two trades involving slugging first baseman Fred McGriff shook the baseball world. The first was a trade of four All-Stars announced at the 1990 winter meetings. That swap sent Joe Carter and Roberto Alomar from the San Diego Padres to the Toronto Blue Jays for McGriff and Tony Fernandez. Three years later, the Padres moved McGriff to Atlanta in a July swap that enabled the Braves, then in the NL West, to overtake the Giants in the last pure divisional race (no wild card).

◇

Jose Canseco was kneeling in the on-deck circle when he was called back to the dugout and told he was traded. The Oakland A's sent the slugger to the Texas Rangers on August 31, 1992, in a waiver trade for Ruben Sierra and Jeff Russell.

◇

Because he was traded from Oakland to St. Louis in the middle of the 1997 season, Mark McGwire was denied a home run crown—even though he led the majors in home runs. Records for the American and National Leagues are kept separately.

◇

The cash-strapped Florida Marlins are famous for selling stars to meet expenses. Like the old Philadelphia A's of Connie Mack, the Fish twice stripped World Championship clubs. They traded 20 of the 25 players from the team that beat the Cleveland Indians in the 1997 World Series, and broke up the ball club that bested the New York Yankees six years later.

◇

Mike Piazza was a member of the Florida Marlins for a week during the Fish feeding frenzy that followed the 1997 season. He arrived from Los Angeles with Todd Zeile in a swap for Bobby Bonilla, Charles Johnson, Gary Sheffield, Jim Eisenreich, and Manuel Barrios, then was traded to the New York Mets before the 1998 season for Preston Wilson, Ed Yarnall, and a player to be named later.

◇

The Yankees acquired Alex Rodriguez from Texas before the 2004 season only after incumbent third baseman Aaron Boone tore up his knee playing basketball in January. Boone's eleventh-inning home run against the Boston Red Sox in the seventh game of the 2003 ALCS had given the Yankees the pennant. The Rangers traded Rodriguez, a shortstop who made a smooth transition to third, and his massive contract, for promising young slugger Alfonso Soriano.

The cost-conscious Florida Marlins sent high-salaried slugger Carlos Delgado to the New York Mets for Mike Jacobs, Yusmeiro Petit, and Grant Psomas on November 24, 2005, but got little immediate return.

The New York Mets returned to contention in 2006 through a series of shrewd signings and trades engineered by general manager Omar Minaya. Among those the team acquired were (left to right) Shawn Green, Carlos Delgado, and Carlos Beltran. Green and Delgado, left-handed sluggers with big salaries, came in trades, while Beltran signed as a free agent after hitting eight home runs for the Houston Astros in the 2004 postseason.
(Bill Menzel)

Josh Beckett and Mike Lowell, acquired from the Florida Marlins for Hanley Ramirez, Anibal Sanchez, and two other prospects, cost the Boston Red Sox more than $52 million. The combined salaries of Ramirez and Sanchez, who outplayed them in 2006, were $754,000.

◇

Randy Johnson was traded from the Arizona Diamondbacks to the New York Yankees a month before 2005 spring training, then returned two years later. The first swap sent the towering left-hander to New York for Brad Halsey, Javier Vazquez, Dioner Navarro, and $8 million cash. Arizona than sent Navarro, William Juarez, Danny Muegge, and Beltran Perez to the Dodgers for Shawn Green and another $8 million—ostensibly to offset Green's salary.

The $103 million the Boston Red Sox spent on Japanese import Daisuke Matsuzaka before the 2007 season was nearly 100 times more than Warner Brothers paid to make *Casablanca*. They were aware of it, too: general manager Theo Epstein's grandfather and great uncle wrote the Humphrey Bogart classic. Matsuzaka, 2006 World Baseball Classic MVP with a 3–0 record and 1.38 ERA for Japan, jumped to the United States when the Sox posted a $51.11 million fee for negotiating rights and signed him to a four-year, $52 million contract. The right-hander had won 57 games and recorded a 2.51 ERA for the Seibu Lions in his final four seasons there.

Japanese import Daisuke Matsuzaka cost the Boston Red Sox more than $100 million in posting and signing fees but responded with 15 wins in his first exposure against AL hitters. He also beat Cleveland in Game 7 of the AL Championship Series.
(Bill Menzel)

One year after the Toronto Blue Jays bestowed B. J. Ryan with a five-year contract worth $47 million, the left-handed closer came down with elbow problems that resulted in season-ending Tommy John surgery. He gave the Jays one good year (1.37 ERA, 38 saves in 2006) before breaking down.

Although he once pitched a no-hitter, A. J. Burnett never won more than a dozen games in a season for the Florida Marlins. But that didn't dissuade the Blue Jays from giving him a five-year, $55 million deal. He won 10 games his first year but spent a third of it sidelined by injury.

◇

While recuperating from a heart attack suffered at the Baseball Winter Meetings in 2006, Chicago Cubs general manager Jim Hendry finalized a $40 million deal for free-agent pitcher Ted Lilly.

◇

When the Yankees signed free agent Roger Clemens on May 6, 2007, his salary was announced at $28,000,022—with the 22 at the end a salute to his uniform number. Though he needed a month to get ready, Clemens earned $18.5 million in 2007, or an average of $153,846 *per day*—highest in the major leagues. The seven-time Cy Young Award winner, who turned 45 in August, had previously pitched for the Boston Red Sox, Toronto Blue Jays, and Houston Astros in addition to an earlier stint with the Yankees. His return to New York was motivated partly by the club's off-season signing of free agent lefty Andy Pettitte, a fellow Texan who had pitched with Clemens in both New York and Houston.

◇

Bad deal: the Philadelphia Phillies got only one win and a big surgical bill from Freddy Garcia, expected to be their ace after his acquisition from the Chicago White Sox prior to the 2007 season. The Phillies had to pay Garcia's $10 million salary and lost the two minor leaguers they traded for him. Garcia, a two-time AL All-Star, finished at 1–5 with a 5.90 ERA for the Phillies, and had shoulder surgery in August.

◇

Third year's the charm: Magglio Ordonez, who moved from the Chicago White Sox to the Detroit Tigers via free agency on February 7, 2005, won his first AL batting title in 2007.

◇

Sammy Sosa, the only man to produce three 60-homer seasons, resurfaced in 2007 after winning a roster spot with the Texas Rangers, his original team, in spring training. Although the Rangers finished last, Sosa reached a major plateau with his 600th career homer.

Sammy Sosa played for the Texas Rangers at the beginning and end of his career. In between, he was swapped to the Chicago White Sox, Chicago Cubs, and Baltimore Orioles.
(Bill Menzel)

After representing the AL in the 2006 World Series but falling short a year later, the Detroit Tigers refortified for 2008 by sending six young prospects to the Florida Marlins for pitcher Dontrelle Willis and third baseman Miguel Cabrera, both rising young stars. The deal was announced during the Baseball Winter Meetings in Nashville.

CHAPTER

7

Big Events

With the exception of the midsummer All-Star Game, an institution since its introduction in 1933, baseball saves its showcase events for the post-season. Before expansion forced leagues to split into divisions, the champions of the American and National Leagues went directly into the World Series without passing "go" or collecting $200. That changed in 1969, when a League Championship Series (LCS) began determining pennant winners and again in 1995 with the advent of a Division Series to produce LCS participants. World champions of the twenty-first century therefore must win three rounds of playoffs—a daunting task.

The All-Star Game

There are three times each year when no other major sports events are played: the day of the baseball All-Star Game and the days immediately before and after.

There was no All-Star Game in 1945 because of wartime travel restrictions, but there were two games apiece during the four-year span from 1959 to 1962—when players wanted to beef up their pension fund. There were two ties—in 1961 (rain) and 2002 (no pitchers left)—and one game shortened to five innings by foul weather (1952). Both leagues also managed winning streaks of at least 10 games.

All-Star Bits

Babe Ruth's two-run homer gave the Americans a 4–2 win in the first All-Star Game, played at Chicago's Comiskey Park in 1933.

AMERICAN LEAGUE ALL-STAR TEAM
1933

(Top Row) SHARKEY, CONROY, GEHRIG, RUTH, HILDEBRAND, MACK, CRONIN, GROVE, SHARKEY, DICKEY, SIMMONS, GOMEZ, WES.FERRELL, DYKES, SHARKEY.

(Bottom Row) SCHACHT, COLLINS, LAZZERI, CROWDER, FOXX, FLETCHER, AVERILL, ROMMEL, CHAPMAN, FERRELL, WEST, GEHRINGER, McBRIDE.

NATIONAL LEAGUE ALL-STAR TEAM
1933

(Top Row) HARTNETT, WILSON, FRISH, HUBBELL, WALKER, WANER, ENGLISH, SCHUMACHER, TRAYNOR, LOTSHAW.

(Middle Row) HALLAHAN, BARTELL, TERRY, McKECHNIE, McGRAW, CAREY, HAFEY, KLEIN, O'DOUL, BERGER.

(Bottom Row) HASBROOK, MARTIN, WARNEKE, CUCCINELLO .

Numerous future Hall of Famers, including Babe Ruth and Lou Gehrig, played in the first All-Star Game, held at Chicago's Comiskey Park in 1933.

(The American League)

The wildest pitcher in All-Star Game history made his mark in the very first Midsummer Classic in 1933. Wild Bill Hallahan of the Chicago Cubs walked five men in two innings.

First All-Star Managers

Lineups for the first All-Star Game, at Chicago's Comiskey Park in 1933, were selected by Connie Mack, the 70-year-old owner/manager of the Philadelphia Athletics, and John McGraw, called out of retirement after winning 10 pennants with the New York Giants.

Lefty Gomez was the American League's (AL) starting pitcher in the first All-Star Game and each of the other four years he made the AL squad.

◊

Screwball specialist Carl Hubbell earned his "Meal Ticket" nickname by striking out five straight future Hall of Famers in the 1934 All-Star Game. His victims were Babe Ruth, Lou Gehrig, Jimmie Foxx, Al Simmons, and Joe Cronin.

◊

Lefty Gomez pitched six innings, an All-Star Game record, in 1935.

Ted's Big Hit

Behind 5–3 going to the bottom of the ninth inning in Detroit, the 1941 AL All-Stars faced Claude Passeau of the Chicago Cubs. A right-hander who had entered the game in the seventh and pitched a perfect inning, Passeau yielded a run in the eighth when Dom DiMaggio's two-out RBI single scored brother Joe, who had doubled. In the ninth, Frankie Hayes led off with a pop fly to second. But pinch-hitter Ken Keltner legged out an infield single, Joe Gordon singled to right, and Cecil Travis walked, loading the bases with one out. Joe DiMaggio grounded to short but the National League (NL), unable to turn two, settled for a force at second. A run scored, narrowing the lead to 5–4, and giving Ted Williams a chance. That's all he needed. Williams homered, scoring Gordon and DiMaggio, as Tiger Stadium erupted. With two outs, the Americans had rallied for a 7–5 victory.

In addition to his game-winning All-Star homer of 1941, Ted Williams had the best single game of any player after returning from wartime military service. His 1946 All-Star performance included two home runs, two singles, a walk, and five RBI. One of his home runs was the only one ever hit against the baffling eephus pitch thrown by Rip Sewell.

En route to a .406 season in 1941, Red Sox slugger Ted Williams took time out July 8 to hit a game-winning, three-run homer with two outs in the bottom of the ninth inning at Detroit's Briggs Stadium. The blow gave the AL a 7–5 win.

(Legends Sports Magazine)

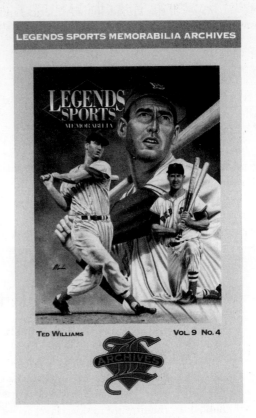

LEGENDS SPORTS MEMORABILIA ARCHIVES

TED WILLIAMS   VOL. 9 No. 4

Only one inning of All-Star history included two pinch-homers. In the eighth inning of the 1954 game, Larry Doby hit a pinch-homer for the AL and Gus Bell connected for the Nationals.

◇

Mickey Owen hit no home runs in 133 games during the 1942 season, but he produced the only NL run in a 3–1 All-Star Game defeat—*with a home run.*

◇

Although Jackie Robinson was the first black player to appear in an All-Star Game, three others played later in the same 1949 contest: Don Newcombe, Roy Campanella, and Larry Doby.

Ralph Kiner not only won seven straight NL home run crowns but also homered in three straight All-Star Games (1949 to 1951). His leadoff shot in the ninth inning of the 1950 game, the first to be nationally televised, forced extra innings and led to the NL's first win in an AL park.

◇

Willie Mays started more All-Star Games (18) than any other player. He holds All-Star records for hits, runs, and stolen bases.

◇

Hank Aaron was an All-Star every season he played except for his first (1954) and last (1976). He shares the mark for All-Star appearances (24) with Willie Mays and Stan Musial.

◇

Warren Spahn not only won more regular-season games than any lefty but also was the only pitcher to start All-Star Games in three different decades.

◇

When Cincinnati fans stuffed the ballot box prior to the 1957 All-Star Game, electing seven Reds plus St. Louis first baseman Stan Musial, angry Baseball Commissioner Ford Frick replaced fan picks Wally Post and Gus Bell with Willie Mays and Hank Aaron and stripped the fans of the right to vote.

◇

Don Drysdale was the starting pitcher in the twenty-sixth and twenty-seventh All-Star Games. They just happened to be in the same summer. The games, at Pittsburgh's Forbes Field and the Los Angeles Coliseum, took place less than a month apart in 1959, the first of four years baseball had two All-Star games to boost the players' pension fund.

◇

Red Sox fireballer Dick "the Monster" Radatz often came into games as early as the seventh inning and worked the rest of the way, but that strategy backfired in the 1964 All-Star Game. Radatz fanned the first two hitters he faced in the top of the seventh, whiffed two more in the eighth, and struck out Hank Aaron for the second out of the ninth. But Johnny Callison, who had popped out in an earlier at-bat against the Monster, connected for a three-run homer, capping a four-run frame that gave the NL a 7–4 victory at New York's Shea Stadium.

◇

The longest All-Star Game ended on a home run by Tony Perez. The Cincinnati slugger hit it in the fifteenth inning of the game at Anaheim on July 11, 1967.

Although their names did not appear on the computerized ballots used by fans to select All-Star lineups, Rico Carty (1970) and Steve Garvey (1974) won election as write-ins.

◇

Pete Rose lived up to his "Charlie Hustle" nickname by bowling over AL catcher Ray Fosse in the 12th inning of the 1970 All-Star Game. The collision won the game for the NL but changed the fortunes of Fosse, who suffered a serious knee injury and was never the same player again.

◇

Versatility rocks: Pete Rose and Paul Molitor both played five different positions in All-Star games.

◇

Reggie Jackson hit a home run worthy of Roy Hobbs in the 1971 All-Star Game at Detroit. One of six future Hall of Famers to connect that night, Jackson belted the ball over the right field wall, through a light tower, and against a generator on top of the Tiger Stadium roof 100 feet above the turf.

Power Show

Players with two homers in an All-Star Game:

Arky Vaughn, NL, 1941
Ted Williams, AL, 1946
Al Rosen, AL, 1954
Willie McCovey, NL, 1969
Gary Carter, NL, 1981

A 1974 reader poll by *The Sporting News* revealed that 74.2 percent of fans preferred the players to pick the All-Star lineups.

◇

Chosen by a meaningless fan vote, Davey Lopes started the 1981 All-Star Game with a .169 batting average, worst in the history of the Midsummer Classic.

◇

The NL won a record 11 straight All-Star Games from 1972–1982.

◇

Fred Lynn hit the only grand slam in All-Star Game history, against Atlee Hammaker at Comiskey Park in 1983.

Cal Ripken Jr. was 40 when he homered in the 2001 All-Star Game at Seattle—his last. That made him the oldest man to connect in All-Star play.

◇

The 2002 All-Star Game ended in a 7–7, 11-inning tie when both teams ran out of fresh pitchers. The ending was especially embarrassing to Baseball Commissioner Bud Selig because it was played at Miller Park in his hometown, Milwaukee. Selig had owned the Milwaukee Brewers before becoming baseball's czar in 1998. To avoid such future debacles, All-Star rosters were expanded to 32 players.

◇

Roger Clemens and Randy Johnson started All-Star Games in both leagues.

◇

Colorado's Matt Holliday got into the 2006 All-Star Game in right field—a position he had never played in a regular-season game.

◇

Eric Byrnes, an active player with the Arizona Diamondbacks, became the first big leaguer to troll McCovey Cove in a kayak during the 2007 All-Star Game in San Francisco. Byrnes, working for Fox-TV as a roving correspondent, wasn't called upon until the middle of the fifth inning.

◇

The father of Russell Martin, starting catcher for the 2007 NL All-Star team, supported his son as a street musician in Montreal. He later played "The Star-Spangled Banner" on his sax before a game in Los Angeles.

◇

Two former MVPs were the only position players picked but not used in the 2007 All-Star Game. Albert Pujols, the 2005 NL MVP, and American Leaguer Michael Young, winner of the 2006 All-Star Game MVP trophy, never appeared.

◇

Tony LaRussa, an attorney as well as a manager, might have made his biggest faux pas in the ninth inning of the 2007 All-Star Game. With the bases loaded and the NL trailing by a run, he let slugger Albert Pujols idle on the bench instead of asking him to pinch-hit for Aaron Rowand. LaRussa later explained that he was saving the versatile Pujols "in case" the game went into extra innings.

◇

Tony LaRussa, manager of the 2007 NL All-Star team, used one pitcher per inning—a first in All-Star annals.

◇

No manager has ever been ejected from an All-Star Game.

There were 166 home runs in All-Star history before Ichiro Suzuki hit the first inside-the-park version in 2007. Ken Griffey Jr. was unable to field the carom of the fifth-inning shot, which struck a corner of the uneven outfield wall in right center field at San Francisco's AT&T Park.

The first inside-the-park home run in Ichiro's big league career was also the first in All-Star history. It helped the AL win the 2007 classic in San Francisco.

(Bill Menzel)

Fan interference may have changed the result of the 2007 All-Star Game. In the sixth inning, a fan reached out from the overhang in right-center field at AT&T Park to catch a ball that might have fallen short. Batter Carl Crawford was credited with a home run, even though the same incident would have provoked a certain argument during the regular season.

The American League extended its winning streak to 11 in the 2007 All-Star Game at San Francisco's AT&T Park.

(Bill Menzel)

No Hanging Chads: How All-Star Voting Changed

All-Star participants have been chosen through a variety of different methods:

1933–1946: Fans "recommended" players but managers picked teams.

1947–1957: Fans voted for starting lineups.

1958–1969: Managers, coaches, and players picked lineups; managers named subs.

1970–2006: Fans named starting lineups using preformulated computerized ballots.

2006–present: Fans picked starters, players picked subs, and managers completed rosters.

The All-Star Game roster size has changed over the years. Each league was allowed 18 men in 1933, 20 in 1934–1935, 21 in 1936, 23 in 1937–1938, and 25 from 1939–1968. Three more slots per league were added from 1969–1997 and two additional ones from 1998–2004, swelling rosters to 30 men each. The current size of 32 players per league was established in 2005.

◊

In 2007, Barry Bonds became the oldest player to start an All-Star Game. On July 10, the date of the game, his age was 42 years, 11 months, and 16 days.

◊

Moises Alou and Gary Sheffield represented five different teams in the All-Star Game.

◊

The 2008 All-Star Game was awarded to the New York Yankees to coincide with their final season in "the House that Ruth Built." The team is scheduled to move into a new building in 2009.

Playoffs

Before the 1969 advent of divisional play added scheduled playoffs to the postseason schedule, NL races ended in a dead heat four times—in 1946, 1951, 1959, and 1962—and the AL season ended unresolved once, in 1948. An unusual make-up game decided the NL's pennant chase after Merkle's Boner in 1908, but it did not fall into the playoff category.

The Dodgers found their way into all four NL playoffs, beating the Braves in 1959 but losing to the Giants twice (1951 and 1962) and the Cardinals in 1946. NL playoffs were best-of-three series, while the AL used a sudden-death format to decide a deadlock in 1948. A victory by the Cleveland Indians over the Boston Red Sox prevented an all-Boston World Series.

The winner-take-all format has also been used to break divisional ties. The first occurred in 1978, when the New York Yankees not only caught the Boston Red Sox in the AL East but won the playoff, the Championship Series that followed, and the World Series.

NL tie-breakers were needed again in 1980, when the Dodgers and Astros shared the top of the NL West; 1998, when the Cubs, Giants, and Mets all lost their final games to force a Giants-Cubs playoff for the wild card spot; 1999, when the Mets won three straight and the Reds dropped two out of three to force a New York-at-Cincinnati playoff for the wild card; and 2007, when the Colorado Rockies hosted the San Diego Padres in a wild card title match.

A pre-playoff playoff was required to settle a divisional deadlock in the AL West in 1995, when the Seattle Mariners caught the Anaheim Angels.

The Championship Series, which originally pitted divisional champions from the East and West, was a best-of-three affair until 1985, when it was expanded to match the best-of-seven format featured in the World Series. The Division Series, created to determine Championship Series opponents, has followed the best-of-five format since its inception in 1995, when Central Divisions were added in both leagues. It includes each league's three divisional winners and wild card champions (the second-place team with the best winning percentage).

Playoff Bits

A pair of home runs by player-manager Lou Boudreau helped Cleveland beat Boston in the only pennant playoff in AL history before the advent of divisional play. The sudden-death contest was played on October 4, 1948. Had Cleveland won its final game against Detroit, the Indians would have won the pennant without a playoff.

Homers That Ended Postseason Series

Bobby Thomson, Giants vs. Dodgers, 1951: ninth-inning homer wins best-of-three playoff.

Bill Mazeroski, Pirates vs. Yankees, 1960: ninth-inning leadoff homer in World Series Game 7.

Chris Chambliss, Yankees vs. Royals, 1976: ninth-inning leadoff homer in ALCS Game 5.

Joe Carter, Blue Jays vs. Phillies, 1993: ninth-inning blast ends World Series in six games.

Todd Pratt, Mets vs. Diamondbacks, 1999: tenth-inning shot wins NLDS in four games.

Aaron Boone, Yankees vs. Red Sox, 2003: eleventh-inning leadoff HR wins ALCS Game 7.

Chris Burke, Astros vs. Braves, 2005: eighteenth-inning homer in Game 4 wins NLDS.

Bobby Thomson's three-run homer in the ninth inning of the last playoff game gave the New York Giants the 1951 NL pennant—even though they occupied first place for fewer days than any other champion, before or since. The Giants were in first place on only on three days: the first day of the season, when they won their opener; the first day of the playoffs, when they beat Brooklyn, 3–1; and on the last day of the playoffs after their 5–4 victory.

Fielding Lapse Blew '51 Flag

Poor defensive positioning cost the Dodgers dearly in the last game of the 1951 NL playoffs against the New York Giants. With Brooklyn up 4–1 in the ninth, Alvin Dark delivered an opposite-field single off the glove of first baseman Gil Hodges. Then Hodges decided to hold the runner, creating an oversized gap between first and second. Don Mueller, a right-handed batter known as "Mandrake the Magician" for his ability to place hits, found the hole, rifling the ball to the opposite field, just beyond the lunging Hodges. Had Hodges not been holding the runner, Mueller's ball might have been a double play. Instead, there were two men on and nobody out. Monte Irvin popped out, but Whitey Lockman doubled home a run, putting runners on second and third with one down. With first base open, Brooklyn manager Charley Dressen could have walked Bobby Thomson—the only Giant with 30 homers— and set up a potential double play. But rookie Willie Mays was in the on-deck circle. Although Ralph Branca had given up a home run to Thomson in the first playoff game, the big right-hander relieved Don Newcombe. Thomson homered again and the Giants won, 5–4.

Although he spent 10 years in the majors, Tom Niedenfuer did nothing to distinguish himself. He had his best year in 1985, when he saved 19 games for the Dodgers, but failed when the team needed him most. In the first best-of-seven NLCS, he threw a game-losing gopher ball to switch-hitting St. Louis shortstop Ozzie Smith, who had *never* before hit a home run batting left-handed. In Game 6, the home run bug bit Niedenfuer again. With the Dodgers up 5–4 in the ninth, the pitcher faced Jack Clark with two on and two out. With runners on second and third, Dodger manager

Tom Lasorda could have walked Clark, the only long-ball threat in the St. Louis lineup. Instead, he elected to let Niedenfuer pitch to him. Home run. End of game. End of series.

◇

The Giants beat the Dodgers with a four-run ninth in another playoff finale 11 years after the Bobby Thomson game. After a late-season slide, Los Angeles lost to NL newcomer Billy Pierce, 8–0, in the opener. The Dodgers came from behind to win the second, 8–7, and took a 4–2 lead into the ninth inning of the deciding third game. But the L.A. bullpen couldn't hold on; the Giants' winning run crossed on a bases-loaded walk by Stan Williams.

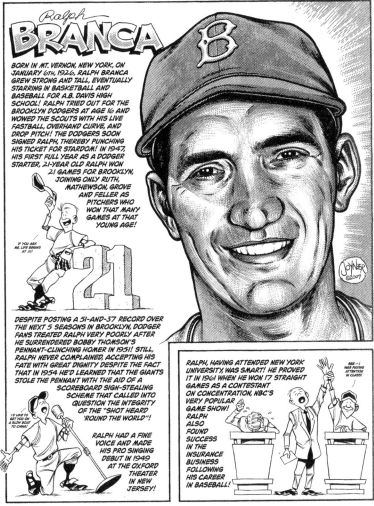

The Dodger goat in the 1951 NL playoffs, Ralph Branca later found a new career touring the card show circuit—with Giants hero Bobby Thomson.

(Ronnie Joyner)

The Los Angeles Dodgers got grand slams in consecutive playoff games in 1977. Ron Cey hit one against Steve Carlton in the NLCS opener against Philadelphia, and Dusty Baker connected the next night against Jim Lonborg.

◇

The 1991 NLCS between the Atlanta Braves and Pittsburgh Pirates featured a record three 1–0 games. After leading the league in batting and runs scored during the regular season, Pittsburgh did not score in its last 22 innings overall and its final 27 innings at home.

◇

Donnie Moore was so devastated by his poor pitching in the 1986 AL Championship Series that he eventually took his own life. The Angels won three of the first four games against the Boston Red Sox and seemed certain to clinch the pennant when they took a 5–2 lead into the ninth inning of Game 5. But Don Baylor hit a two-run homer, making it a 5–4 game, and Moore entered with a man on first and two outs. With a 2–2 count, Dave Henderson homered, putting Boston up, 6–5. After the Angels tied it, Henderson delivered an eleventh-inning sacrifice fly to win the game. The Sox won the next two games and the pennant.

◇

Steve Avery, a 21-year-old Atlanta southpaw, capped his first full year in the majors by pitching a record 16⅓ consecutive scoreless innings in the 1991 NLCS against Pittsburgh. That earned him MVP honors for the seven-game series.

◇

In the seventh game of the 1992 Braves-Pirates NLCS, Pittsburgh starter Doug Drabek took a 2–0 lead into the bottom of the ninth but couldn't hold it. Drabek, defeated in the first and fourth games, left after Atlanta loaded the bases with nobody out. Ron Gant greeted reliever Stan Belinda with a long sacrifice fly that was nearly his second grand slam of the series. One out later, seldom-used Francisco Cabrera, who had three hits in just 10 at-bats during the regular season, lined a pinch-hit single to left that scored two runs and kept the pennant in Atlanta for the second straight season. Drabek, Pittsburgh's biggest winner during the season, was the loser in three of the four Pittsburgh defeats in the playoffs.

◇

The AL needed a divisional playoff to determine the AL West champion in 1995. The race went down to the wire when the California Angels lost 27 of their last 39, blowing a 13-game August lead and matching Seattle's

78–66 record. The Mariners won the playoff to reach the postseason for the first time, then defeated the favored Yankees in the first AL Division Series before losing to Cleveland in a six-game ALCS.

◇

Andruw Jones was the youngest player to hit a home run in postseason play. The Atlanta outfielder was only 19 when he connected against the St. Louis Cardinals in the 1996 NLCS.

◇

Getting to the playoffs via the wild card route did not discourage the Anaheim Angels in 2002. After dropping the first game of the AL Division Series at Yankee Stadium, they scored successive come-from-behind wins to take three straight and knock out the favored Yankees, who had won 103 games during the regular season and four world championships in six seasons. An eight-run fifth inning in the decisive Game 4 proved to be the knockout punch for the Angels, who went on to win a pennant and the World Series for the first time.

◇

The 2003 Chicago Cubs were confident of reaching the World Series for the first time since 1945. But the Florida Marlins had other ideas. Chicago needed to win only one of the last three NLCS games, with the final two scheduled for Wrigley Field and aces Mark Prior and Kerry Wood scheduled to pitch. But the wild card Marlins won three straight to take their second NL pennant—even though they had never won a divisional championship. The turning point came in the eighth inning of Game 6, when Cub fan Steve Bartman knocked a catchable foul ball away from left fielder Moises Alou, setting up an eight-run outburst that turned a 3–0 Cub lead into an 8–3 deficit. With five outs to go, Prior couldn't close the deal, allowing Florida to stretch the series to a seventh game.

◇

The 2004 New York Yankees are the only team in baseball history to blow a 3–0 lead in a best-of-seven series. On October 16, they ripped the Boston Red Sox, 19–8, at Fenway Park and seemed set to sweep the ALCS. Instead, the Red Sox rebounded to win the last four ALCS games and then sweep the World Series against the St. Louis Cardinals.

◇

Carlos Beltran, then with the Houston Astros, hit *eight* postseason homers in 2004.

David "Big Papi" Ortiz and Manny Ramirez provided a devastating double whammy for pitchers facing the Red Sox line-up. Batting third and fourth, respectively, they helped Boston batter opponents during world championship seasons in 2004 and 2007.

(Bill Menzel)

Late Lightning

Players with late postseason homers:

Billy Hatcher, Astros, fourteenth inning, Game 6, 1986 NLCS
Jim Leyritz, Yankees, fifteenth inning, Game 2, 1995 ALDS
Chris Burke, Astros, eighteenth inning, Game 4, 2005 NLDS
Geoff Blum, White Sox, fourteenth inning, Game 3, 2005
    World Series

The 1973 New York Mets and 2005 San Diego Padres reached postseason play with just 82 wins, fewest of any team that reached the playoffs. The only postseason game featuring two grand slams was Game 4 of the 2005 NL Division Series between the Braves and Astros. Adam LaRoche connected in the third inning, giving the Braves a 4–0 lead, but Lance Berkman returned the favor in the eighth, cutting Atlanta's lead to 6–5 in a game the Braves eventually lost, 7–6 in 18 innings.

◇

The 2007 Arizona Diamondbacks were the first team in baseball history to vault from last place one year to first place the next, then lose the League Championship Series. The 1991 Atlanta Braves, 1991 Minnesota Twins, 1993 Philadelphia Phillies, 1998 San Diego Padres, and 2007 Colorado Rockies all reached the final round in their worst-to-first seasons.

◇

How sweep it is! The 2007 Colorado Rockies were not only the seventh wild card team to win a pennant but the first to sweep both the Division Series and the LCS since that format was adopted in 1995. The only other team to win its first seven postseason games was the 1976 Cincinnati Reds of Big Red Machine vintage. Colorado went into the '07 World Series with 21 wins in 22 games dating back to the regular season.

The World Series

Although World Series contestants must survive two rounds of playoffs first, baseball insiders insist the best-of-seven classic between league champions retains its traditional role as the highlight of the baseball year.

Critics contend the advent of the wild card (1995) and interleague play (1997) cheapens the World Series, since rivals might have met a few months earlier as interleague opponents. There's no longer a guarantee that the best teams will be World Series opponents. A slump, injury, or hot opposing pitcher can fell great teams during the playoffs even before they reach the final round. With wild card winners now part of the postseason equation, it's even possible that a World Series could pit two teams that failed to finish first (see Giants vs. Angels, 2002).

Getting to the World Series is hard; winning it is harder.

World Series Bits

In the first World Series, played two years after the 1901 birth of the AL, the Boston Red Sox beat the Pittsburgh Pirates, 5–3, in a best-of-nine affair. An estimated 100,000 fans paid double the going rate (50 cents for general admission and $1 for reserved seats) to watch.

No World Series has ever gone nine games—but it could have. The first Fall Classic, in 1903, and the World Series of 1919, 1920, and 1921 were all played with a best-of-nine format.

◇

There was no World Series in 1904 because John McGraw, manager of the NL champion Giants, refused to acknowledge the major status of the AL and shunned its champion. But the Series was renewed to stay in 1905, under the supervision of the three-man National Commission that governed the game. Revenue was divided among players, owners, and the commission.

◇

Christy Mathewson threw a record three shutouts against the Philadelphia Athletics in the 1905 World Series. A fourth shutout, by Joe McGinnity, gave the Giants a team ERA of 0.00 in the five-game Fall Classic.

The $30,000 Muff

The 1912 Boston Red Sox won the World Championship when the careless Giants blew a 2–1 lead in the tenth inning of the seventh game. With Christy Mathewson on the mound, Clyde Engle led off with a fly ball to center fielder Fred Snodgrass. He dropped it, allowing Engle to reach second. Harry Hooper then lined to Snodgrass, who caught it for an out, but Steve Yerkes walked. Tris Speaker popped up wide of first, but Fred Merkle failed to move from his position and catcher Chief Meyers could not reach the foul fly. Given another chance, Speaker singled to score Engle with the tying run. Yerkes went to third and scored when Larry Gardner hit a sacrifice fly to left. Snodgrass' error was labeled "the $30,000 muff" because he denied his 16 teammates (only 17 players were then eligible for the Series) the difference between the winner's share of $4,025 and the loser's share of $2,566.

In one of the most boneheaded plays in World Series history, Giants third baseman Heinie Zimmerman botched a rundown play that cost his team the 1917 world championship. Instead of throwing the ball home, he held it while hoping to tag White Sox baserunner Eddie Collins. Collins had other ideas: he crossed home plate with the winning run.

Babe Ruth's record string of 29⅔ scoreless World Series innings (later topped by Whitey Ford) ended the day after he fought a Red Sox teammate on the team train. Ruth hurt the middle finger of his pitching hand in the fracas.

◇

Cincinnati won the 1919 World Series, five games to three, after eight White Sox players allegedly sold out to gamblers. Although acquitted in court after evidence disappeared, the "Black Sox" conspirators were banned from the game by Commissioner Kenesaw Mountain Landis when word leaked out in 1920.

◇

Triple plays in the World Series seldom happen. But an unassisted triple play has happened once: Bill Wambsganss did it for Cleveland vs. Brooklyn on October 10, 1920.

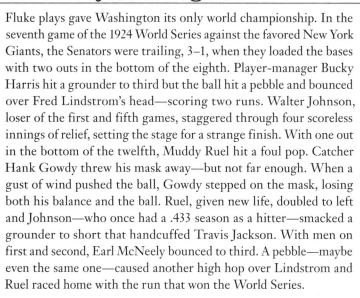

Why Washington Won

Fluke plays gave Washington its only world championship. In the seventh game of the 1924 World Series against the favored New York Giants, the Senators were trailing, 3–1, when they loaded the bases with two outs in the bottom of the eighth. Player-manager Bucky Harris hit a grounder to third but the ball hit a pebble and bounced over Fred Lindstrom's head—scoring two runs. Walter Johnson, loser of the first and fifth games, staggered through four scoreless innings of relief, setting the stage for a strange finish. With one out in the bottom of the twelfth, Muddy Ruel hit a foul pop. Catcher Hank Gowdy threw his mask away—but not far enough. When a gust of wind pushed the ball, Gowdy stepped on the mask, losing both his balance and the ball. Ruel, given new life, doubled to left and Johnson—who once had a .433 season as a hitter—smacked a grounder to short that handcuffed Travis Jackson. With men on first and second, Earl McNeely bounced to third. A pebble—maybe even the same one—caused another high hop over Lindstrom and Ruel raced home with the run that won the World Series.

Casey Stengel's home run settled the first 1–0 game in World Series history, on October 10, 1923. Stengel, then with the New York Giants, would later manage the team he beat, the New York Yankees. Stengel hit the first two World Series homers at Yankee Stadium; all three Babe Ruth homers in the 1923 World Series came at the Polo Grounds.

Although Walter Johnson went on to win two World Series games in 1925, he never won another ring. Forced to retire three years after a broken leg and a severe bout with influenza, Johnson finished his illustrious career with 417 wins, a record 110 shutouts, and a dozen 20-win seasons. He once pitched 56 consecutive scoreless innings, a record that stood for 55 years; led the AL in victories six times; won a dozen strikeout crowns; and proved himself such an intense competitor that he won 38 times by the score of 1–0.

◇

The first all-New York World Series was played in 1921, when the Giants faced the Yankees.

◇

Babe Ruth did not hit a World Series homer in Yankee Stadium until 1926, three years after the ballpark opened.

Alexander's Last Hurrah

Grover Cleveland Alexander won 373 games, an NL record shared by Christy Mathewson, and had more shutouts (90) and complete games (437) than any other NL hurler. But the biggest moment of his career came long after his best days were behind him. After winning the second and sixth games of the 1926 World Series for the Cardinals against the Yankees, the 39-year-old righty hardly expected to work again. Dumped by Cubs manager Joe McCarthy because of his penchant for drinking, Alexander was recuperating from a nocturnal binge in the seventh inning of the finale when St. Louis starter Jesse Haines raised a blister. Alexander, a control artist who warmed up quickly, inherited a bases-full, two-out situation with slugging rookie Tony Lazzeri at the plate and the Cards nursing a 3–2 lead. Lazzeri hit a long foul to left on an 0–1 pitch, then fanned. Alexander retired the next five men but walked Babe Ruth on a 3–2 pitch with two outs in the bottom of the ninth. With Bob Meusel batting, Ruth tried to steal second and was thrown out to end the Series.

Nothing might have helped the Pittsburgh Pirates avoid a 1927 World Series sweep by Babe Ruth's Yankees, but manager Donie Bush certainly contributed: he kept Pirate star Kiki Cuyler benched because of an ongoing feud.

Howard Ehmke was a surprise starter in the 1929 World Series opener. Out with a sore arm that summer, Ehmke scouted the Chicago Cubs at the suggestion of Philadelphia A's manager Connie Mack. Healthy by the time the clubs met in the Fall Classic, Ehmke not only won 3–1, but struck out 13 batters.

◇

The biggest rally in World Series history occurred on October 12, 1929, when the Philadelphia Athletics exploded for a 10-run seventh *after being shut out by the Chicago Cubs in six previous innings.* The Game 4 rally gave the A's a 10–8 win, reversed Chicago's momentum, and spurred the A's on to the world championship.

◇

After the Philadelphia A's beat the St. Louis Cardinals in the 1930 World Series, the Cards rode a rookie performance to the title in the seven-game World Series of 1931. Center fielder Pepper Martin collected 12 hits (including a homer and four doubles) in 24 at-bats, scored five runs, knocked in five, and stole five bases with the leaping, head-first slide that won him the nickname "Wild Horse of the Osage."

◇

Mel Ott was a teenager when he became the first future 500 Home Run Club hitter to homer in his first World Series at-bat. It happened in the opener of the 1933 World Series between the New York Giants and Washington Senators.

Dizzy Dean was the ace of the staff for the "Gashouse Gang" Cardinals. A 30-game winner in 1934, he also took two of the club's four World Series wins against the Detroit Tigers.
(National League)

The stars of the 1934 World Series, won by the "Gashouse Gang" Cardinals, were the Dean brothers. Dizzy and Paul split the four St. Louis wins over the Detroit Tigers. Dizzy won Game 7, 11–0, after boasting to the Tiger hitters that he would use only fastballs against them.

◇

Mickey Owen, catching for the 1941 Brooklyn Dodgers, made the most damaging error in World Series history when he failed to hold Hugh Casey's game-ending third strike against the New York Yankees in Game 4 at Brooklyn. Instead of a 3–2 Dodger win and a Series tied at two games each, the Yankees scored four runs and took a three games to one lead. They wrapped up the World Championship the next day.

◇

The 1946 Red Sox may have lost the World Series because the *NL* pennant race ended in a tie. When the Dodgers and Cardinals finished with identical records, forcing the NL's first best-of-three pennant playoff, the Red Sox decided to stay in shape by playing three exhibition games against teams of AL "All-Stars." In the very first game, a pitch hit Ted Williams in the elbow, knocking him out of the remaining two games and silencing his bat throughout the seven-game World Series against St. Louis. He delivered just five hits—one of them a rare bunt single—and one RBI as the Cards won the world title.

◇

The 1947 World Series between the Yankees and the Dodgers is remembered for the no-hit game Floyd "Bill" Bevens took into the ninth inning of Game 4, the Cookie Lavagetto pinch-hit that ruined it with two outs, and the Al Gionfriddo catch of a titanic Joe DiMaggio drive in Game 6. Bevens, Lavagetto, and Gionfriddo all left the majors after that, but a rookie named Jackie Robinson—who had seven hits in a losing effort for the Dodgers—remained.

◇

After making all 74 of his regular-season appearances in relief during the 1950 season, Jim Konstanty started the World Series opener for the Philadelphia Phillies against the Yankees. He wound up with the loss by the thinnest of margins: 1–0.

◇

The 1951 World Series matched 19-year-old Mickey Mantle (Yankees) against 20-year-old Willie Mays (Giants). Mantle hurt his knee in the second game, sidelining him for the duration, but the Yankees won in six games.

Although knee problems plagued Mickey Mantle for much of his career, he still hit 536 home runs in the regular season and a record 18 in the World Series.

(John Pennisi)

Mickey Mantle might have reached greater heights had he not torn up his knee during the 1951 World Series. The switch-hitting slugger, completing his rookie season, tripped over an exposed drainage pipe in the Yankee Stadium outfield, tore cartilage, and missed the rest of the series.

◇

Joe Black was the first black pitcher to win a World Series game: the 1952 opener for the Brooklyn Dodgers vs. the New York Yankees.

◇

During the New York Giants' sweep of the highly favored 1954 Cleveland Indians, Vic Wertz lost a potential inside-the-park home run when Willie Mays made a back-to-the-plate catch of his 450-foot drive to deep center field in the horseshoe-shaped park—and then pegged a throw to third to double up the runner. The 2–2 tie then lasted until the tenth inning.

◇

Dusty Rhodes delivered the game-winning home run for the Giants in the 1954 opener and two pinch-hit singles later on. The home run, against Cleveland ace Bob Lemon, was a 260-foot fly ball that barely cleared the short right field wall of the Polo Grounds.

THIS is Next Year

Virtually every time the Brooklyn Dodgers faced the New York Yankees in the World Series, they lost. The Yankees won in 1941, 1947, 1949, 1952, and 1953, and were supremely confident in 1955—especially after winning the first two games. But Brooklyn won three straight, putting the Yankees in an unfamiliar hole, before Whitey Ford evened things up in Game 6. With 62,465 Yankee fans howling in his ear, Johnny Podres responded with a 2–0 win, highlighted by a Sandy Amoros catch. In the bottom of the sixth, Amoros was inserted as a defensive replacement in left field. He was soon tested. With two men on, Yogi Berra sliced an opposite-field drive that looked like a sure double. But Amoros, shaded toward center, switched gears and made a mad dash to the left field line, arriving just in time to snare the ball. With both runners moving, Amoros was able to hit cutoff man Pee Wee Reese with his throw. Reese's relay to Gil Hodges completed a double play that preserved the Dodgers lead.

Using his newly mastered no-windup delivery to perfection, Don Larsen delivered a 2–0 perfect game against the Brooklyn Dodgers in Game 5 of the 1956 World Series. Five of his seven strikeouts came on called third strikes. Larsen, who had been knocked out in the second inning of the second game that fall, had only 81 wins (less than six per season) during his 14-year career. The righty even posted an embarrassing 3–21 record with the 1954 Baltimore Orioles (née St. Louis Browns) before moving to the Yankees, where he went 45–24 in five seasons.

◇

The Yankees locked up the 1956 World Series when Johnny Kucks followed Don Larsen's perfect game with a three-hit shutout of his own. The six-game set against the Brooklyn Dodgers was the last Subway Series until the Mets and Yankees met in 2000.

◇

Between 1921 and 1956, there were 13 World Series involving two of the three New York teams, the Yankees, Dodgers, and Giants.

World Series Pitching Gems

No-hitter

Don Larsen, Yankees vs. Dodgers, October 8, 1956 (perfect game)

One-hitters

Ed Reulbach, Cubs vs. White Sox, October 10, 1906
Claude Passeau, Cubs vs. Tigers, October 5, 1945
Floyd Bevens, Yankees vs. Dodgers, October 3, 1947
Jim Lonborg, Red Sox vs. Cardinals, October 5, 1967
Tom Glavine and Mark Wohlers, Braves vs. Indians,
    October 28, 1995

The fourth game of the 1957 World Series, played in Milwaukee County Stadium on October 6, 1957, turned in favor of the Braves because of shoe polish. With the Braves trailing the Yankees, 5–4, little-used Nippy Jones came up as a pinch-hitter. Bob Grim's pitch hit his foot, but umpire Augie Donatelli didn't see it. But Jones knew his shoes had just been polished and asked the arbiter to examine the ball. He did and sent Jones to first base. After Red Schoendienst bunted him to second, Johnny Logan doubled home the tying run. Yankee manager Casey Stengel, realizing Hank Aaron was on deck, elected to pitch to the slumping Eddie Mathews rather than issue an intentional walk and set up a righty/righty confrontation. The left-handed Mathews suddenly sprang to life, uncorking a long home run and tying the Series at two games apiece.

◇

Lew Burdette of the Milwaukee Braves pitched as many shutouts against the Yankees in the 1957 World Series (2) as the entire AL managed during the 154-game regular season. With matching seven-hit shutouts, Burdette became the first pitcher since Christy Mathewson in 1905 to throw two shutouts in one World Series.

◇

Gene Conley was the only pro athlete to play for world champions in two different sports: baseball, with the 1957 Milwaukee Braves, and basketball, with the 1959 to 1961 Boston Celtics.

Joe Torre, then 17, accompanied brother Frank when he played for the 1957 Milwaukee Braves. The younger Torre cleaned equipment, did the laundry, and helped with other clubhouse chores. According to Frank, "That was the year he got the dream for himself. He saw the excitement of us winning the World Series. He really had that ambition. He wanted to be part of it."

◇

Frank Torre gave his 1957 Milwaukee Braves world championship ring to brother Joe. "Fine," said Torre the Younger. "I'll give you one when I win the World Series." It took a while but Joe returned the favor by giving Frank the 1996 world championship ring he won with the New York Yankees—against the Atlanta Braves, who had moved from Milwaukee 30 years earlier.

◇

Hank Aaron won the only Most Valuable Player award of his career in 1957 by leading the NL with 44 home runs, 132 RBI, 118 runs scored, and 369 total bases. He then topped the two World Series teams, the Braves and the Yankees, in runs, hits, homers, average, and RBI.

Although Hank Aaron hit half of his six postseason homers against Tom Seaver's Mets in the 1969 NLCS, he couldn't keep New York from advancing to the World Series against the Baltimore Orioles.

(Dan Schlossberg)

After hitting only 11 home runs during the 1960 season, Bill Mazeroski wasn't expected to put on a power show in the World Series. But the Pittsburgh second baseman connected twice in the seven-game set against the New York Yankees. His last one was a leadoff shot against Ralph Terry in the bottom of the ninth in Game 7 that gave the Pirates a 10–9 victory and their first world title in 35 years.

◇

In October 1960, Yankee second baseman Bobby Richardson became the first player from a losing team to win a World Series MVP award.

◇

Powered by Mickey Mantle, Roger Maris, and Yogi Berra, the New York Yankees outscored the Pittsburgh Pirates 55–27 in the 1960 World Series, but wound up losing in seven games.

◇

Pitching wins: the Los Angeles Dodgers proved the point in the 1963 World Series, winning the first and fourth games for Sandy Koufax, the second for Don Drysdale, and the third for Johnny Podres. The Yankees scored a grand total of four runs during the four-game sweep.

◇

The 1964 New York Yankees had more wins, more homers, and a better ERA than their World Series opponents, the St. Louis Cardinals. They also had more homers and more runs scored in the World Series. All of that didn't help, however: St. Louis won in seven games.

◇

The Boyers—Ken and Clete—were the first brothers to homer in the same World Series game. They did it as opponents for the Cardinals and Yankees, respectively, in 1964.

◇

The Dodgers scored their two only runs of the 1966 World Series against Baltimore ace Dave McNally in the first game. Journeyman Moe Drabowsky pitched 6⅔ innings of shutout relief in the opener, fanning 11 during his time on the mound, and the O's followed with consecutive shut-outs by Jim Palmer, Wally Bunker, and McNally. The last two scores were 1–0 and 1–0.

◇

Bob Gibson and Dave McNally are the only pitchers to hit two World Series home runs.

BOB GIBSON

pitcher ST. LOUIS CARDINALS

Crack Cardinal right-hander Bob Gibson had a record 17 strikeouts in the 1968 World Series opener against the Detroit Tigers.
(Ronnie Joyner)

Detroit manager Mayo Smith took a huge gamble by moving outfielder Mickey Stanley to shortstop for the 1968 World Series against St. Louis. That move allowed him to deploy an outfield of Willie Horton, Jim Northrup, and Al Kaline, and bench weak-hitting shortstop Ray Oyler.

◇

Pitcher Mickey Lolich hit the only home run of his career while pitching Detroit to an 8-1 victory over the St. Louis Cardinals in Game 2 of the 1968 World Series.

◇

After beating Tom Seaver in the 1969 World Series opener, the Baltimore Orioles looked for an easy mark in the New York Mets, appearing in their first Fall Classic. But the Mets parlayed strong pitching, tight defense, and timely hitting into four straight wins and the world championship. The most memorable plays were diving catches by outfielders Tommie Agee and Ron Swoboda.

◇

Dazzling defense by Brooks Robinson was a major factor in Baltimore's defeat of Cincinnati in the 1970 World Series. The Orioles third baseman acquired the nickname "Hoover" that fall for his flawless fielding.

◇

The Orioles were at Pittsburgh for the first night game in World Series history on October 13, 1971. The Pirates won, 4–3.

*Brooks Robinson demonstrated
the importance of dynamic defense
during the 1970 World Series,
when his glovework at third base
helped the Baltimore Orioles beat
the Cincinnati Reds.*

(John Pennisi)

Playing in his second and final World Series in 1971, Roberto Clemente
batted .414, with 2 homers and 4 RBIs, to help the Pirates win the title.
Two months after the Pirates lost the 1972 NLCS to Cincinnati, Clemente
was killed in a plane crash.

◇

The Oakland A's won the first of three straight world titles in 1972 when
second-string catcher Gene Tenace became the first man to homer in
his first two World Series at-bats. The red-hot Tenace, who hit .225 with
five homers during the regular season, hit four during the seven-game set
against Cincinnati.

◇

According to Hall of Famer Rollie Fingers, the highlight of his career
was getting Pete Rose to fly out to Joe Rudi for the last out in the seventh
game of the 1972 World Series.

◇

A three-run, pinch-hit homer in the eighth by Bernie Carbo at Boston's
Fenway Park tied 1975 World Series Game 6 between the Reds and Red
Sox, setting the stage for a memorable finish in the twelfth. The first

Boston batter, Carlton Fisk, hit Pat Darcy's first pitch down the left-field line, gestured at ball to stay fair, then pranced around the bases with the winning run in a 7-6 game. Although the Sox had an early 3-0 lead in the finale, Cincinnati rallied for a 4-3 win, scoring the winning run in the ninth.

◇

Reggie Jackson of the 1977 Yankees needed only three swings to produce a three-homer game in the World Series—a feat done twice previously only by Babe Ruth (twice). With two homers in the previous five games of that clash with the Dodgers, the Yankee slugger became the first man to hit five home runs in one World Series.

◇

Although world champs do it every year since the creation of the wild card format, the 1978 Yankees were the first team to take three postseason titles: a playoff for the AL East crown, a Championship Series victory, and the world championship.

◇

The Philadelphia Phillies won their only world championship by winning four of six from the Kansas City Royals in 1980.

◇

Proof that anything can happen in a short series: Yankee reliever George Frazier compiled a 1.29 ERA during the 1981 season but a 17.17 ERA in a six-game World Series loss against Los Angeles. The losing pitcher in three of the last four games, Frazier tied the record for most defeats by a pitcher in a World Series and set his own mark for most losses in a Series shorter than seven games.

◇

Bob Stanley *never* threw a wild pitch during the 1986 AL season. But the Boston right-hander *did* throw one in the tenth inning of World Series Game 6 at Shea Stadium. After three singles reduced the Red Sox lead over the Mets to 5–4, Stanley succeeded Calvin Schiraldi and got two quick strikes on Mookie Wilson. The wild pitch followed, allowing the tying run to cross and moving runner Ray Knight from first to second. Then Wilson's multi-bounce grounder found its way through the legs of first baseman Bill Buckner and the Mets won, 6–5, to tie a Series they would win the next night.

◇

A rare Dennis Eckersley walk to the weak-hitting Mike Davis set up the game-winning Kirk Gibson homer in the 1988 World Series opener. A master of control, Eckersley issued only three walks in 58 innings in 1989 and four in 73 innings a year later. But he let the count on Davis reach 3–2 and couldn't get the final strike, setting the stage for the gimpy Gibson, side-lined with a knee injury. The lefty slugger limped to the plate, worked the count to 3–2, then hit his home run and hobbled around the bases. Although Gibson did not bat again in the Fall Classic, his shot set the tone for the underdog Los Angeles Dodgers, who beat the Oakland A's in five games.

◇

When you're hot, you're hot: Orel Hershiser pitched 67 consecutive score-less innings—a record 59 to finish the 1988 season and eight more in the NLCS opener against the New York Mets. The Dodgers right-hander reaped his rewards after the season with a Cy Young Award plus MVP honors in both the NLCS and World Series.

◇

Gene Tenace and Andruw Jones are the only players to homer in their first two World Series at-bats.

◇

The 1996 Yankees were the third team to win a world title after losing the first two games *at home*, joining the 1985 St. Louis Cardinals and 1986 New York Mets.

◇

Back-up catcher Jim Leyritz became an instant Yankees legend in Game 4 of the 1996 World Series with a three-run, game-tying, eighth-inning homer against Braves closer Mark Wohlers. Atlanta blew a 6-0 lead to lose, 8–6 in 10 innings, and square a series they eventually lost in six games.

◇

The 1997 Yankees extended their World Series winning streak to a record-tying 12 games with consecutive sweeps of the Padres in 1998 and the Braves in 1999. Baseball's first repeat champion since the 1992 to 1993 Toronto Blue Jays, they were also the first team with successive sweeps since the 1938 to 1939 Yankees.

◇

From 1947 to 2000, the Bronx Bombers never lost a postseason game they led after eight innings.

◇

The Bronx Bombers took their third straight world championship in 2000, winning the first two games to extend their winning streak to a record 14, and then defeating the crosstown Mets in a five-game Subway Series.

◇

Yankees pitcher Roger Clemens was fined for throwing a broken bat in the general direction of Mets catcher Mike Piazza during the 2000 World Series.

Roger Clemens drew a $50,000 fine for heaving a jagged piece of broken bat at Mike Piazza during the first inning of the second game in the all-New York World Series of 2000. After the pitcher's action, Piazza glared at him and the benches emptied. The Yankees won the game and the Series.

(John Pennisi)

The oldest pitcher to start the seventh game of the World Series was 39-year-old Roger Clemens in 2001. Starting for the Yankees against the Arizona Diamondbacks, Clemens did not get a decision.

◇

With closer Mariano Rivera on the mound, the New York Yankees were confident they could hold their 2–1 lead in Game 7 of the 2001 World Series. But Mark Grace singled and Damian Miller followed with a bunt back to the mound. Rivera, hoping for a double play, wheeled toward second but threw the ball into center field. Jay Bell then bunted into a force before Tony Womack sliced a game-tying double. Craig Counsell was hit by a pitch, loading the bases with Luis Gonzalez at bat. With the infield drawn in, Gonzalez hit a broken-bat fly just over the head of shortstop Derek Jeter to score Bell with the winning run and end the Yankees' bid for a fourth straight world championship.

◇

Barry Bonds not only homered in his first World Series at-bat but hit eight home runs in the same postseason (2002). It didn't help: his San Francisco Giants still lost.

Late-Inning Lightning

One reason the 2001 World Series went seven games was the propensity of Arizona pitcher Byung-Hyun Kim to throw gopher balls at critical moments. In Game 4, he fanned all three Yankees he faced in the eighth and seemed certain to sew up a save when he had one man on and two men out in the ninth. But Tino Martinez hit Kim's first pitch for a game-tying homer, erasing a 3–1 Arizona lead. With two outs and two strikes in the tenth, Derek Jeter delivered the game-*winning* homer against Kim.

Then, though he'd worked three innings and threw 62 pitches the previous night, Kim got the call again in Game 5. Arizona led 2–0 in the ninth when Kim entered. Two quick outs followed a Jorge Posada leadoff double and the game seemed over. But Scott Brosius, hardly a home run hitter, had other ideas: he homered to left, tying a game the Yankees won in the twelfth. Only once before had a team tied a World Series game with a home run after trailing by two runs in the bottom of the ninth.

Derek Jeter's game-winning homer against Arizona in Game 4 of the 2001 World Series helped cement his reputation as a clutch hitter.
(Bill Menzel)

Maybe age helps: Jack McKeon, the oldest manager in World Series history, also won it with the 2003 Florida Marlins over the New York Yankees. McKeon was 72 years and 303 days old when that Fall Classic opened.

◇

McKeon took a calculated gamble in the sixth game of the 2003 World Series: he could start star starter Josh Beckett on three days of rest or use him on normal rest in Game 7. McKeon went for the gold immediately, and the move paid off. Beckett pitched a five-hit shutout to make the Fish World Champions for the second time in seven seasons.

◇

The 2004 Boston Red Sox not only won their last eight postseason games but never trailed in any game of the World Series against the St. Louis Cardinals.

◇

During the 86 years between Red Sox world championships, there were 15 presidents, 11 Boston mayors, and 7 popes. Oh, yes: the price of a World Series ticket skyrocketed from $3.30 in 1918 to $140 in 2004.

◇

The surprise Red Sox win in the 2004 World Series moved heaven and earth: a lunar eclipse occurred while the Bosox were wrapping up their victory over the Cardinals.

◇

The Chicago White Sox were the only team to get game-deciding homers in the ninth inning or later *twice* in the same postseason series, their 2005 World Series win over the Houston Astros.

◇

The longest game in World Series history consumed 5 hours and 41 minutes, 14 innings, and 43 players, including 17 pitchers. In that third game of the 2005 Fall Classic, the White Sox beat the Astros, 7–5.

◇

Scott Podsednik of the White Sox had more homers (1) and more triples (2) in the four-game World Series sweep of the Astros in 2005 than he did during the regular season (no homers and one triple).

◇

The first game of the 2006 World Series marked the first time both teams started rookie pitchers in the opener. Anthony Reyes, who had gone 5–8 during the regular season for the Cardinals, outpitched 17-game winner Justin Verlander of the Tigers for a 7–2 victory.

The Cardinals pulled an upset when they swept the AL champion Tigers in the 2006 World Series. Although 12 teams had better regular-season records than the Cardinals, and no previous world champion had fewer regular-season wins (83), the Cards proved that experience trumps enthusiasm in trouncing the young Detroit Tigers.

◊

Wild card teams may not win divisional titles, but they *do* seem to win World Series. The wild card, awarded to the second-place team in each league with the best winning percentage, was introduced in 1995, the first year of the three-division format, to provide a fourth team in the first-round Division Series (three divisional champs plus a wild card) in each league. In 13 seasons since, 5 wild card teams have become world champions: the 1997 Marlins, 2002 Angels, 2003 Marlins (again), 2004 Red Sox, and 2006 Cardinals.

◊

Although Joe Torre's Yankees once won a record 14 straight World Series games and made the playoffs every year of his 12-year tenure, they failed to survive the first round Division Series in 2005, 2006, and 2007, costing the manager his job.

◊

The New York Yankees have *won* more World Series than any other team has even *played*.

◊

Twice in four years, the Boston Red Sox swept a World Series after overcoming an enormous deficit in the AL Championship Series. It happened in 2004, when Boston beat St. Louis, and again in 2007, when the Red Sox refrigerated the red-hot Colorado Rockies.

CHAPTER

8

BallTalk

Without BallTalk, baseball would be a silent movie—a black-and-white newsreel in an era of digitally produced colors. Much of the game's glory would be lost in the process.

BallTalk comes in many forms. Players, coaches, and managers have their own language—a lingo with a rich legacy that ranges from nicknames to unforgettable and sometimes inadvertent quotations. Entire books have been written about memorable baseball quotes, although only one of the quotes is contained in *Bartlett's Familiar Quotations.* Some of the best things ever said about baseball are included in induction speeches at the Baseball Hall of Fame. Since 1939, that is where greats of the game have been honored—assuming that they can muster 75 percent of the vote from the writers, officials, and members who serve as electors. Some of the most memorable lines have come from the press box or broadcast booth, where coverage of the game has slowly shifted its emphasis from print to electronic media during the game's 150-year history.

Language and Terminology

The heritage of baseball is reflected by its colorful language, which has influenced American culture and speech patterns for generations. Teams and players have nicknames, personalities have a penchant for popping off, and every corner of the ballpark and equipment rack has a name that has withstood the test of time. Writers, managers, and players create phrases that stick like pine tar, providing pundits with words they borrowed for general usage. For example, a businessperson whose deal went sour has *struck out* or a speaker unable to keep an engagement might ask for *a rain check*.

The quotes are just as memorable. Writer Grantland Rice once said, "It's not whether you win or lose, it's how you play the game." Connie Mack, whose worst season in a 50-year managerial career might have been 1916 when his A's lost 117 games, contributed another classic: "Well, you can't win them all." (The 1914 A's had finished first.) And Babe Ruth, after an embarrassing strikeout, summarized the game succinctly: "You're a hero one day and a bum the next."

Even casual fans have a basic knowledge of the baseball lexicon—the list of words and terms that describe the various nuances of the game.

Language Bits

The star of any team effort is called the "ace"—because of Asa Brainard, who pitched every game for the unbeaten Cincinnati Red Stockings of 1869. Whenever a pitcher of that time did well, he was called an "asa," later shortened to ace.

 # How the Bullpen Got Its Name

Several conflicting theories try to explain the origin of the word "bullpen." One says the area where pitchers warm up won its name because early parks featured large outfield billboards advertising Bull Durham tobacco. Not only did pitchers warm up under the sign—usually deep in fair territory—but the company popularized its name by offering $50 to any player who hit the bull with a ball. Another possible derivation pinpoints the log enclosure used by pioneers to fend off Indian attacks. "Bullpen" later described any makeshift jail and jumped to baseball after Connie Mack began the practice of having his pitchers warm up in a secluded area in 1909. The term could have come from bullfighting, where bulls are kept in separate pens, or railroading, where workers took breaks in shanties with benches located at intervals along the roadbed. Pitchers who weren't working sat on similar benches in foul territory.

The horseshoe-shaped Polo Grounds, longtime home of the New York Giants, lent credence to the term "Chinese home run." The stadium stretched just 258 feet from home to the right field line and 279 to left. In the early 1920s, *New York Tribune* sports editor Bill McGeehan noted that the close right field fence looked thick, low, and not very formidable— like the Great Wall of China. T. A. Dorgan of the *Journal,* also in the 1920s, used the phrase to mean a home run that wasn't worthy of being a home run. He disliked the Giants, especially manager John McGraw, and enjoyed deprecating Giant victories. A native of San Francisco, which had the largest Chinese population in the United States but did little to make it feel welcome, he knew Chinese immigrants were barred from voting and often worked for small wages. The analogy followed: cheap Chinese labor became cheap "Chinese" home runs.

◇

Who was the first baseball "fan"? During the late 1880s, German-born Chris Von der Ahe, owner of the St. Louis Browns of the American Association, was discussing a St. Louis spectator who never missed a game. "Dot feller is a regular FAN-a-tic," he said, accenting the first syllable of the word "fanatic."

◇

The letter "K" is used in baseball to designate a strikeout victim, especially in scoring after the single initial was introduced by *New York Herald* baseball writer M. J. Kelly in 1868. Kelly, who used a system of letters to cover most situations in the game, hit upon "K" because it is the last letter of the word "struck." The letter "S" could not have been used because it might have been confused with shortstop or sacrifice.

◇

Great slugging teams, like the 1927 Yankees, were said to have a "Murderer's Row" (hitters who kill pitchers). The phrase dates back to 1858, when an early baseball writer borrowed it from the isolated Death Row at The Tombs prison in New York.

◇

The word "rookie" was first used by the *Chicago Record-Herald* in 1913. The unflattering term for a first-year player may have stemmed from chess, where the rook must wait its turn and is often the last piece to be used after the game opens.

◇

Rhubarb is more than a vegetable. Garry Schumacher of *The New York Journal-American* used the word to describe a 1938 Dodger/Giant brawl. He explained that winners of fights during his boyhood in Brooklyn would invariably force the losers to swallow terrible-tasting rhubarb tonic.

In baseball today, a "scout" is an observer who watches games and evaluates players. Before the 1845 Cartwright rules, however, a scout was something else: a second catcher who played far to the rear of the regular catcher. He grabbed passed balls and wild pitches and fielded "hits" that landed near him. (There were no fouls then, and batters could run on hits behind the plate as well as in front of it.)

◇

Because left-handers are a small minority (7 percent of the U.S. population), right-handers in baseball began calling them "southpaws." The name stemmed from the fact that early ballparks were laid out in such a way that the afternoon sun was behind the batter but in the eyes of the right-fielder. That alignment made the home to first base line run almost directly east and west, so a left-hander's arm faced south.

◇

An extra man—called in when two persons disagreed—was called a *noumper* in Middle English. The "n" was eventually dropped, and "umpire" became part of baseball's phraseology when Cartwright's rules were written in 1845.

Nicknames

Nicknames have always been an integral part of baseball. Before the Civil War, newspapers were referring to teams like the New Yorks, the Brooklyns, or the Bostons. After professional baseball introduced the concept of placing more than one team in a given city, nicknames became a necessity.

Player nicknames come mostly from the animal kingdom, with strong players named after strong animals. Jimmie Foxx was not only known as "Double-X" because of his name but also "The Beast" because of his brawn. Jim "Hippo" Vaughn, who weighed 230 and pitched half of the famed double no-hit game of May 2, 1917, was opposed in the classic by 260-pound Fred Toney, the "Man Mountain from Tennessee." And Dick "The Monster" Radatz dazzled rivals with a sizzling fastball as a Red Sox reliever of the 1960s.

Nickname Bits

When the Athletic Club of Philadelphia was formed in 1864, it kept the shortened name of Athletics active with the team after it joined the American League in 1901 and through franchise shifts to Kansas City and Oakland. Headline writers eventually adopted the abbreviated "A's."

◇

The Cincinnati club was called the Red Stockings two years before it began paying players in 1869, and press box occupants—seeking to save time and space—shortened that to Reds. "Redlegs" was used during periods when it was politically dangerous to be identified as "Reds," however.

◇

Baltimore has hosted a half dozen different teams called Orioles (named after the bird). The city had an American Association club from 1882 to 1891, a National League (NL) team from 1892 to 1899, an American League (AL) entry that lasted two years (1901 and 1902) before moving to New York, a Federal League team in 1914, and another AL team starting in 1954 after the relocation of the St. Louis Browns. The city had two teams in 1884, when the Union Association was a one-year wonder and there was a successful independent minor league team that later sent Babe Ruth, Lefty Grove, and other stars to the majors.

◇

The New York Giants had other names before 1885 when manager Jim Mutrie, thrilled with a spectacular play, jumped to his feet shouting, "My Giants!" The club had previously been called Green Stockings, and after making its NL debut in red-tinged uniforms in 1876, they were dubbed the Mutuals.

◇

The Chicago Cubs were originally the Chicago White Stockings—a name assumed and shortened by the AL team of 1901. Before the advent of the AL, the NL team's nickname morphed from White Sox to Colts after manager Cap Anson appeared on stage in *A Runaway Colt*, a play written for him in 1896. Cowboys and Broncos, natural derivatives, followed, and Rainmakers was used briefly. Sportswriters Fred Hayner and George Rice coined "Cubs" when the team had many young players in 1901.

◇

The Pittsburgh Pirates have had their nickname longer than most. They got it in 1891, when management successfully signed a deserting Players League star who rightfully belonged to another club.

The Dodgers weren't always Dodgers. Called the Brooklyn Bridegrooms because three of their players got married in 1888, the team won the 1889 American Association flag and took the title Superbas after the "Hanlon's Superbas" vaudeville troupe, whose director had the same surname as the Brooklyn manager. Also called Atlantics, Kings, and Robins—after colorful manager Wilbert Robinson—the name "Dodgers" is an abbreviated version of Trolley Dodgers, an unkind nickname given to Brooklynites by New Yorkers at the turn of the twentieth century.

◇

The St. Louis Cardinals, often dubbed Cards or Redbirds, acquired their nickname after changing their uniform colors just before the turn of the century. A female fan near the press box noticed the new suits and declared, "What a lovely shade of cardinal!" Writers heard her, spelling the end of the St. Louis Maroons.

◇

Because Michigan is the Wolverine State, the Detroit team had that nickname before *Detroit Free Press* newsman Phil J. Reid said its blue-and-orange striped stockings matched the colors of Princeton University, which called its teams Tigers.

◇

The future Yankees were first called Highlanders because of the elevation of their park at the entrance to Manhattan Island. They were also called Hilltoppers before moving into the Polo Grounds, which they shared with the Giants before Yankee Stadium opened in 1923. *New York Press* sports editor Jim Price and *New York Globe* newsman Mark Roth decided both names were too log to fit into a headline, prompting them to create the name Yankees.

◇

Although the Red Sox nickname is one of the oldest in baseball, the Boston team was previously called Pilgrims, then Puritans, then Somersets (after owner Charles Somers).

◇

Where did the Cleveland Indians get their nickname? The team was first called Forest City but later Molly McGuires (for many Irish players), Blues (for uniforms), Spiders (for players' dexterity), and Naps (for player-manager Napoleon Lajoie) before writers labeled the club "Indians" in an informal poll. The apparent reason: Indians once lived on the shores of Lake Erie.

◇

Because Phillies was once spelled "Fillies" (as in horses), the Philadelphia NL club took its alliterative nickname from the world of horse-racing.

The Futile Phillies

In 1944, exasperated Philadelphia executives tired of hearing their club called the "Futile Phillies" conducted a name-change contest and renamed the team "Blue Jays." The winning entry in a contest that produced 5,064 letters and 634 different suggestions was submitted by a Philadelphia woman who received a $100 war bond as a prize. One of the more appropriate losing names was "Stinkers."

Before becoming the Baltimore Orioles in 1954, the St. Louis Browns were named for the brown trimmings on their uniforms but were often called "Brownies" because of their inept play.

◇

The Minnesota Twins were the first team named after a state. The transplanted Washington Senators didn't want to offend either of the Twin Cities (Minneapolis or St. Paul) and did not play in either because their stadium was located in Bloomington. So they incorporated both into their name.

◇

The New York Mets, officially called the Metropolitan Baseball Club of New York, actually borrowed their nickname from an American Association team of the 1880s.

◇

Houston's 1962 expansion team was first called the Colts (after horses) and then the Colt .45s (after guns) before moving into the Astrodome. The third name change was a natural because Houston had become the home of the Manned Space Flight Center by 1965, the year the domed ballpark opened.

◇

The late, lamented Montreal Expos—an NL expansion team created two years after the city hosted Expo '67—were the only team ever named for a World's Fair.

◇

When the second-edition Washington Senators shifted to the Dallas/Fort Worth area after the 1971 season, they faced the same problem as the Minnesota Twins, who had left Washington 11 years earlier: they did not wish to offend either "host" city but actually played elsewhere (in Arlington). So they took the traditional name of the state's famous lawmen.

The Kansas City Royals and Toronto Blue Jays got their nicknames in fan contests.

◇

Some players were known only by their nicknames: Yogi Berra, Whitey Ford, Gabby Hartnett, Catfish Hunter, Sparky Lyle, Blue Moon Odom, Pee Wee Reese, Preacher Roe, Duke Snider, Dazzy Vance, Rube Waddell, and even Turk Lown (whose favorite holiday was Thanksgiving).

◇

Emil Frederick "Irish" Meusel, who played for Irishman John McGraw with the New York Giants of the early 1920s, was Irish only in appearance. In reality, he was of German extraction.

◇

Ken "Hawk" Harrelson got his name because of his nose. "Turkey Mike" Donlin was nicknamed after his walk, and Ron Cey suffered the same fate 50 years later when he was first called "The Penguin."

◇

Elwin Charles "Preacher" Roe was a pitcher—primarily for the Brooklyn Dodgers of the early 1950s—while Lynwood Thomas "Schoolboy" Rowe toiled for the Tigers of the 1930s. The former was quiet and introverted but the latter was a comedian.

◇

Mickey Cochrane's first name was a nickname, but Mickey Mantle's wasn't. The latter was named after the former, whose real name was George Stanley Cochrane.

◇

The media referred to Ted Williams as the "Splendid Splinter," to Joe DiMaggio as the "Yankee Clipper," and to Tom Seaver as "the Franchise," but the names did not catch on among players. At least George Thomas Seaver convinced teammates to use the shortened version of his middle name.

◇

Because his curly hair resembled a nest, and because he seemed to make pecking motions around the pitching mound, it was no surprise that 1976 AL Rookie of the Year Mark Fidrych was called "The Bird."

◇

Shorter nicknames that stuck included Hazen "KiKi" Cuyler, Edwin "Duke" Snider, Edward "Whitey" Ford, Willie "Stretch" McCovey, and Lawrence Peter "Yogi" Berra. Harold "Pee Wee" Reese was a whiz with marbles; Charles Leo "Gabby" Hartnett talked a lot; and Harold Joseph "Pie" Traynor used to run grocery errands for his mother with a list in hand that invariably ended with "pie."

A penchant for clubhouse and bullpen pranks produced the "Sparky" nickname for Albert Walker Lyle. His specialty was sitting on birthday cakes *sans* uniform.

◇

Baseball has had famous Rubes (notably George Edward Waddell and Richard Marquard) and dozens of Docs, including medical doctors Bobby Brown and George Medich, dentists G. Harry White and James Prothro, and even a pitcher—Dwight Gooden —who bore the moniker because he "cured" sick ballgames.

Famous Quotations

Because baseball's history links three centuries and spans more than 150 years, the game has generated more than its share of famous quotations. Dizzy Dean, Casey Stengel, and Yogi Berra were masters of malapropos and twisted syntax, while Branch Rickey and Leo Durocher were well-read individuals whose stated observations have become part of baseball lore.

Quoted Bits

Wee Willie Keeler, whose flood of hits between 1890 and 1910 seemed to have eyes, explained his prowess by saying, "I hit 'em where they ain't."

◇

Ty Cobb once fought with a roommate over first rights to the hotel bathtub. "I got to be first—all of the time," said Cobb, whose .367 lifetime batting average tops the lifetime list.

◇

When White Sox star "Shoeless" Joe Jackson emerged from the courtroom where game-fixing charges were being heard in 1920, an adoring youngster blurted, "Say it ain't so, Joe."

◇

Yankees pitcher Lefty Gomez, asked to explain his success, said, "I'd rather be lucky than good."

◇

Babe Herman was a better batter than speaker. Asked whether he'd buy his young son an encyclopedia for his birthday, he said, "Buy an encyclopedia for my kid? He'll learn to ride a two-wheeler or walk!"

◇

Kiner's Corner: Slugger Ralph Kiner always insisted, "Home run hitters drive Cadillacs; singles hitters drive Fords."

"Nice Guys Finish Last"

"Nice guys finish last" came from Leo ("The Lip") Durocher, longtime player and manager, in 1948. Never at a loss for words, Durocher was talking to a group of Brooklyn writers when he gazed across the field and noticed his contemporary, Giants manager Mel Ott. "Look at Ott," he told the reporters. "He's such a nice guy and they'll finish eighth for him." Spying Bobby Thomson, Sid Gordon, and other Giants home run stars, Durocher added, "All nice guys … and they'll finish eighth." The NL had eight teams until 1962, when expansion swelled the circuit to 10, but it wasn't long after he made the statement that writers had delivered the classic quote to the American public. Since its quick adoption into everyday usage, the substitution from "eighth" to "last" was immediate. But the meaning never changed.

Executive Branch Rickey, talking about the controversial Leo Durocher, described the fiery manager in no uncertain terms: "He can take a bad situation and make it immediately worse."

The Rickey Quotebook

Brooklyn executive Branch Rickey inspired player Chuck Connors, later TV's *Rifleman*, to talk about his reputation for tight economics: "It was easy to figure out Mr. Rickey's thinking about contracts. He had both players and money and didn't like to see the two of them mix." Although stingy with a dollar, Rickey was quick with a compliment—particularly for his own men. Of Eddie Stanky, Rickey said, "He can't hit, he can't run, and he can't throw—all he can do is beat you." A shrewd trader, Rickey was also credited with saying, "The trades you don't make are your best ones."

Casey Stengel, a huge success with the Yankees after previous failures with the Dodgers and Braves, explained his fortunes, good and bad: "I couldn't have done it without my players."

Roger Maris and Mickey Mantle kept swinging in 1961 and closed with home run totals of 61 and 54, respectively—the best teammates have done in one season. Talking about his senior partner, Maris said, "It's smarter to give the big man four balls for one base than one ball for four bases."

◇

Pitcher Mudcat Grant, who won 20 games for the 1965 Twins after adopting some tips from legendary pitching coach Johnny Sain, praised his tutor: "That man Sain sure puts biscuits in your pan."

Traditions

Because of its long history, baseball has acquired many traditions. A rules change, such as the introduction of the designated hitter by the AL in 1973, may seem radical—but even that idea was percolating (since its conception by NL President John Heydler in 1928).

Traditional Bits

Admitting women without charge was a baseball promotion designed to lure more men into the park. The custom began when executives of the 1889 Cincinnati Reds noticed more females in the stands whenever handsome hurler Tony Mullane worked. The team advertised he would pitch every Monday, which would be Ladies' Day. Mullane, who had thick black hair and a wavy mustache, won 283 games in his career—helped in part by his loyal band of female supporters.

◇

Rain checks have been part of baseball for more than a century. Early clubs sold heavy cardboard tickets but collected them during each game and used them again. When a game was shortened by rain one day in 1889, New Orleans owner Abner Powell saw numerous fence-jumpers and complimentary guests join the paying customers in line for new tickets. He devised the idea of a perforated rain check stub, and the innovation was so successful it is still in use.

◇

Sunday used to be a day off for baseball—sometimes because blue laws in certain cities prohibited playing on the Christian Sabbath. When the AL was founded in 1901, only Chicago played games on Sunday. St. Louis allowed Sunday ball the next year, but Boston didn't approve until 1929 and Philadelphia until 1934.

The Seventh-Inning Stretch

The 1882 Manhattan College baseball team played under a coach named Brother Jasper. Before each game, he told spectators not to move or leave their seats with the game in progress. One hot afternoon, however, the fans got restless—and as the team came to bat in the seventh inning, Brother Jasper told them to stand and stretch their legs. Because Manhattan College often played in the park of the New York NL club, Giants fans picked up on the "seventh-inning stretch." Other sources say the stretch began when fans of the 1869 Cincinnati Red Stockings stood to gain temporary relief from the hard wooden benches of the day. Another theory credits U.S. President William Howard Taft, who rose to stretch in the seventh inning of the 1910 Washington opener. Thinking he was leaving, fans stood out of respect for the office.

The tradition of retiring uniform numbers is relatively young. Babe Ruth's No. 3, for example, was not retired until long after the end of his Yankee career in 1934. In the 13 years it remained active, it was worn by George Selkirk, Allie Clark, Bud Metheny, Cliff Mapes, and (in spring training) Joe Medwick.

Players and managers in Yankee Stadium's Monument Park wore numbers retired by the club in their honor.

(Bill Menzel)

Before the home-run era triggered by Babe Ruth in the 1920s, fans returned balls hit into the stands. The practice of returning balls was reinstated during World War II to benefit the Army Relief Fund.

◇

Five NL teams dressed their players in identical No. 42 uniforms on April 15, 2007, to honor the 60th anniversary of Jackie Robinson's debut. They were the Dodgers, Astros, Phillies, Pirates, and Cardinals.

Jackie Robinson's widow, Rachel, shown here with blind sportswriter Ed Lucas, was honored at New York's Shea Stadium on April 15, 2007—the 60th anniversary of her husband's first game with the Brooklyn Dodgers. Robinson's debut marked the end of the baseball color line.

(Bill Menzel)

Opening Days and Farewells

Many people consider Opening Day the official start of spring. Temperatures are still low in many cities, but fans, players, and team executives have a special warmth inside on the eve of the season. Unlike the always-festive Opening Days, farewells are invariably sad—whether the retiring star enjoys a good final season or a bad one.

Opening and Closing Bits

Because it's the nation's capital, Washington's team traditionally opened at home one day ahead of the other clubs. Cincinnati enjoyed annual advance-opener honors in the NL—a tradition that began in 1876 (the league's first season) as a tribute to the Cincinnati Red Stockings, the first professional team.

◇

Opening Day games have been marked by unusual events on the field. In 1900, the Phillies beat the Braves 19–17—the highest score ever recorded in an NL opener. A year later, in the first AL game for both clubs, Detroit scored 10 runs in the ninth inning to beat Milwaukee 14–13.

◇

The 1909 season opened with Leon "Red" Ames of the New York Giants no-hitting the Brooklyn Dodgers for the first nine innings but losing in the thirteenth, 3–0. The following April, Walter Johnson lost a no-hitter because right fielder Doc Gessler tripped over a child who was sitting in front of an overflow crowd behind outfield ropes. The ball, which should have been an out, dropped for a double. Washington still won, however.

◇

Although the Cleveland Indians scored the most Opening Day runs with a 21–14 victory over the St. Louis Browns in 1925, Cleveland also registered the only no-hitter on Opening Day 15 years later—a 1–0 triumph pitched by Bob Feller over the Chicago White Sox. That same day, Lefty Grove of the Boston Red Sox worked seven perfect innings at Washington but gave up a one-out single to Cecil Travis in the eighth.

◇

At age 45, Cy Young pitched a masterful game in his last appearance, with the Boston Braves on September 7, 1911, but wound up a 1–0 loser. The winning pitcher was Phillies rookie Grover Cleveland Alexander, who not only won 28 games that year but also went on to win 373 lifetime—tied with Christy Mathewson for tops in the NL.

◇

Mordecai "Three-Finger" Brown and Christy Mathewson ended their careers by special agreement on September 4, 1916. Brown, 37, was working for the Cubs while Mathewson, 39, was player-manager of the Reds— a club he took over after leaving the New York Giants in midseason. Mathewson won 10–8 to register his only decision for Cincinnati.

Ted Williams knew when to quit. In 1960, his final season, he hit .316 with 29 homers in just 310 at-bats—including a home run in his last trip. Baltimore's Jack Fisher, who would give up No. 60 to Roger Maris a year later, was the victim of the Williams shot.

Superstitions

Ballplayers have practiced strange rituals since the game began. Players doing well, for example, may wear the same clothes while their hot streaks continue. Some maintain the same daily regimen—eating, driving, and even sleeping the same way during hot streaks. Many follow widely accepted routines of not stepping on the foul lines but deliberately touching a base while running out to a defensive position. Some players and broadcasters even feel that they will jinx a no-hitter in progress merely by mentioning it.

Superstitious Bits

Longtime New York Giants manager John McGraw believed that seeing empty beer barrels would bring good luck. Just before the 1905 World Series, he hired a mule team to drag a wagon of barrels past the Polo Grounds, where the Giants were playing the Philadelphia Athletics. New York won the World Series four games to one.

◇

As a group, pitchers don't like to be bothered before a start, considering it "bad luck" to do anything that will disturb their concentration.

◇

Hugh Casey, Vic Raschi, and Chief Bender refused to be photographed before a game—and Bender grew so indignant when the ban was broken that he smashed the offender's camera.

◇

Washington Senators manager Bucky Harris realized that his team won every time 11-year-old schoolboy Bradley Wilson was in the ballpark. During the 1924 World Series, Harris sent a chauffeured limousine to bring the boy to the stadium. The Senators went on to win their only world championship.

◇

Ralph Branca, one of the few players who dared to wear No. 13, threw the most infamous pitch of all time. His last-of-the-ninth pitch to Bobby Thomson with one out and two men on became a three-run homer that erased a 4–2 Dodgers lead and gave the New York Giants their miracle pennant of 1951. Branca was crushed. Although he switched to No. 12, he was slowed by a sore arm the next season and was never again the pitcher he had been before the Thomson home run. He was through before he turned 30.

◇

Sal Maglie, ace of the 1951 Giants, believed it was bad luck to shave before he pitched. Maglie was called "The Barber" not only because his pitches passed ominously close to rival hitters' heads but also because he needed one.

◇

Wade Boggs not only collected batting titles but superstitions. The five-time AL batting champion had to run wind sprints at a specific time and had other set times for batting practice and infield practice. Although he was not Jewish, he invariably carved the Hebrew letters for life (*chai*) in the dirt of the batter's box. And he was such an ardent believer that chicken helped him perform that he actually wrote a recipe book called *Fowl Tips*.

Broadcasting

Before Harold Arlin of Pittsburgh radio station KDKA did the first broadcast of a baseball game in 1921, fans followed the game through newspapers, magazines, and candy store window displays that conveyed pitch-by-pitch descriptions of the World Series. Arlin's August 5 broadcast of a Phillies-Pirates game changed all that and opened new worlds of communication that eventually included television and the Internet.

Broadcasting Bits

In the old days, when baseball press boxes were open and play-by-play men could be heard by writers, one New York scribe told another, "I don't know which game we went to—the one we saw or the one we heard Graham McNamee broadcast."

◇

Cleveland's Jack Graney started a trend in 1932 when management decided that ex-players on the air would attract listeners.

◇

Few fans had TV sets when Red Barber hosted the first televised game from Brooklyn's Ebbets Field on August 24, 1939. Within a dozen years, however, baseball had taken full advantage of the TV boom. Suddenly able to see the faces behind the voices, fans gave broadcasters celebrity status, making Mel Allen, Ernie Harwell, and Vin Scully as famous as Willie, Mickey, and the Duke.

◇

The National Broadcasting Company (NBC) launched network television coverage of the World Series in 1947 and the All-Star Game three years later. The network's New York affiliate handled the first major-league broadcast as well as the first sporting event ever televised—a Princeton/ Columbia baseball game that drew an audience estimated at 5,000 (also in 1939).

◇

Early television was primitive. Announcers making the transition from radio to TV often had as much trouble as actors switching from silents to talkies. They didn't know whether to talk more or less and realized their mistakes would become painfully obvious to fans who could see as well as hear.

◇

Mel Allen's tenure as "Voice of the Yankees" ran from 1940 to 1965 with three years out for wartime Army duty. Discovered as a public address announcer at college football games, the one-time Birmingham lawyer not only made a smooth transition from radio to television but also convinced general manager George Weiss to lure Red Barber from Brooklyn to the Yankees broadcast booth. Phil Rizzuto, the team's star shortstop, joined them after his retirement in 1956 and outlasted both Allen and Barber. Rizzuto spent 40 years in the Yankees broadcast booth.

◇

Announcers have always had trademarks. Mel Allen popularized the home run call, "Going … going … gone," but the phrase was originally used by Cincinnati radio man Harry Hartman in 1929. Russ Hodges said "Bye-bye, baby" when someone connected, while Vin Scully simply said, "Forget it." Milo Hamilton said "Holy Toledo!" while both Phil Rizzuto and Harry Caray accented their accounts with exclamations of "Holy cow!"

◇

Before television made such calls impossible, Pittsburgh's Rosey Rowswell reported Ralph Kiner home runs by yelling, "Open the window, Aunt Minnie … here it comes!" He then smashed a light bulb, suggesting the little old lady failed to get her apartment window open in time.

Bob Prince, who joined Rowswell as a $50-a-week assistant in 1948, soon won recognition for his slow, nasal twang—coupled with his knowledge and passion for the game. He called the Pirates "Bucs" or "Buccos," shortened versions of Buccaneers, and openly rooted for "a bloop and a blast" when the team trailed by a run.

◇

Vin Scully was born in the Bronx, grew up a fan of the New York Giants, and spent his professional career as "Voice of the Dodgers" in both Brooklyn and Los Angeles. He became a Giants fan at age nine when he passed a candy store where a World Series linescore was posted showing that the Giants had beaten the Yankees 18–4.

◇

Vin Scully began with the Brooklyn Dodgers in 1950, stayed with the team when it went to California, and is still the voice of the Los Angeles Dodgers.

◇

Ernie Harwell was doing the game on television when Bobby Thomson's "shot heard 'round the world" ended the 1951 Dodger-Giants playoff and sent radio announcer Russ Hodges into a frenzy of "The Giants win the pennant! The Giants win the pennant! The Giants win the pennant!" Uttering the most famous words ever spoken behind a baseball microphone, Hodges said it nine times without giving the final score. His score sheet had disappeared in a gust of wind. Because Harwell kept his description simple on television, the frenetic Hodges radio version is invariably coupled with newsreel film of the event.

◇

Ernie Harwell, who ended his 55-year career in the broadcast booth in 2002, had a press box named in his honor (at Detroit's Comerica Park). The soft-spoken southerner began in Brooklyn when Branch Rickey acquired him from the minor league Atlanta Crackers for minor league catcher Cliff Dapper in 1948. He later worked for the Giants and Orioles before joining the Tigers in 1960.

◇

Sixty-six songs written by Ernie Harwell have been recorded by various artists.

◇

In the early days of the Mets, catcher Choo Choo Coleman appeared on Kiner's Korner after a game. Host Ralph Kiner asked, "What's your wife's name, and what's she like?" Coleman replied, "Her name is Mrs. Coleman, and she likes me."

This Week in Baseball became the highest-rated syndicated show in television history after hiring former "Voice of the Yankees" Mel Allen as host in 1976.

◇

Three famous broadcasters called Hank Aaron's 715th home run on April 8, 1974, but the one replayed most—superimposed over footage of the historic event—is the local radio broadcast done by Milo Hamilton for Atlanta's WSB. He called the game on the Braves network while Vin Scully called it for his Los Angeles audience, and Curt Gowdy did the television network version for NBC.

Broadcasters are a bulwark of stability in an age of unprecedented player movement. Both Vin Scully of the Dodgers (left) and Milo Hamilton of the Astros worked well past their 80th birthdays, following the leads of Ernie Harwell (Tigers), Herb Carneal (Twins), Jerry Coleman (Padres), and Ralph Kiner (Mets).

(Milo Hamilton Collection)

Red Barber and Mel Allen never lost their credibility. In 1978, they became the first recipients of the Ford C. Frick trophy for broadcast excellence.

◇

Yankees radio voice Suzyn Waldman spoke the first words on WFAN when the New York sports talk station went on the air on July 1, 1987.

One of the best one-liners came from Fran Healy, who was in the broadcast booth less than a month when a flock of ducks landed on the field during a game in Toronto. "That's the first time I've ever seen a fowl in fair territory," he told his New York audience.

◇

Although he started with the St. Louis Cardinals, Harry Caray was with the Cubs in 1992 when he joined his son Skip and grandson Chip to become the first three-generation family to announce the same game.

◇

Longtime Milwaukee Brewers broadcaster Bob Uecker won Hollywood roles in baseball comedies plus more than 100 appearances on *The Tonight Show with Johnny Carson*.

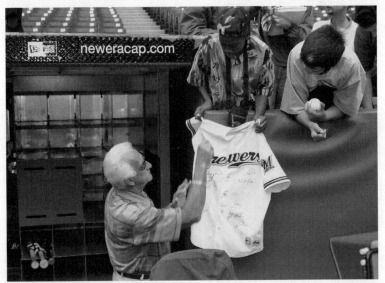

Who me? Milwaukee Brewers broadcaster Bob Uecker, beloved for his self-deprecating humor, signs autographs before a game against the Toronto Blue Jays.
(Wanda Chirnside)

Although Japan has nine daily baseball newspapers, media members are not allowed into baseball clubhouses there.

A Presidential Pastime

Presidents of the United States have always had close associations with "America's national pastime," particularly when a club was located in the nation's capital. Some 40 openers were preceded by a president throwing out the first ball from a box adjacent to the field, with more than a dozen taking part in the ceremonies.

Presidential Bits

The first sitting president to attend a game was Benjamin Harrison, who watched Cincinnati edge Washington 7–4 in 11 innings in an NL game on June 6, 1892.

◇

William Howard Taft, once a standout pitcher at Yale, liked the baseball Senators much more than those on Capitol Hill. An ardent fan of Walter Johnson, Taft became the first U.S. president to throw out the first pitch of a game on April 14, 1910.

◇

Woodrow Wilson not only threw out the first ball three times but also attended games regularly—even after leaving office.

When Woodrow Wilson threw out the first pitch for the Washington Senators on Opening Day 1916, it fueled the tradition of presidents throwing out the first ball.

(Library of Congress)

One-time Ohio sportswriter Warren G. Harding succeeded Woodrow Wilson in office and maintained an avid interest in the game, but Calvin Coolidge was cool to baseball. He considered the first-ball assignment a task rather than a privilege and once left a game in the second inning.

◇

Ambidextrous Harry Truman was the most unorthodox Opening Day pitcher; he threw two balls—one with each arm.

President John F. Kennedy and Vice President Lyndon B. Johnson, elected in 1960, knew baseball thoroughly. Kennedy discussed detailed aspects of the game with George Selkirk, general manager of the "new" Senators, when the baseball executive presented the president with the traditional gold season's pass in 1963. Kennedy attended all three Opening Day games during his short-lived administration.

◇

Senator Henry Jackson, an unsuccessful candidate for president, threw out the first pitch for both the 1969 Seattle Pilots, who lasted only one season, and the new Seattle Mariners, in 1977.

◇

Before he became president, Ronald Reagan had close ties to baseball: he broadcast Cubs games over WHO radio in Des Moines, Iowa, and played Grover Cleveland Alexander (named for President Grover Cleveland) in a movie called *The Winning Team*.

◇

George H. W. Bush attended 10 games during his one-term presidency. They included the 1991 All-Star Game in Toronto, the 1992 inaugural opener in Oriole Park at Camden Yards, and the 1992 All-Star Game in San Diego. After leaving office, he went to the Hall of Fame induction and the first game pitched by Roger Clemens in Houston, home to both men.

By playing in more consecutive games than anyone else, Cal Ripken Jr.
ensured his enshrinement in the Baseball Hall of Fame. The durable infielder,
who spent his entire career with the Baltimore Orioles, was admitted in his
first try along with Tony Gwynn in 2007.
(Baseball Hall of Fame)

During his two-term tenure in the White House, Bill Clinton attended several Orioles games, including the 1995 contest in which Cal Ripken Jr. broke Lou Gehrig's record for consecutive games played.

◇

George W. Bush, owner of the Texas Rangers before becoming governor of Texas in 1994, later worked on presidential speeches while listening to baseball broadcasts.

The Baseball Hall of Fame

The Baseball Hall of Fame is more than just a museum; it's a shrine to American history. From the outside, the shrine to baseball looks unimposing. The plain brick building could pass for a post office or police precinct if not for the glass-enclosed display board showing the latest major league scores. Inside, however, the contents of the four-story museum evoke a sense of the majesty and mystery of the game.

Babe Ruth, larger than life when he played, comes to life again at the Baseball Hall of Fame. An entire room is devoted to the game's first home run king.

(Baseball Hall of Fame)

Throughout the museum, rare photos and displays of artifacts, accompanied by concise explanations, whisk viewers through a time tunnel from the pre-Civil War "sandlot" period to the post-World War II era of integration, expansion, divisional playoffs, and interleague play.

Plaques in the Hall of Fame gallery honor former players, pioneers, executives, Negro Leaguers, managers, and umpires. Among them are the Hall of Fame's only father-and-son combination, executives Larry and Lee MacPhail, and the first two men to top 700 career homers: Hank Aaron and Babe Ruth. Willie, Mickey, and the Duke are there, too, but neither they nor anyone else won by unanimous vote.

Cooperstown Bits

Cooperstown, New York, home of the Baseball Hall of Fame, was founded by the father of *The Last of the Mohicans* author James Fenimore Cooper. The town of five square blocks, lined by homes and structures built in the nineteenth century or earlier, seems like midtown Manhattan during Hall of Fame Induction Weekend in July.

◇

The 1907 Mills Commission, created to determine the origins of baseball, issued a report that concluded, "The first scheme for playing baseball, according to the best evidence obtainable to date, was devised by Abner Doubleday at Cooperstown, New York, in 1839." More fiction than fact, that statement was used as the rationale for placing America's first sports museum in Cooperstown.

◇

The 1934 discovery of an old, homemade baseball in a Cooperstown farmhouse attic gave new life to the idea that baseball was first played in the Central New York village. Singer sewing machine magnate Stephen C. Clark purchased the "Abner Doubleday ball" and conceived the idea of putting it on display, along with other baseball artifacts. NL president Ford Frick welcomed the idea, enlisted the support of AL president Will Harridge and Baseball Commissioner Kenesaw Mountain Landis, and triggered the first wave of donations. Because the game's executives were already thinking about ways to mark the game's centennial in 1939, Frick suggested that a Hall of Fame gallery be part of the baseball museum. The Baseball Writers Association of America (BBWAA) agreed, set up guidelines, and conducted the first vote.

Five men were chosen when balloting results were announced on February 3, 1936. Ty Cobb drew 222 of 226 votes, Babe Ruth and Honus Wagner polled 215 each, Christy Mathewson 205, and Walter Johnson 189. No one else received the required 75 percent. By the time the building was dedicated more than three years later on June 12, 1939, 20 more players had been selected. All 11 living Hall of Famers attended that initial induction ceremony.

Except for Ty Cobb, who was delayed in transit, all living members of the Baseball Hall of Fame made it to Cooperstown for the first induction photo in 1939. In back, left to right: Honus Wagner, Grover Cleveland Alexander, Tris Speaker, Napoleon Lajoie, George Sisler, and Walter Johnson. In front, left to right: Eddie Collins, Babe Ruth, Connie Mack, and Cy Young.
(Baseball Hall of Fame)

Legendary Yankee P.A. announcer Bob Sheppard, who held his job more than 50 years, helped Reggie Jackson write his Hall of Fame induction speech.

◇

Bruce Sutter's plaque in the Baseball Hall of Fame gallery is the only one that portrays a bearded player.

Mike Schmidt made a political point at his 1995 Cooperstown induction, wearing a No. 14 pin to honor former Phillies teammate Pete Rose. Six years earlier, Rose had been banned for life for gambling and was disqualified from the Hall of Fame ballot.

◇

So many people jammed Cooperstown for the 2007 inductions of Tony Gwynn and Cal Ripken Jr. that a state of emergency had to be declared. An estimated 70,000 people packed the tiny central New York hamlet for the late-July induction ceremony.

◇

Through 2007, the Baseball Hall of Fame had 285 members. Included are 198 former major league players, 35 Negro Leaguers, 26 executives or pioneers, 18 managers, and 8 umpires. The BBWAA elected 105 former players to the Hall of Fame while the Hall of Fame Committee on Baseball Veterans elected 153 candidates (92 major leaguers, 26 pioneers/executives, 18 managers, 9 Negro Leaguers, and 8 umpires). The defunct Committee on Negro Leagues selected nine members between 1971 and 1977.

Willie, Mickey, and the Duke? Hank Aaron had them all beat with more home runs, more RBI, a 30/30 season, and three Gold Gloves for fielding excellence. But nine writers still managed to leave him off their Hall of Fame ballots.

(Baseball Hall of Fame)

HENRY "HANK" L. AARON
MILWAUKEE N.L., ATLANTA N.L.,
MILWAUKEE A.L., 1954-1976
HIT 755 HOME RUNS IN 23-YEAR CAREER TO
BECOME MAJORS' ALL-TIME HOMER KING. HAD
20 OR MORE FOR 20 CONSECUTIVE YEARS, AT
LEAST 30 IN 15 SEASONS AND 40 OR BETTER
EIGHT TIMES. ALSO SET RECORDS FOR GAMES
PLAYED (3,298), AT-BATS (12,364), LONG HITS
(1,477), TOTAL BASES (6,856), RUNS BATTED
IN (2,297). PACED N.L. IN BATTING TWICE
AND HOMERS, RUNS BATTED IN AND SLUGGING
PCT. FOUR TIMES EACH. WON MOST VALUABLE
PLAYER AWARD IN N.L. IN 1957.

Cooperstown's Top 10

The following players received the highest percentages in voting for the Hall of Fame:

	Player	Year	Votes	Percentage
1.	Tom Seaver	1992	425/430	98.84
2.	Nolan Ryan	1999	491/497	98.79
3.	Cal Ripken Jr.	2007	537/545	98.53
4.	Ty Cobb	1936	222/226	98.23
5.	George Brett	1999	488/497	98.19
6.	Hank Aaron	1982	406/415	97.83
7.	Tony Gwynn	2007	532/545	97.61
8.	Mike Schmidt	1995	444/460	96.52
9.	Johnny Bench	1989	431/447	96.42
10.	Steve Carlton	1994	436/455	95.82

Baseball fans can change the game. The Society for American Baseball Research (SABR) proved that point by convincing Major League Baseball to change several long-standing records, including the long-standing assumptions that Ty Cobb won 12 batting crowns and that fellow Hall of Famer Rogers Hornsby had the best single-season average. Started by a group of 16 rabid fans who met in Cooperstown in 1971, SABR grew to more than 7,000 members by the end of 2007. Although the primary field of members is education, many are writers, researchers, historians, or work in Major League Baseball.

Hallowed ground: visitors speak in hushed tones as they read the plaques in the Hall of Fame gallery. Nearly 300 players, managers, executives, and pioneers have been enshrined.

(Baseball Hall of Fame)

CHAPTER 9

Palms and Cacti: Spring Training

Whenever the calendar inches toward mid-February, baseball throws its fans a valentine: pitchers and catchers report to sunny climes and start to clear away the cobwebs of winter. Frozen fans from points north and west flock to Florida and Arizona even before the exhibition games begin in March. For them, watching ballplayers do jumping jacks beats shoveling snow.

Florida has been a bastion of spring training for nearly a century, but teams have been increasingly attracted to Arizona by ballpark proximity and new facilities. By 2009, Florida will host 16 teams while the other 14 will train in Arizona. All fields have natural grass, most games are played in daylight, and nobody cares who wins or loses during the 30-game exhibition season. Fans follow their favorite teams through daily won-lost standings listed under the Grapefruit League, the nickname of the Florida clubs, or the Arizona-based Cactus League.

Spring Training Bits

Spring training traces its roots back to February 1870, when Tom Foley took his newly organized touring club, the Chicago White Stockings, south to New Orleans to train for the task of toppling the undefeated 1869 Cincinnati Red Stockings.

After the National League (NL) was founded in 1876, NL teams trained under the stands of their home parks until A. H. Roden took his Boston Nationals to New Orleans, the first stop of a pre-season exhibition swing, in 1884.

◇

The first journey southward for the specific purpose of entering a period of preseason training came in 1886, when White Stockings manager Cap Anson, concerned about his team's portly condition, decided to force off the suet with sweat under the broiling sun—and in the therapeutic baths—of Hot Springs, Arkansas.

◇

The 1888 Washington Senators, with Connie Mack as catcher, went south for the spring with a 15-man contingent. Overnight accommodations were in third-class hotels because the better inns refused ballplayers, then considered a rowdy bunch. Two men shared a lower berth when the team traveled during its two weeks of training.

◇

In 1906, John McGraw's New York Giants became the first team to train in California, but the experiment was short-lived. Heavy rains had made fields in the Los Angeles area unplayable, so McGraw headed east in search of suitable surroundings. He set up headquarters in San Antonio.

◇

The Giants established the first permanent training base in Marlin Springs, Texas, in 1908. The team received not only an annual subsidy from the town but the deed to the ballpark. Soon after, the Chicago Cubs set up the second regular training site when they pitched camp on Catalina Island, 26 miles from Los Angeles.

◇

Four foreign capitals—Mexico City, Havana, Ciudad Trujillo, and Panama City—spent at least one season hosting big-league spring training.

◇

Teams could not always afford spring training. The 1919 St. Louis Cardinals could not pay for the trip south, so Branch Rickey moved them indoors—to the Washington University gymnasium in St. Louis. Out-of-town players tripled up at a nearby hotel, while residents rode the streetcar. When weather permitted, the Cards practiced on the college's outdoor diamond, which had no outfield fence.

◇

Al Lang's letters inspired teams to train in Florida. A one-time batboy, clubhouse boy, and errand boy for ballplayers, Lang retained his baseball ties after establishing a successful laundry business. The Pittsburgh native, who went south for his health at age 41 in 1911, was close to Pirates owner Barney Dreyfuss. But his pleas to bring the Bucs to St. Pete, then a sleepy fishing village of 3,000 people, fell upon deaf ears—even after snow killed three days of spring exercises in Hot Springs, Arkansas. Instead, the 1922 Boston Braves took the bait, moving to St. Pete from Galveston, Texas, and the New York Yankees, who had been in New Orleans, later joined them—establishing Florida as a great place to train.

◇

Some spring-training sites were chosen for frivolous reasons. Augusta, for example, was a Detroit spring base because it was the hometown of manager Ty Cobb, the Georgia Peach. When Cobb left Detroit, Detroit left Augusta.

Ty Cobb was player-manager of the Detroit Tigers until 1928.

(The Topps Company)

Babe Ruth nearly ate himself out of the league during 1925 spring training. Fined $5,000 by manager Miller Huggins for breaking training rules, Ruth endured a miserable season, losing 88 points from his 1924 batting average.

He hit 21 fewer home runs and knocked in 55 fewer runs. The embarrassed slugger paid attention to conditioning that winter and engineered a strong comeback in 1926, returning the Yankees to the top after a seventh-place finish in 1925.

◇

Wartime travel restrictions forced major-league teams to train close to home from 1943–1945.

◇

The Brooklyn Dodgers made Bear Mountain, New York, their spring port o' call during the war years. The club also had an option to use the West Point fieldhouse for a minimum of three hours per day—and did that when bad weather prevailed.

◇

Brooklyn pitcher Clyde King loved beating GM Branch Rickey in checkers. "Beating Mr. Rickey was like winning the World Series," King said. "He took so much pride in the game."

◇

The Pittsburgh Pirates learned to cope with unpredictable conditions when they trained in Muncie, Indiana. Manager Frankie Frisch told his players, "If you can see your breath when you walk out of the hotel in the morning, don't go to the field. Go to the high school gym. We'll play basketball instead of baseball." Pitcher Rip Sewell put a potted palm in the team hotel as a hint of better things to come.

◇

The Dodgers trained in Havana in 1947 because of Jackie Robinson. Hotels in Florida refused to accommodate black players and the team did not want to house players separately.

◇

The New York Yankees and New York Giants swapped 1951 training camps with the Yanks training in Phoenix and the Giants in St. Petersburg. The changing-of-the-guard training camp marked the last spring training for Joe DiMaggio and the first for Mickey Mantle. It also allowed Yankee co-owner Del Webb a chance to keep tabs on his ballclub as well as his burgeoning real-estate empire.

◇

A two-game exhibition series in Phoenix gave the Chicago Cubs impetus to leave their longtime spring base on Catalina Island, off the California coast. The team moved to Mesa for 1952 spring training and has stayed there since.

Holman Stadium was the last spring training ballpark to add outfield fences. Instead, the Vero Beach diamond featured an incline that warned outfielders they were approaching the ring of palms that circled the outfield perimeter. Only after Dick Allen nearly collided with one of the trees were fences added. Players did not have covered dugouts, however: they sat on open benches in the hot sun with wet towels on their heads.

◇

Though other spring-training sites have merged into their urban surroundings, Dodgertown occupied a peaceful preserve at the edge of Vero Beach, a tiny citrus-producing community. The 450-acre site had a 70-acre orange grove, 27-hole golf course, country club, restaurant, practice fields, and a handsome, well-groomed, 110-acre baseball facility. The Dodgers left their Florida home for Arizona in the middle of 2008 spring training. The move was made primarily to please the club's California-based fans.

◇

Longtime Cleveland star Bob Feller was coaxed into wearing a Houston uniform to help welcome the expansion Houston Colts to the 1962 Cactus League. The team trained at Apache Junction.

Welcoming the Houston Colts to the Cactus League are Ted Williams, then a hitting instructor for the Boston Red Sox; Bob Feller, who was inducted into the Hall of Fame that Year; and Hotel Valley Ho owner Robert Foehl, whose Scottsdale property housed some of the players.

(Hotel Valley Ho)

Clubhouses in Jupiter, home of the Cardinals and the Marlins, are not connected to dugouts. Instead, they're located beyond the center-field fence of Roger Dean Stadium. The only shared stadium in the Grapefruit League, Roger Dean Stadium has exhibition games virtually every day.

◇

Scottsdale Stadium, where the San Francisco Giants prep for the season, was the first spring training facility designed to resemble a major-league ballpark.

◇

Legends Field looks like a smaller version of Yankee Stadium—even down to outfield façade and the miniature Monument Park. Pinstriped plaques featuring numbers of retired stars greet visitors at the gate of the Tampa ballpark, which is not far from the year-round home of majority owner George Steinbrenner.

◇

The Phillies opened two new ballparks in 2004: Brighthouse Networks Field in Clearwater and Citizens Bank Park in Philadelphia. Pitchers described both as hitter-friendly bandboxes.

Brighthouse Networks Field replaced Jack Russell Stadium as the Phillies' spring training home in 2004.

(Dan Schlossberg)

Before moving to Port Charlotte, the Tampa Bay Devil Rays trained in Progress Energy Park in St. Petersburg, 1.2 miles from Tropicana Park, their regular-season home.

◇

The 275 Grapefruit League exhibition games played in 2007 drew a record 1,716,840 fans. Ten of the 18 Florida-based teams reached new peaks.

Combined attendance of the 12 Cactus League clubs topped 1.2 million in 2007. The three biggest draws were the Cubs, Giants, and Mariners, who sold at least 60 percent of their exhibition game tickets to out-of-towners.

◇

Proximity is a plus in the Cactus League: the Texas Rangers are so close to the Peoria facility shared by the Mariners and Padres that the Rangers often take batting practice at home in Surprise before exhibition games in Peoria.

Arizona Trumps Florida, Says San Diego GM

San Diego GM Kevin Towers is a big booster of the Cactus League. "Training in Arizona is much more efficient than in Florida," he said. "The weather and travel in Florida are brutal. I spent two years there as a player and two more there as a scout. There's nothing like Arizona. Everything in Florida is a two-hour commute. Every time I call a GM of a team that trains in Florida, he's in his car. Teams over there just don't get as much work because of all the travel. And the front-office people don't get to look at their minor-leaguers like we do in Arizona because they're always on the road."

The $48.3 million spring training complex in Surprise, Arizona, cost its major-league tenants nothing. The city received $32 million from the state of Arizona and found private capital for the rest. The Surprise complex is shared by the Texas Rangers and Kansas City Royals, both former Florida denizens.

◇

Two teams also share spring training parks in Peoria, Arizona, where the Mariners and Padres have been partners since 2003, and Jupiter, Florida, shared by the St. Louis Cardinals and Florida Marlins since 1998.

◇

The Marlins, the only team to go *north* for spring training, traded spring sites with the Montreal Expos in 2003 when that team was owned and operated by Major League Baseball. The Expos went to Space Coast Stadium in Viera, while Florida got closer to its South Florida fan base by moving from Viera to Jupiter.

Roger Dean Stadium, shared by the Cardinals and Marlins in Jupiter, is one of the more picturesque Florida ballparks.
(Dan Schlossberg)

Tampa is the ranking veteran of spring training in Florida. The 2009 season will mark its 90th anniversary as the winter home of a big-league team. Behind Tampa are Bradenton and Clearwater (79 years), Lakeland (78), Sarasota (77), Fort Myers (67), Palm Beach County (66), and Orlando (65).

◇

After training in Vero Beach, Florida, for 60 years, the Dodgers will move closer to their Los Angeles fan base by switching to Glendale, a Phoenix suburb that already hosts the NFL Cardinals and the NHL Coyotes. The $77 million Dodger headquarters, perched on the Phoenix-Glendale line north of Peoria, will hold 12,000, nearly double the capacity of Holman Stadium in Vero.

◇

All but 6 of the 30 current clubs have trained in Florida. The absentees were the Angels, Brewers, Mariners, Padres, Rockies, and Diamondbacks— all expansion teams in the West.

◇

Tucson was the only town occupied by three teams before the Chicago White Sox said they would move to Glendale and share the new facility there with the Los Angeles Dodgers. The Colorado Rockies, who occupy old Hi Corbett Field, and the Arizona Diamondbacks, who play in Tucson Electric Park, are the other local clubs. Tucson is two hours south of the Phoenix metro area.

◇

Scottsdale Stadium has been the spring training home of the Baltimore Orioles, Boston Red Sox, Chicago Cubs, Oakland A's, and San Francisco Giants.

Spurred by a local civic group called the HoHoKams, the Chicago Cubs pack 'em into HoHoKam Park, largest of all the spring-training parks (capacity 12,500). The ballpark opened in 1977. No matter how poorly the Cubs do on the field, they often lead the majors in spring attendance. Their streak may end in 2009, however, when the Los Angeles Dodgers start training in a slightly bigger Glendale park within driving distance of Los Angeles.

CHAPTER 10

Color, Clout, and Controversy

Baseball changed dramatically after World War II, with the era of integration followed by the era of expansion. Three cities that had two teams (Boston, St. Louis, and Philadelphia) lost one of them and the one city that had three teams (New York) wound up with one—at least before baseball expanded to counteract the threat from the proposed Continental League. The majors expanded in 1961, 1969, 1977, 1993, and 1998, increasing from 16 teams to 20, then to 24, 28, and finally to 30. There were two 10-team leagues until 1969, when the leagues split into East and West divisions. An extra round of playoffs was added in 1995, when the Central Division was created along with the wild-card champion (the second-place team with the best record), producing four playoff contestants from each league. Limited interleague play started two years later.

The biggest change of the postwar era was the signing of Jackie Robinson by the Brooklyn Dodgers on August 28, 1945. Hand-picked to break the color line by Brooklyn general manager Branch Rickey, Robinson had been a shortstop with the Kansas City Monarchs, a Negro Leagues team. In his first year in organized ball, Robinson won the International League batting title with the Montreal Royals and advanced to Brooklyn. He played his first National League (NL) game on April 15, 1947.

Although he had to overcome enormous obstacles, Robinson succeeded—changing not only the face of baseball but also the face of the nation. Black players eventually claimed many records, including single-season and career marks for home runs and stolen bases; strikeouts by a pitcher in a World Series game; and saves by a relief pitcher.

Next to the integration of the game, interleague play was the most radical innovation in baseball history. Although critics contended it would cheapen the World Series, hurt the integrity of divisional title chases, and muddy player records, baseball introduced the formula in 1997. Except for the few games where teams in the same city faced each other, however, fan enthusiasm faded once the novelty wore off.

The postwar period was full of novelties: colored uniforms, coast-to-coast travel, night World Series games, the emphasis on relief pitching, and exploding scoreboards to name a few. All would be foreign to Ty Cobb or Babe Ruth. So would the astronomical salaries that players received after winning the right to free agency. Such things came at a price: work stoppages shut the game down eight times since the players formed a union and the lure of big money made some players use artificial means to boost performance. Whether new records were tainted remains to be decided by future historians—and those who vote for the Hall of Fame.

During all the changes, baseball lost its balance. The 2008 season opened with two leagues of different sizes (16 in the National, 14 in the American); six divisions of different sizes; and schedules that did not have all teams playing the same opponents. In addition, the American League (AL) continued to operate with a designated hitter (DH) batting for the pitcher, a 1973 innovation designed to boost the offense. Pitchers still batted in the older, more traditional NL.

Postwar Bits

Jackie Robinson found an unexpected helping hand in longtime AL slugger Hank Greenberg. After spending his entire career with the Detroit Tigers, Greenberg joined the Pittsburgh Pirates in 1947, the same year Robinson broke in. In one early-season game, Robinson reached first while Greenberg was playing there for the Pirates. The Jewish star told Robinson he had endured similar abuse because he too was different. Greenberg's advice assured the rookie infielder that he could silence critics with his play on the field.

Next to the integration of the game, a second seismic event shook the baseball world when the Brooklyn Dodgers and New York Giants decided to continue their rivalry in California. Both moved after the 1957 season, leaving New York with only one team for the next four seasons.

◇

Baseball Commissioner Ford Frick did not attend the game in which Roger Maris broke Babe Ruth's record of 60 home runs in a season. Frick, a former sportswriter who served as ghostwriter of Ruth's autobiography, later placed an asterisk after Maris' name in the record book to signify his 61-homer season occurred during the expanded 162-game schedule, as opposed the 154-game schedule in effect when Ruth hit 60 in 1927.

The only time Roger Maris reached the 40-homer plateau in his career was the year he hit 61.

(John Pennisi)

Not counting home runs nullified by rainouts before games became official, Hank Aaron actually hit 757 home runs. He lost his first when he was called out on appeal after failing to touch first base and lost another when Cardinals catcher Bob Uecker complained that Aaron's foot had been out of the batter's box when he hit the ball onto the roof of Sportsman's Park, St. Louis. Umpire Chris Pelekoudas agreed with the appeal and called Aaron out.

Atlanta slugger Hank Aaron became the career home run king on April 8, 1974, when he connected against Dodger lefty Al Downing.

(Atlanta Braves)

Heartbreak for Haddix

Harvey Haddix won 136 games for five major-league teams from 1952–1965. But he's remembered most for one he lost. On May 26, 1959, a night when fog and mist made conditions at Milwaukee County Stadium more suitable for ducks, the compact left-hander took the mound for Pittsburgh against Lew Burdette of the Braves. Through 12 innings, Haddix was perfect: 36 up, 36 down. Burdette scattered 12 hits but, like Haddix, allowed no runs. In the home twelfth, Felix Mantilla reached on an error by Pirate third baseman Don Hoak. Eddie Mathews sacrificed and Hank Aaron drew an intentional walk, setting up a potential double play. Joe Adcock then got the first clean hit—sending the ball over the fence. Aaron, stunned at the sudden turn of events, ran to second, then headed for the Milwaukee dugout. Adcock, into his home-run trot, didn't see that he passed the spot Aaron vacated, and was called out for passing a preceding runner. Mantilla scored and Adcock's "home run" was ruled a double, making the final score 1–0.

Hank Aaron and Eddie Mathews homered in the same game 75 times, more than any other teammates.

◇

Hank Aaron hit his only inside-the-park home run against a future U.S. senator. The future home run king, then an outfielder for the Atlanta Braves, did it on May 10, 1967, against Jim Bunning of the Philadelphia Phillies.

Expansion Bits

When baseball added new teams, it provided players from existing clubs through expansion drafts. Teams were permitted to protect up to 15 players, then to add three more after each round of the draft. The first draft pick of the 1962 New York Mets was Bob Miller, a right-handed relief pitcher who promptly proceeded to post a 1–12 record.

DEAR FRIEND:

UNDOUBTEDLY YOU KNOW THAT THE NICKNAME SELECTED FOR NEW YORK'S NEW NATIONAL LEAGUE BASEBALL TEAM IS "METS".

AS WE EXPLAINED TO THE PRESS, OUR CHOICE WAS BASED ON THE FOLLOWING FIVE FACTORS:

1. IT HAS RECEIVED PUBLIC AND PRESS ACCEPTANCE.

2. IT IS CLOSELY RELATED TO OUR CORPORATE NAME—METROPOLITAN BASEBALL CLUB, INC.

3. IT IS DESCRIPTIVE OF OUR ENTIRE METROPOLITAN AREA.

4. IT HAS THE DESIRED BREVITY.

5. THE NAME HAS HISTORICAL BASEBALL BACKGROUND.

WE WANT TO THANK YOU FOR YOUR GREAT INTEREST IN OUR EFFORTS TO FIND A NAME, AND FOR THE SUPPORT THAT YOU VOICED IN OUR ENDEAVOR TO BRING YOU A TEAM IN 1962 OF WHICH WE WILL ALL BE PROUD.

METROPOLITAN BASEBALL CLUB, INC.

Charles A. Hurth

GENERAL MANAGER

This card was sent to everyone who submitted a suggestion in the public contest to name New York's new NL team.

(Dan Schlossberg)

Hobie Landrith's lone home run as a member of the Mets was a ninth-inning fly ball that narrowly cleared the Polo Grounds fence in right field, just 257 feet from home plate. It came against future Hall of Famer Warren Spahn, still the star pitcher of the Milwaukee Braves at the time, and helped the Mets beat the Braves twice on May 12, 1962. New York had only 38 other wins that year.

◊

After he retired in 1966, Sandy Koufax said his toughest hitter was fellow pitcher Lew Burdette. Come again? Burdette not only went 5–0 against Koufax in his career, but won *three* of those games with home runs.

◊

Baseball purists complained that the LCS made it more likely that the team with the best record over the 162-game regular schedule would not reach the World Series. A team with a hot hitter or pitcher might be more likely to win, while a sudden slump or critical injury could deprive a deserving team of a trip to the Fall Classic. That first year, the "Miracle" Mets roared down the stretch in the original NL East and upset the favored Atlanta Braves, sweeping the NLCS, while the Baltimore Orioles beat the Minnesota Twins in the AL. After seven losing seasons, New York capped its drive with the 1969 world title.

Divisional Play

From 1962–1968, the two major leagues had 10 teams each—thanks to expansion that added two teams to each circuit early in the decade. Winners went directly to the World Series but also-rans complained that it was embarrassing to finish ninth or tenth when eighth place was equivalent to last under the old format. When the leagues expanded again, they created two 12-team formats that were split in half, with divisions loosely based upon geography. A best-of-five "League Championship Series" was created to determine pennant winners, as well as to raise more revenue. The second wave of baseball expansion brought baseball to Montreal and San Diego, which joined the NL, and Seattle, which won a short-lived franchise called the Pilots (it moved to Milwaukee a year later). The other expansion franchise went to Kansas City, which had lost the Athletics to Oakland in 1968.

When arbitrator Peter M. Seitz declared ace Oakland pitcher Catfish
Hunter a free agent on a contractual technicality in 1974, the resulting bidding war was won by the Yankees—and Hunter. His $3.5 million,
multi-year deal was the best ever given a player. Seitz also sided with the
players after the 1975 season, freeing pitchers Andy Messersmith and Dave
McNally, who had refused to sign contracts containing the reserve clause.
After court rulings upheld the decision, McNally retired but Messersmith
migrated from Los Angeles to Atlanta with a seven-figure deal. The age of
free agency had begun.

◇

Under the reserve clause, teams maintained perpetual rights to their
athletes. Players could be sold, traded, or released but could not jump to
other teams.

◇

With experienced stars able to play out their contracts and sell their services to the highest bidder, owners engaged in bidding wars that made
many players millionaires. Reggie Jackson joined the Yankees in 1977 after
signing a five-year deal worth $4.293 million. A year later, Dave Parker
became the first man to make a million a year when the Pirates gave him
a five-year, $5 million pact. Pete Rose was a hot potato on the sizzling free
agent market. At age 37, the future all-time hits king, paid $375,000 by
the 1979 Reds, inked a four-year Philadelphia contract that would pay him
$3.225 million.

◇

Even though more than 30 years have passed since the advent of free
agency, owners have never figured out how to stop the salary spiral. When
they tried, at the suggestion of Commissioner Peter Ueberroth in 1984,
they were found guilty of collusion and fined heavily.

◇

Ron Blomberg became the first designated hitter by accident. Batting sixth
in the Yankee lineup at Fenway Park on April 6, 1973, he came to bat in
the top of the first because his team had loaded the bases with two outs.
Blomberg thus stole the spotlight from Orlando Cepeda, batting third for
Boston and certain of coming to the plate in the bottom half of the inning.
Blomberg drew an RBI walk and the bat he used as the first DH is the only
one given to the Hall of Fame because of a walk rather than a hit.

◇

Only Babe Ruth won more home run titles than Mike Schmidt. The
Philadelphia third baseman led the NL eight times, three of them in consecutive seasons from 1974–1976, and won three MVP awards. He was

also the only man in baseball history to hit four consecutive home runs twice—once in the same game (an 18–16 Philly win at Chicago's Wrigley Field on July 17, 1976).

As the scoreboard suggests, the wind was blowing out at Wrigley Field on April 17, 1976. The Phillies won, 18–16, but couldn't have done it without Mike Schmidt. He homered in the fifth, seventh, eighth, and tenth innings to tie a record for most home runs in a game.

(Philadelphia Phillies)

The Pete Rose Streak

Pete Rose started the 1978 season needing 34 hits to reach 3,000. He reached that plateau May 5 with a single against Montreal's Steve Rogers. But a new pressure would soon surface: between June 14, when Rose stroked a first-inning single against the Cubs, and the end of July, Rose found himself approaching Joe DiMaggio's 56-game hitting streak of 1941. He passed Tommy Holmes, whose 1945 streak of 37 straight had been the NL standard for 33 years, and set his sights on Wee Willie Keeler, whose 44-game streak in 1897 occurred when the Baltimore Orioles were in the NL. On August 1, however, Atlanta pitchers Larry McWilliams and Gene Garber stopped the streak. While it lasted, Rose batted .385.

"Do-overs" don't happen in the big leagues—not usually, anyway. On July 24, 1983, Kansas City slugger George Brett hit a two-out, ninth-inning home run against Goose Gossage to put the Royals up, 5–4. But the Yankees protested that Brett had too much pine tar on his bat handle and

the umpires agreed, nullifying the blow and giving the Yankees a controversial victory. When AL president Lee MacPhail upheld Kansas City's
protest, the game was restarted from the point of interruption. When
completed on August 18, the Royals won.

◇

Dale Murphy, a devout Mormon, believed in the theory that one should
speak softly but carry a big stick. After Atlanta manager Joe Torre convinced the slugger he could hit to all fields with power, Murphy won
consecutive NL MVP awards in 1982–1983. He and Roger Maris remain
the only men with back-to-back MVP awards but no Hall of Fame plaque.

*The youngest man to win
consecutive MVP awards,
Dale Murphy had more total
bases during the decade of the
1980s than any other player.
The seven-time All-Star
also finished second in both
home runs and RBI during
that same time frame.*

(The Topps Company)

During a 25-year career that included stints with nine different teams,
Rickey Henderson had more stolen bases (1,406) and runs scored (2,295)
than any other player. He also was a member of the 3,000 Hit Club.

100-Steal Seasons

Stolen Bases	Year	Player, Team
130	1982	Rickey Henderson, A's
118	1974	Lou Brock, Cardinals
110	1985	Vince Coleman, Cardinals
109	1987	Vince Coleman, Cardinals
108	1983	Rickey Henderson, A's
107	1986	Vince Coleman, Cardinals
104	1962	Maury Wills, Dodgers
100	1980	Rickey Henderson, A's

After a player strike produced the eighth work stoppage in baseball history on August 12, 1994, Acting Commissioner Bud Selig announced the cancellation of postseason play, including the World Series. Only a court ruling on March 31, 1995, brought the striking players back. The 232-day walkout, baseball's longest labor dispute, shortened the 1995 season to 144 games.

◇

Bud Selig engineered expansion to four new cities and the transfer of the Milwaukee Brewers franchise, which his family owned, across league lines. His office also eliminated league offices, consolidated umpiring staffs, and gave home-field advantage in the World Series to the All-Star Game winner. Selig did nothing to fix a format that had leagues and divisions of different sizes competing for the same post-season prize while playing different schedules.

◇

Fan reaction to the seven-month player strike was fast and furious. After the games resumed, average attendance fell and TV ratings dropped. One bright spot, however, was the warm welcome given Cal Ripken Jr. on September 6, 1995, when he passed Lou Gehrig's record of 2,130 consecutive games played.

◇

Willie Mays, Ted Williams, and Mark McGwire went only one at-bat between their 499th and 500th home runs.

◇

For five years, Sammy Sosa was the most prolific slugger in baseball history. He averaged 58.4 home runs per season from 1998–2002, a record for any five-year span.

The Baseball Hall of Fame kept track of the Great Home Run Race of 1998 with a daily scoreboard. Eventual winner Mark McGwire hit 70, a record that lasted three seasons, while Sammy Sosa also topped the 1961 Roger Maris record of 61.

(Milo Stewart, Baseball Hall of Fame)

The 2001 season will always be remembered as a year great records fell. Barry Bonds hit 73 home runs, three more than previous record-holder Mark McGwire; fellow outfielder Ichiro Suzuki duplicated Fred Lynn's feat of winning the Rookie of the Year and MVP awards in the same season; and the Seattle Mariners won an AL-record 116 games, two more than the 1998 Yankees, to tie the 1906 Chicago Cubs atop the lifetime victory list.

◇

Barry Bonds stamped himself as a serious contender for the career home run record in 2001 with a 73-homer season—the only time in his career he topped 50. Six years later, he seized the crown from Hank Aaron while denying swirling rumors about steroids abuse. After the 2007 season ended, he was indicted for perjury when a federal grand jury determined he had lied about taking steroids.

◇

Though known primarily as a starting pitcher, John Smoltz reached 100 saves more quickly than any closer in baseball history. He needed only 151 games, of which 108 were save opportunities. Smoltz and Dennis Eckersley are the only pitchers with 150 wins and 150 saves. Before returning to his erstwhile role as a star starter for the Braves, Smoltz pitched in a record 73 straight games that his team won.

Mr. Moneybags: After sign-
ing the biggest contract in
baseball history with the
Texas Rangers after the
2000 season, Alex Rodriguez
found even greener pastures
with the New York Yankees
three years later. An escape
clause in his contract made
him even richer after the
2007 campaign.
(John Pennisi)

Agent Scott Boras received $12.6 million as his 5 percent *commission* for negotiating the $252 million, 10-year contract shortstop Alex Rodriguez signed with the Texas Rangers after the 2000 season.

◇

Voters for AL Most Valuable Player bypassed Alex Rodriguez in both of his 50-homer seasons with Texas, in 2001 and 2002, but twice gave him the award when he failed to hit 50, in 2003 (with Texas) and 2005 (with the Yankees). His 2007 MVP award was the first to coincide with a 50-homer season by A-Rod.

◇

Ordinarily, a player with 3,000 hits and 500 home runs is considered a lock for the Hall of Fame. But Rafael Palmeiro probably blew his chances by violating baseball's drug policy. The Baltimore slugger, who had vehe-mently denied substance abuse in televised testimony before Congress, was suspended in August 2005 and never played again.

◇

Trevor Hoffman worked more games for one team (the San Diego Padres) than any other pitcher.

Carlos Delgado, playing for the New York Mets at Houston's Minute Maid Park, hit a home run at 7:07 on 7/7/07.

◇

Of all the players who delivered back-to-back-to-back-to-back home runs, J. D. Drew is the only one to do it twice. He was part of the Dodger quartet that hit four straight homers in the ninth inning of a game against San Diego in 2006 and was with the Red Sox when they powered four in a row against the Yankees on April 22, 2007. The 1961 Braves, 1963 Indians, and 1964 Twins also did it.

◇

Carl Pavano paid few dividends on the four-year, $39.95 million contract he signed with the Yankees as a free agent. The right-handed pitcher, formerly with Florida, was injured for virtually all four years.

◇

Jewish-American players Ken Holtzman, Ron Blomberg, and Art Shamsky were three of the six managers in the Israel Baseball League that started play with a 45-game slate in 2007. The league opened with 120 players, including 77 Americans, 15 Dominicans, 13 Israelis, nine Canadians, six Australians, two Colombians, and one Japanese. Some 40 percent of players in the league were Jewish.

◇

Less than a year after leading AL pitchers in hits allowed during the 2006 season, White Sox left-hander Mark Buehrle pitched the first AL no-hitter in five years.

◇

After a dreadful postseason in 2006, Yankees third baseman Alex Rodriguez began 2007 with 14 home runs and 34 RBI in April.

◇

Derek Jeter passed Joe DiMaggio on the Yankees' career hit list when he collected No. 2,215 on May 23, 2007. Only Bernie Williams, Mickey Mantle, Lou Gehrig, and Babe Ruth remain ahead of him.

◇

Derek Jeter had more hits on his 33rd birthday than all-time hits king Pete Rose did at the same age.

◇

Greg Maddux is the only pitcher in baseball history to post double-digit wins for 20 straight years. He topped Cy Young, who had 19 straight seasons with at least 10 wins from 1891–1909, on August 24, 2007, while pitching for the San Diego Padres at age 41.

*The first man to win four consec-
utive Cy Young Awards, control
artist Greg Maddux proved
he had longevity by winning in
double digits for 20 consecutive
seasons, a baseball first. Maddux
had his best years with the Braves
but also pitched for the Cubs
(twice), Dodgers, and Padres.*

(Legends Sports Magazine)

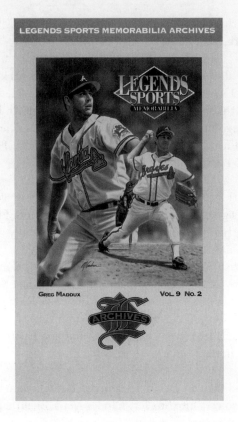

When 44-year-old Roger Clemens started on Old-Timers Day in Yankee Stadium in 2007, he was older than five of the old-timers being honored.

◊

After Mets lefty Tom Glavine won his 300th game in August 2007, the Atlanta Braves took out ads in the New York papers congratulating him—and reminding Mets fans that Glavine won 80 percent of his games in a Braves uniform. That percentage should jump: the Braves signed Glavine again for 2008.

◊

The strength of both New York teams in 2007 was the left side of the infield: Derek Jeter and Alex Rodriguez with the Yankees and Jose Reyes and David Wright with the Mets. All four were All-Stars as well as candidates for the Most Valuable Player awards given after the season (Rodriguez was the AL MVP).

◊

Angels outfielder Reggie Willits was named after former Angels slugger Reggie Jackson.

Most Runs in a Game

Teams that have scored 25 or more runs in a Major League game since 1900:

American League

Runs	Team and Opponent	Date
30	Texas vs. Baltimore	August 22, 2007
29	Boston vs. St. Louis	June 8, 1950
29	Chicago vs. Kansas City	April 23, 1955
27	Cleveland vs. Boston	July 7, 1923
26	Cleveland vs. St. Louis	August 12, 1948
26	Texas vs. Baltimore	April 19, 1996
26	Kansas City vs. Detroit	September 9, 2004
25	Cleveland vs. Philadelphia	May 11, 1930
25	New York vs. Philadelphia	May 24, 1936
25	Boston vs. Florida	June 27, 2003

National League

Runs	Team and Opponent	Date
28	St. Louis vs. Philadelphia	July 6, 1929
26	Cincinnati vs. Boston	June 4, 1911
26	Chicago vs. Philadelphia	August 25, 1922
26	New York vs. Brooklyn	April 30, 1944
26	Philadelphia vs. New York	June 11, 1985
26	Chicago vs. Colorado	August 18, 1995
25	New York vs. Cincinnati	June 9, 1901
25	Brooklyn vs. Cincinnati	September 23, 1901

Fans convinced that steroids helped Barry Bonds break Hank Aaron's home run record during the 2007 season set up a website called Boycottbarry. com. They also passed out Bondsfolds—blindfolds for fans who didn't want to see Barry bat.

◇

Although his home run record is gone, Hank Aaron remains No. 1 on the career RBI list (2,297).

Barry Bonds belted his 756th home run, making him the career home run champion, in 2007. The shot was tinged with controversy, however, because of speculation that the seven-time MVP boosted his chances by using illegal steroids. He finished the 2007 season with a career total of 762 and an uncertain future.
(Bill Menzel)

By hitting 54 home runs in 2007, Alex Rodriguez silenced skeptics who considered Yankee Stadium a tough target for right-handed power hitters. The three-time AL MVP also stamped himself as the leading contender for the career home run crown.

◇

The only father-and-son tandem in the 50 Home Run Club is the Fielders. Cecil hit 51 for the 1990 Detroit Tigers while Prince hit a league-leading 50 for the 2007 Milwaukee Brewers. At 23, he also became the youngest man to hit 50 home runs in a season.

◇

Tips from former slugger Mark McGwire helped Colorado outfielder Matt Holliday win the 2007 NL batting crown. During an August visit to Coors Field, McGwire told Holliday to add a leg-kick to his swing. Holliday wound up leading the league in hits, doubles, and average.

◇

As a boy, Matt Holliday was such a fan of Cal Ripken Jr. that he named his dog Cally.

Yankees general manager Brian Cashman got his start in baseball as batboy for the Dodgers.

◇

Jamie Moyer, the 44-year-old southpaw who pitched the NL East title clincher for the 2007 Phillies, was a high school student playing hooky when he attended the parade honoring the team's only world championship in 1980.

◇

After searching all season for a bullpen bridge to closer Mariano Rivera, the 2007 New York Yankees captured late-summer lightning by promoting Joba Chamberlain from the minors and converting the erstwhile starter into a short reliever.

Rookie fireballer Joba Chamberlain, who surfaced with the Yankees near the end of the 2007 campaign, became the perfect set-up man for closer Mariano Rivera.

(John Pennisi)

Although he pitched a no-hitter in his second big-league start, Clay Buchholz was withheld from postseason play by the 2007 Boston Red Sox because of arm fatigue.

◇

CitiField, scheduled to become the new home of the Mets in 2009, will have a strong architectural resemblance to Ebbets Field, one-time home of the Brooklyn Dodgers. Mets owner Jeff Wilpon, who played baseball with Sandy Koufax at Brooklyn's Lafayette High School, was a Dodgers fan.

The devil made them do it: after 10 seasons, Tampa Bay's 1998 AL expansion franchise dropped the "Devil" from their nickname and substituted sunlight for the flapping stingray on their logo. They opened the 2008 season as the Tampa Bay Rays.

BIBLIOGRAPHY

Billheimer, John. *Baseball and the Blame Game: Scapegoating in the Major Leagues.* Jefferson, NC: McFarland, 2007.

Bodendieck, Zach, ed. *2007 Baseball Register.* Chesterfield, MO: Sporting News, 2007.

Cohen, Richard M., David S. Neft, and Michael L. Neft. *The Sports Encyclopedia: Baseball 2007.* New York: St. Martin's Griffin, 2007.

Enright, Jim, ed. *Trade Him: 100 Years of Baseball's Greatest Deals.* Chicago: Follett, 1976.

Hoppel, Joe, ed. *Official Major League Baseball Fact Book, 2005 Edition.* Chesterfield, MO: Sporting News, 2005.

Kuenster, John, ed. *The Best of Baseball Digest.* Chicago: Ivan R. Dee, 2006.

Light, Jonathan Fraser. *The Cultural Encyclopedia of Baseball, Second Edition.* Jefferson, NC: McFarland, 2005.

Lyons, Jeffrey, and Douglas B. Lyons. *Curveballs and Screwballs—Over 1,286 Incredible Baseball Facts, Finds, Flukes, and More.* New York: Random House, 2001.

———. *Short Hops & Foul Tips: 1,734 Wild and Wacky Baseball Facts.* Lanham: Taylor Trade, 2005.

Mandell, David. *The Suspension of Leo Durocher, The National Pastime: A Review of Baseball History.* Issue No. 27. Cleveland: SABR, 2007.

Markusen, Bruce. *Tales from the Mets Dugout*. Champaign, IL: Sports Publishing, 2007.

Palmer, Pete, ed. *The ESPN Baseball Encyclopedia*. New York: Sterling, 2007.

Pietrusza, David, Matthew Silverman, and Michael Gershman. *Baseball: the Biographical Encyclopedia*. New York: Total Sports Illustrated, 2000.

Reidenbaugh, Lowell. *The Sporting News Selects Baseball's 50 Greatest Games*. St. Louis: The Sporting News, 1986.

Shatzkin, Mike, and Jim Charlton. *The Ballplayers*, New York: Arbor House, 1990.

Smith, Ron. *The Sporting News Selects Baseball's 100 Greatest Players*. St. Louis: The Sporting News, 1998.

Spatz, Lyle, ed. *The SABR Baseball List & Record Book*. New York: Scribner, 2007.

Thorn, John, ed. *Total Baseball: The Ultimate Baseball Encyclopedia, 8th edition*. Toronto: Sports Classic Books, 2004.

Total Baseball Trivia. New York: Total Sports Illustrated, 2001.

Weiss, Peter. *Baseball's All-Time Goats as Chosen by America's Top Sportswriters*. Holbrook, MA: Bob Adams Inc., 1992.

Woods, Bob, ed. *The Baseball Timeline*. New York: DK Publishing, 2001.

Wonham, Linc, ed. *Subway Series 2000*. Bannockburn, IL: H&S Media, 2000.

Periodicals:

Baseball America

Baseball Digest

ChopTalk

The Sporting News

Sports Illustrated

USA Today

USA Today Sports Weekly

Websites:

Baseball-reference.com

Baseballhalloffame.org

Baseballguru.com

Cactusleague.com

Goodsportsart.com

LibraryofCongress.com

Retrosheet.com

INDEX